THE MODERN LIBRARY

of the World's Best Books

Livy: A History of Rome

SELECTIONS

The publisher will be pleased to send, upon request, an illustrated folder listing each volume in

THE MODERN LIBRARY

Livy : A History of Rome

SELECTIONS

translated, with an introduction by

MOSES HADAS

and

JOE P. POE

THE MODERN LIBRARY · NEW YORK

Library of Congress Catalog Card Number: 62-9689

THE MODERN LIBRARY
is published by
RANDOM HOUSE, INC.

CONTENTS

Chronological Table

IN SOME CASES DATES ARE ONLY APPROXIMATE.

B.C.

1184 Legendary arrival of Aeneas in Italy

753 Founding of Rome by Romuius

715-672 Numa Pompilius

672-640 Tullus Hostilius

640-616 Ancus Martius

616-578 Tarquinius Priscus

578-534 Servius Tullius

534-510 Tarquinius Superbus

510 Ejection of Tarquins, establishment of republic

499 Battle of Lake Regillus

494 First secession of plebeians

458 Dictatorship of Cincinnatus

451 Establishment of Decemvirate

449 Valerian-Horatian laws

445 Canuleian law

444 Office of military tribune with consular power established

396 Capture of Veii

390 Battle of Allia; Rome sacked by Gauls

367 Licinian-Sextian laws

366 Establishment of praetorship

343-341 First Samnite War

340-338 Latin War

327-304 Second Samnite War

321 Battle of Caudine Forks

281-272 War with Tarentum and Pyrrhus

264-241 First Punic War

Livy: A
History
of Rome

SELECTIONS

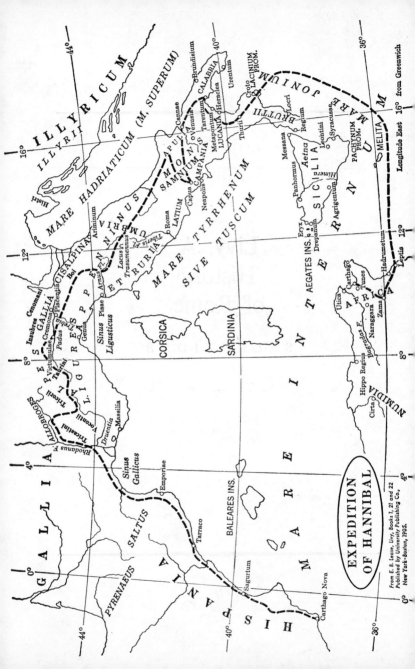

EXPEDITION OF HANNIBAL

From E. B. Lease, Livy, Book I, 21 and 22
Published by University Publishing Co.,
New York-Boston, 1905.

Introduction

Roman history and the Roman ideal, for which Roman history is the incarnation and the vehicle, are central ingredients in the complex of European political ideals and practices. Our fullest and most attractive presentation of the history of Rome in its formative centuries is the work of Livy, and Livy is also our most effective instrument for communicating the ideal of Rome.

In a very real sense the Romans regarded their own history as a kind of national charter, almost as a scripture. From the earliest times the Romans cherished a profound reverence for national tradition, a conviction of being the special object and instrument of destiny, and a sense of responsibility to the obligations of that tradition and that destiny. These attitudes and convictions are implicit in every serious writer of Rome, from Ennius onwards. But in the Augustan age piety to history was systematized as an instrument for promoting moral regeneration and responsible citizenship, and a number of Augustan writers, Livy among them, contributed to shaping and propagating the Roman ideal.

In the case of Livy we cannot be sure, as we are in the case of Vergil and Horace, that he received official encouragement for his enterprise, but none of the three can be dismissed as a hireling in the service of a conspiracy. Object as they might, and as we with fuller experience may, to the concentration of power in the hands of a single individual, it is hard to think of any solution

other than Augustus' to restore order in a world which
had been torn by a century of civil dissension and two
decades of bloody civil war. Any sensitive writer might
sincerely lend himself to a program which promised an
end to bloodshed and misery. The wars, like those Vergil
describes in the *Aeneid,* could be looked upon as a necessary prelude for the inauguration of an era of enduring
and fruitful peace, and Augustus, whose genealogy was
made to derive from Aeneas, could be regarded as the
legitimate heir of Aeneas' charismatic prestige and his
mission to realize the Roman ideal.

LIVY'S LIFE AND BOOK

Of Livy's life we know little more than the two facts
essential for understanding his outlook—his dates, and
the circumstance that he was personally acquainted with
Augustus and members of the imperial household. He
speaks of receiving one piece of antiquarian information
from Augustus himself, and Tacitus mentions an encounter
between the two men. Suetonius reports that he advised
the young Claudius concerning his studies. We know little
of Livy outside his writing because unlike other eminent
Latin prose writers—Caesar, Sallust, and Cicero, Seneca,
the Plinys, and Tacitus—he had no military or political
career; if he had personally been involved in the world
of action his descriptions of battles and of constitutional
developments might have been more precise. His sole
occupation seems to have been his history, which is indeed
a spacious enough enterprise to have occupied a long and
busy life.

Livy was born in Patavium (modern Padua) in 59
B.C., and doubtless received his early education there.
Contemporaries criticized his language as showing traces
of "Patavinity"; his Latin does not show marked differ-

ences from the Latin of the capital and perhaps the gibe referred to his pronunciation. When he went to Rome, and whether he spent the greater part of his time at Rome or Padua is not clear. He cannot have traveled much, for he shows little direct knowledge of terrain he describes. In his youth he wrote dialogues patterned after those of Cicero (who was still writing when Livy was adolescent); these appear not to have been highly regarded, but they seem to have established him as a writer.

When Caesar crossed the Rubicon and so started the Civil War, Livy was ten years old, and he was twenty-eight in 31 B.C. when the victory over Antony and Cleopatra at Actium gave Octavian sole authority to reconstitute the commonwealth. The first book of the history must have been published between 27 and 25 B.C., for at 1.19 he tells us that Augustus closed the temple of Janus for the second time; Octavian did not assume the title of Augustus until 27, and the temple was closed for a third time in 25. Livy continued to work on his history for forty years, and died in A.D. 17. The history ran from the founding of Rome in 753 B.C. to the death of Drusus in 9 B.C. Of its 142 books only 35 have survived complete—1-10 and 21-45, which cover the years 753-793 and 219-167 B.C. It is no accident that the survivals, like the survivals of other long works, are in multiples of five books. Because of the bulkiness of papyrus rolls, which was the ordinary writing material in the Greco-Roman world, long works were regularly published in blocks of five or ten books, called pentads and decades. Authors took cognizance of these divisions; so of the extant books of Livy the first pentad comes to a logical conclusion with the establishment of the republic, and Book 6 begins with a new preface. There is a new preface, similarly, at Book 21, which begins the account of the Second Punic or Hannibalic War.

The scope and distribution of materials in the books that are lost we know from ancient summaries called Periochai or Epitomes. The bulk and cost of the complete work encouraged abridgements; one such is referred to by Martial (14.90) before the end of the first century: "These little skins contain great Livy, whom my whole library would not hold." No systematic abridgement (other than the Epitomes) has survived, but we do have a number of later authors—Florus, Aurelius Victor, Eutropius, Orosius, and Julius Obsequens—who drew largely, and in some cases exclusively, on Livy.

The use of Livy by these and other writers shows that until the end of antiquity and beyond, Livy was regarded as the standard historian of Rome; perhaps the reason the ordinary student's knowledge of Roman history stops where it does is that Livy stopped where he did. And it was not merely as a chronicler that Livy was valued, but as a spokesman for the Roman ideal. The fact that we possess as much of Livy as we do is possibly due, as colopha to certain manuscripts suggest, to the effort of Symmachus, a noble Roman of the fourth century A.D., to propagate the work. Symmachus was concerned to defend Roman tradition against the "subversiveness" of the Christians, and apparently felt that the best way to inculcate loyalty to the Roman ideal was to broadcast the text of Livy.

THE HELLENISTIC PATTERN

But when scientific historiography came into vogue, estimates of Livy were reduced. If what we expect of the historian is laboratory accuracy, which involves critical examination of original documents, complete objectivity, straightforward presentation, then Livy is not a first-class historian, and it is natural for scientific scholars who must perforce have recourse to him to grumble at his short-comings. But it is unjust to condemn Livy for being different from modern historians or even from Thucydides or Polybius, for his objectives and his standards belong to a different order of historical writing.

From its beginnings onward Latin literature is dependent upon Greek models. Sometimes, as in the early tragedies or in some of Vergil's *Eclogues,* the dependence is so close as to be tantamount to translation. Sometimes, as in the *Aeneid,* Greek models are digested and transformed into a new work with independent art and independent meaning; but even so the *Aeneid* is inconceivable without the models of Homer and Apollonius of Rhodes. A poet like Horace might seek his models among the most ancient Greek writers of lyric, but most poets, and all prose writers concerned with ideas, were naturally more impressed with Greek writers and thinkers nearer their own time—that is to say, with those of the Hellenistic age.

From the end of the fourth century B.C. onwards, and largely as a result of the teaching of Isocrates, to whom the historians of the age went to school, the writing of history took a new direction. History came to be regarded less and less as a science and more and more as a species of oratory or of belles lettres. The characteristics of the historiography of the Hellenistic age, which is to say of the third and following centuries B.C., may be summarized under three heads. In the first place there was an effort to assimilate history to the norms of drama. This was effected by emphasizing sudden reverses of fortune, inserting pathetic descriptions of ruined cities and peoples, elaborating the psychological reactions of participants in dramatic crises. A natural concomitant of the dramatic mode, secondly, was a heightened interest in the individual agents and victims of history, and a tendency to glorify those individuals conceived of as heroes and to denigrate those conceived of as villains. This, finally, made pronounced partisanships inevitable. Indeed, it came to be expected of the historian that he should advocate a cause, a set of attitudes, an individual who symbolized a favored ideal.

All of these characteristics are exemplified, abundantly and admirably, in the work of Livy. Against the background of the traditional annalistic texture he inserts dramatic panels, each tightly constructed, frequently with a set debate between the protagonists, and with a striking reversal of fortune. The early books, on the legendary period, give Livy fullest scope for his dramatic art, and here comparison with Dionysius of Halicarnassus, who wrote at about the same time as Livy and used the same materials, is an instructive demonstration of Livy's mastery. An insert in Livy, like those of the Horatii and Curiatii, of Mettius Fufetius, of the Faliscan schoolmaster, of Coriolanus, of Lucretia, is much shorter and more effective than similar things in Dionysius. The *dramatis personae* are reduced to the leading actors, the matter of speeches is concentrated, usually into a single pair, the story is rounded, with a beginning, a high point, and an end. Like all classical historians after Thucydides Livy follows the practice of inserting fictive speeches, but though his speeches serve historical understanding or patriotism, their most obvious function is to serve the drama.

Livy's patriotic interest, as well as his dramatic bent, can best be seen in his treatment of national heroes. Polybius had said (1.14.8), "We must disregard the actors in our narrative and apply to the actions such terms and such criticisms as they deserve." In Livy the heroes of the republic receive a kind of reverence which the Greek historians do not give even a Solon or a Lycurgus, a Themistocles or a Pericles. The Roman analogues of these Greeks are represented as not merely lawgivers, statesmen, generals; their lives constitute a kind of hagiographa. Numa, Camillus, even Scipio Africanus are hedged about with a kind of sanctity. Horatius Cocles, Mucius Scaevola, Cloelia, to take characters from a single episode (2.10), are each made to embody a properly lofty, if not quite credible, patriotism. When we know that Polybius (6.55) has Horatius die in the Tiber, and Dionysius of Halicarnassus (5.33) has Cloelia and her companions effect their escape by prevailing upon the Etruscans to turn their backs while the girls bathe, Livy's hagiologic design becomes clear.

Romans had, indeed, always venerated the heroes and heroism of the past, as the much-quoted line of Ennius, their first great poet shows: *Moribus antiquis res stat Romana virisque:* "It is by the ways of old that Rome stands fast, and by the heroes of old." But when Livy was writing, a special emphasis seems to have been placed on reverence for ancient worthies as part of the Augustan program. In the *Aeneid* the shade of Anchises solemnly announces the roll of great heroes-to-be, and Aeneas carries representations of their great deeds on his divinely wrought shield. In his magnificent new Forum Augustus put before the eyes of Livy's readers an actual gallery of all the Roman triumphators from Aeneas down, done in bronze, and placed in a double row of niches fitted with inscriptions detailing the career and achievements of each figure.

For those who are accepted as national heroes there is a natural tendency to exaggerate merits and gloss over failings in order to produce a uniformly favorable picture. This tendency may be seen, for example, in the characterizations of the heroes of the Second Punic War, Fabius Cunctator, Marcellus, and Scipio Africanus, for each of whom, however, Livy incidentally provides enough unfavorable information to render suspect the wholly favorable picture it is his manifest intention to give. Conversely, and perhaps to underline the merits of the saints, unsuccessful generals are exaggerated into villains. In the same war Flaminius and Minucius and Varro, who are the scapegoats, were certainly not all rash incompetents solely responsible for Roman defeats. For posterity the images are more important than the actuality. We can find, if we look carefully, that Cincinnatus was a wealthy man and had held high office before he was made dictator, but the name suggests, as Livy intended it should, a simple rustic who wipes the sweat from his face and lays his hoe aside in order to guide the state in its need.

In his creation of heroic images and in his drama Livy is surely superior to his predecessors; in the third of the characteristics of Hellenistic historiography, the promotion of particular outlooks and attitudes, his superiority is more marked. His conviction of Roman destiny and of Roman superiority obligated to this destiny was earnestly held and a potent instrument for improving human welfare. Livy's treatment of Roman defeats makes the position clear. If Rome is the object and instrument of destiny, defeats must be explained, and we find that the explanations are almost in the nature of a theodicy. The Gallic invasion, for example, was a divine means for *proving* the Romans and serving as a rod of chastisement.

It is in their courage, discipline, and ability to rule that the Romans are preëminent, and they have a virtual monopoly on such moral traits as *fides, pietas, clementia*—which Augustan propaganda stressed as peculiarly Roman virtues. By corollary the lesser breeds without the law are assumed to be not only deficient in these traits but generally inferior. The Romans are, in a word, in the natural order of things children of destiny, lords of creation, fated to prevail over all other peoples. Livy cannot marvel at

Roman expansion as Polybius does any more than he could marvel at water running down hill. From the beginning heaven guided Rome to its destiny (1.4.1): "The fates were resolved, I believe, upon the founding of this great city and the beginning of the mightiest of empires, next after that of heaven." Rome's first king, immediately upon his translation to heaven, sends word (1.16.7): "Go, said he, and declare to the Romans the will of Heaven that my Rome shall be the capital of the world; so let them cherish the art of war, and let them know and teach their children that no human strength can resist Roman arms." From the circumstances of its occurrence it is no exaggeration to say that this quotation is intended to serve as a sort of text for Livy's whole enterprise.

HISTORICAL VALIDITY

What gives force to Livy's patriotic doctrine and a voucher to his own professional integrity is his concern for truth. In view of his patriotic objectives and his adherence to the modes of Hellenistic historiography, the remarkable thing about Livy is not his shortcoming as a scientific historian but his mature critical sense and his generally high reliability. He records such miraculous tales as those of the birth and exposure of Romulus and Remus and the apotheosis of Romulus, as any patriotic historian must, but he indicates his own rationalist skepticism clearly enough. When he tells us, for patriotic reasons, that it was the young Scipio Africanus and not a slave that saved the elder Scipio's life at Ticinus (21.46), he is careful to say that good authorities attribute the exploit to a slave.

But Livy is under no delusions about the trustworthiness of his sources for the early period and does not conceal his misgivings from his readers. "It is not easy," he writes at the end of Book 8, "to prefer one account over another or one authority over another. The record has been vitiated, in my belief, by funeral eulogies and by falsified inscriptions on family busts. With a mendacity deceptive at all points, the great families draw credit for achievements and honors to themselves; this is surely a source of confusion in the official memoirs of individual personages and in the public records. No writer who was contemporary with the events and who can therefore be relied upon as an authority has survived." At several other conjunctures Livy voices his suspicion that the received account of certain extraordinary achievements may have been falsified by family pride.

Another source of falsification in his authorities of which Livy was apparently not aware are stories calculated to explain the origin of certain religious rituals or legal formulae (so-called aetiological stories) and those supporting certain political attitudes which antiquarians and partisan politicians had retrojected into the past to give them authority. Among the many aetiological stories a good example is the account of the combat of the Horatii and Curiatii and of the trial of the surviving Horatius for slaying his sister (1.24.26). This not only provides an archetypal case for a complicated legal procedure but also explains the sanctity of certain spots. An example of the latter process is the agitation concerning agrarian reforms, which is anachronistic in its fourth-century context and which was doubtless elaborated by partisans of the Gracchan reforms in the late second century.

As the history moves into better documented periods not only is the scale enlarged, so that a single year occupies as much space as a century had done in the earlier period, but the literary approach is more factual. In the early books vocabulary and style have more of a poetic coloring, and this in itself gives the reader the sense that he is moving in an area of legend.

SOURCES

In an apology for the scarcity of reliable sources for the early period, in the preface to Book 6, Livy remarks that most of the official records were destroyed when the city was burned by the Gauls in 390 B.C. On the basis of this remark hypercritical historians of the nineteenth century declared that nothing certain could be known of the history of Rome anterior to 390. The accounts upon which Livy drew were believed to have been based on popular ballads, and in his *Lays of Ancient Rome*, Macaulay thought he was providing specimens of what such ballads must have been like. Later scholars have adopted a more reasonable view and have held that certain official records had in fact been preserved in later compilations. There were the *Annales Maximi*, a chronicle of public events compiled in the late second century from pontifical records; the *Libri Lintei*, which contained lists of magistrates and were kept in the temple of Juno Moneta; a register of decrees of the senate; and finally semi-official private archives.

None of these, apparently, were consulted by Livy, though they appear to have been used by his secondary sources. Of none of these (with the exception of the Greek Polybius) do we have considerable remains, but on the basis of citations in later authors scholars have determined the character of each and the portions or aspects of Livy's work which derive from each. The first Roman prose historian was Q. Fabius Pictor, who fought in the Second Punic War. Livy cites him several times, and probably drew from him the annalistic arrangement and something of the color of the whole work. Others who are drawn upon for the first decade are L. Calpurnius Piso, Valerius Antias, Claudius Quadrigarius, Licinius Macer, and Aelius Tubero. Piso, who was consul in 133, is cited only for additions or alterations to the main account; his interest seems to have been largely ethical, and he praises the puritan virtues of the ancients. Valerius Antias' history, in at least seventy-five books, went down to the early first century B.C. He is turgid, sensational, and given to exaggeration, especially where anyone named Valerius is involved. He is much used by Livy. Claudius Quadrigarius' work, in at least twenty-three books, went down to the time of Sulla; he was a better writer than Valerius Antias and a more critical historian. Much of Livy's material on the Claudii derives from him. Licinius Macer, who was tribune in 73, was a strong supporter of the popular party, and much of the pro-plebeian matter in Livy doubtless derives from him. Aelius Tubero, who was his immediate predecessor, Livy may have known personally. Tubero's main interest was in constitutional development; Livy made large use of him, especially in sections on the struggles of plebeians to attain political equality with patricians.

For the third decade Livy had two writers who had not been used in the first, the Greek Polybius (203-120 B.C.), and the Latin Coelius Antipater, who himself used Polybius. Of Polybius, as compared with other historians of early Rome, the eminent Theodor Mommsen had this to say: "His books are like the sun: at the point where they begin the veil of mist which envelopes the Samnite and Pyrrhic Wars is raised, and at the point where they end a new and, if possible, still more vexatious twilight begins." Since Polybius is so careful a writer, a comparison of the parts of Livy which run parallel to his account, whether drawn directly from Polybius or through an intermediary, affords an excellent gauge of Livy's own

standards of historical accuracy. We can see that Livy
used good judgment in following one source or another,
that he supplemented real gaps in one account with ma-
terials from another, that he made an honest if not always successful effort to reconcile discrepancies in such
details as the length of time required for a certain operation or the numbers of combatants involved. On the other
hand, he heightens dramatic conflict by sharpening the
differences between opposing viewpoints, and will say that
all officers favored a certain course of action where Polybius says some did. He gives much space to the psychol-
ogy of combatants in a crucial battle and of the populace
in a threatened city. He is least reliable, perhaps, in descriptions of battles and other military operations; these
often sound like the commonplaces taught in schools of
rhetoric, and might be interchangeable.

But this is only to say that Livy is a literary man, not
a scientist; not a strategist or constitutional lawyer or
economist or antiquarian, but a Roman who was moved
by the panorama of almost a millennium of his people's
history and who wished to set his findings forth, as attrac-
tively as he could, so that other Romans might be similarly moved. To find answers to the questions which only
modern historians ask, the professional student must seek
supplements to his Livy. But for the humanist and the
historian of ideas it is important to know what the Romans
themselves thought of their history and in what form they
transmitted it to posterity. For such ends Livy remains
the most useful book as it is surely the most agreeable.

It is with such a view of Livy's work that the selections
presented in this volume have been made. To sense his
sweep and movement not snippets but large continuous
masses are wanted; and to show Livy's approach in both
the legendary and the better documented periods these
masses should be chosen from the first and the third

decade. Books 1 and 21 (which are incidentally the two usually studied in college) are best for these purposes, and they are, therefore, included with only slight omissions. On the other hand, for a fuller conspectus of the whole of Livy all of his books need to be represented. From the remaining books, therefore, only such passages as present significant stories or important historical conjunctures have been selected for inclusion, and the interstices filled out with transitional sentences, printed in italics, or, where whole books are omitted, with translations of their ancient Epitomes. Short omissions are indicated by the usual dots; where whole sections are omitted the reader can gauge their extent by the chapter numbers which precede each section.

No equivalents for official titles and coinage are given because precision is impossible without long commentary and the appearance of precision without its substance is misleading. It may be mentioned, however, that the phrase "master of horse" (*magister equitum*) signifies a dictator's second in command.

Book 1

7 5 3 - 5 1 0 B C
Preface

Is it worth my pains to write the history of the Roman people straight through from the inception of the city? I cannot be sure, and would not venture an affirmative answer even if I were. The enterprise, I realize, has had a long vogue, and people of all sorts have essayed it. A constant stream of new writers believes either that they can introduce greater factual accuracy or that their style will surpass the crudities of the past. But however it may turn out, I shall have the satisfaction of having contributed personally, so far as in me lies, to propagating the record of the foremost nation in the world; and if, in such a crowd of writers, my own reputation is eclipsed, I can console myself with the distinction and stature of those who obscure my light.

Another deterrent is the enormous scope: there is a span upwards of seven hundred years to retrace, and growth from frail beginnings to our present state, where sheer mass is an embarrassment. Moreover the early beginnings and the period ensuing are hardly likely to entertain the generality of readers, who are impatient to get to the contemporary situation, where the very energies of a people long dominant are compassing its own ruin. But for me this will afford another compensation for my labor: it will distract me from the melancholy spectacle our age has been witnessing these many years; for as long, at least, as my mind is absorbed in recalling the heroic past I shall be free of the anxieties which can beset a writer even if they do not divert him from the truth.

The traditions of the founding of the city and its preliminaries are more appropriate to poetic saga than to
strict historical record; these it is my purpose neither to
affirm nor refute. Indulgence may be granted to antiquity
to mingle elements of divine and human in order to enhance the prestige of a city's origins. And if license is allowed any nation to exalt its inception and make the gods
its sponsors, so towering is the military glory of Rome
that when it avows that Mars himself was its father and
the father of its founder, the races of mankind can submit to the claim with as little qualm as they submit
to Rome's dominion. But of matters of this sort, however
they are to be criticized or esteemed, I shall myself make
no great issue. The aspects to which I would have every
reader apply himself most attentively are the levels of life
and morality and the character of men and policies, in
peace and in war, by which our realm was acquired and
expanded. Then let him observe how when discipline
wavered morality first tottered and then began the headlong plunge, until it has reached the present level when
we can tolerate neither our vices nor their remedies.

It is this in particular that makes the study of history
salutary and profitable: patterns of every sort of action
are set out on a luminous monument for your inspection,
and you may choose models for yourself and your state to
imitate, and faults, base in their issue as in their inception,
to avoid. If partiality for my own enterprise does not deceive me, there has never been any commonwealth
grander or purer or richer in good examples, none into
which greed and luxury were naturalized so late, none
where lowly means and frugality were so long and so
highly esteemed. In the degree that possessions were scant
so was avarice also; it is only lately that riches have introduced greed and pleasures overflowing have imported a
passion for individual and general ruin.

But plaintiveness is disagreeable even where it may prove necessary; at the outset of our large enterprise, at least, let us have none of it. Let us rather begin with good omens and, if we may adopt the usage of the poets, with prayer and supplication to gods and goddesses to vouchsafe good success to our undertaking.

1. At the fall of Troy, according to generally accepted tradition, the Greeks exercised their fury against other Trojans but exempted Aeneas and Antenor from the rules of war because of ancient ties and because they had advocated restoring Helen and making peace. After various adventures Antenor attached to himself a crowd of Eneti who had lost their king Pylaemenes at Troy, had been ejected from Paphlagonia in a revolution, and were therefore seeking a home and a leader. Eneti and Trojans migrated to the inmost bay of the Adriatic, drove out the Euganei who lived between the sea and the Alps, and occupied the region. The spot where they landed is named Troy and the district is called Trojan; the people as a whole is called Venetian.

Aeneas was made a refugee by a similar disaster, but him the fates summoned to higher enterprises. First he reached Macedonia, then his search for a home carried him to Sicily, and from there he voyaged to the Laurentian country. That place too is called Troy. The Trojans who disembarked had nothing left but their weapons and their ships after their interminable wandering, and while they were collecting plunder from the countryside King Latinus and the Aborigines who occupied the area swarmed out under arms from city and field to repel the invading foreigners. . . . *After a battle, according to one tradition, or without one, according to another, the leaders made peace, and Aeneas married Latinus' daughter Lavinia, after whom the Trojans named the town they founded Lavinium. To Aeneas and Lavinia was born Ascanius.*

2. Next Aborigines and Trojans were attacked together. Turnus king of the Rutuli, to whom Lavinia had been betrothed before Aeneas came, was indignant at being supplanted by a newcomer and made war upon both Aeneas and Latinus. The outcome rejoiced neither side: the Rutuli were vanquished, but the victorious Aborigines and Trojans lost their leader Latinus. Mistrusting their own strength Turnus and the Rutuli resorted to the powerful Etruscans and their king Mezentius, who ruled at Caere, a rich city at the time. From the beginning Mezentius had been irked by the establishment of a new city, and now he felt that Trojan power was growing too rapidly for the security of its neighbors; he was therefore very willing to join forces with the Rutuli. To secure the devotion of the Aborigines in the face of so formidable a war, Aeneas called them and Trojans alike Latins; all shared the same designation as well as the same privileges, and thenceforth the natives were no less loyal to King Aeneas than the Trojans. The increasingly close amalgamation of the two peoples heartened Aeneas, and though the fame of Etrurian power had pervaded not only the land but even the whole stretch of Italian sea from the Alps to the Sicilian straits, Aeneas led his forces out to battle though he might have taken the defensive behind his walls. The battle which followed was a victory for the Latins; for Aeneas it was also the last of his mortal achievements. The site commemorating him, however it is proper and pious to style him, lies above the river Numicus; his title there is Jupiter Indiges.

3. Aeneas' son Ascanius was not yet ripe for authority, but it awaited his adulthood undiminished; under a woman's regency—so competent was Lavinia—the Latin polity and the throne his grandfather and father had held stood firm. I shall not question whether this was Lavinia's Ascanius or an elder brother born of Creusa while Troy

was intact who shared his father's wanderings, the one whom the Julian clan calls Iulus and claims as the founder of their line; in matters so ancient who can be positive? Ascanius then, who was certainly Aeneas' son, whatever his birthplace and whoever his mother, left Lavinium, by now a populous and flourishing city by current standards, to his mother or step-mother, and himself founded a new city under the Alban Mount. Its site along a ridge gave it the name Alba Longa. From the founding of Lavinium to the planting of Alba Longa thirty years elapsed, but resources had so multiplied, especially after the rout of the Etruscans, that not even the death of Aeneas, the subsequent regency of a woman, nor the faltering rule of a boy tempted Mezentius and the Etruscans or any other natives to aggression. The boundary between Etruscans and Latins specified by treaty was the river Albula, now called Tiber. . . . The successors of Ascanius were Silvius, Aeneas Silvius, Latinus Silvius, Alba, Atys, Capys, Capetus, Tiberinus, Agrippa, Romulus Silvius, Aventinus, Proca. Proca had two sons, Numitor and Amulius. To Numitor, because he was eldest, he bequeathed the ancient realm of the Silvian line. But force proved stronger than a father's wish or the respect due an elder. Amulius drove his brother out and ruled instead. Adding crime to crime, he destroyed Numitor's male issue, and deprived his daughter Rhea Silvia of the hope of children by the specious honor of appointing her a Vestal, which obliged her to perpetual virginity.

4. But the establishment of this great city, the inception of this empire next in might to heaven's, was determined, I hold, by the fates. The Vestal was ravished and produced twins; as the father of this doubtful issue she named Mars, whether she believed it was so or whether a god's responsibility gave the fault decency. But neither gods nor men screened mother or children from the king's

cruelty. The priestess was manacled and thrown into prison, the boys he ordered flung into the river. Providentially the Tiber had overflowed its banks into stagnant pools, which made the regular channel inaccessible and led the messengers to expect the infants would be drowned even in still water. So, as if discharging the king's orders fully, they set the boys down in the nearest overflow, where the Ruminalis fig tree now stands; formerly, it was said, the name was Romularis. In those days the neighborhood was wild and desolate. The prevalent story is that, when the floating basket which carried the children was left on dry ground by the receding water, a thirsty she-wolf from the nearby hills was attracted by the infants' wails and very tenderly gave them her teats; the keeper of the king's herds—his name is said to have been Faustulus —found her licking the boys with her tongue. Faustulus, the story adds, carried them home to his wife Larentia to rear. Some hold that Larentia was called "She-wolf" by the shepherds because she was free of her body: hence the origin of the fabulous tale. Such being their birth and rearing, they grew up to be stout farmers and shepherds and ranged over the forests for game. And when they had grown stalwart in body and spirit they not only faced wild beasts but attacked robbers loaded with booty and distributed their takings among the shepherds. With these shepherds they shared their pursuits, serious and playful, and their band increased daily.

5. Once when they were known to be preoccupied with celebrating the Lupercalia they were ambushed by robbers who were incensed at the loss of their plunder. Romulus defended himself, but Remus was taken captive and delivered to King Amulius with the charge that they had raided Numitor's fields; they had collected a band of young fellows, it was alleged, and had pillaged like an invading enemy. Consequently Remus was handed over to

Numitor to be punished. Even from the beginning Faustulus had suspected that the children he was bringing up were of the blood royal. He knew that the babes had been exposed at the king's order, and that the time when he had taken them up corresponded exactly; but he had resolved to avoid hasty disclosure unless opportunity offered or necessity compelled. Necessity came first: under the compulsion of fear he imparted the facts to Romulus.

As it happened Numitor too, when he had Remus in custody and heard that the brothers were twins, noticed their age and their far from servile character and was struck with the thought of their being his grandchildren. His inquiries led to the same conclusion, so that he was on the point of acknowledging Remus. From all sides, then, a plot was woven against the king. Romulus ordered his shepherds to come to the palace at an appointed time by diverse routes—he was not equal to open violence—and Remus supported him with another party procured in Numitor's house. And so they attacked and slew the king.

6. At the beginning of the tumult Numitor shouted that an enemy had invaded the city and attacked the palace, and so had drawn the Alban youth off to defend the citadel as an armed garrison. When he saw the young men approaching to congratulate him, after they had dispatched the king, he instantly convoked a council and set forth his brother's crimes against himself; the origin, rearing, and discovery of his grandchildren; the death of the usurper; and his own responsibility for the deed. The brothers marched through the crowd with their band and hailed their grandfather king, and the unanimous shout of approval from the entire multitude ratified the new king's title and authority.

When the Alban state was in the hands of Numitor, Romulus and Remus conceived a desire to build a city in the area where they had been exposed and reared. The population of Albans and Latins was excessive, and there were also the shepherds; their combined numbers made it likely that Alba and Lavinium would be eclipsed by the city which they would build. But these plans were interrupted by their hereditary curse, lust for rule, which resulted in shameful rivalry. The beginning was innocent enough. Since they were twins and consideration of age could give no priority, they agreed that the guardian gods of the place should choose which should give his name to the new city and rule it when it was built. For awaiting the auguries Romulus took the Palatine and Remus the Aventine hill.

7. Remus is said to have received the first augury—a flight of six vultures. The omen had already been announced when double the number appeared in Romulus' quarter. Each was hailed king by his own followers, the one party claiming kingship on the basis of priority, the other on the number of the birds. The altercation proceeded from angry taunts to blows, and in the broil Remus was struck down. A commoner story is that in derision of his brother Remus jumped over the new walls, whereupon Romulus slew him in a rage, adding the imprecation: "Any other who leaps over my walls shall have the same!" Thus Romulus acquired sole power, and the city thus founded was called by its founder's name. . . .

Romulus regularized the worship of Hercules which had been established by Evander in ancient times when Hercules stopped by the Tiber when he was driving cattle from Spain. 8. He also adopted, from the Etruscans, the use of the curule chair, the purple-bordered toga, and the official beadles called lictors; chose a hundred leading citizens to be designated Fathers; and established the Asylum for landless men from outside in order to increase the strength of the city.

9. Now the Roman state was strong enough to be a match for any neighboring nation in war, but from the scarcity of women its greatness could last for one generation only, for there was neither hope of progeny at home nor marriage rights with neighboring states. Upon the advice of the Senate, therefore, Romulus sent emissaries to the states round about to solicit alliances with the privilege of intermarriage for his new subjects. . . . Nowhere did the envoys receive a favorable hearing. Men despised them and at the same time feared that a power growing great in their midst would endanger themselves and their posterity. Frequently they were dismissed with the query: "Are you welcoming female rabble too? That is the kind of marriage suitable for you." This the Roman youth resented bitterly, and the business pointed to inevitable violence. To provide a time and place appropriate for its exercise Romulus dissembled his resentment and set on foot ritual games to Equestrian Neptune which he called Consualia. Then he gave orders that the show should be advertised among the neighbors, and the Romans made the celebration as sumptuous as their taste and resources allowed so that it should engage attention and raise expectation. A view of the new city was an added attraction, and crowds gathered, especially from the nearest places, Caenina, Crustumium, and Antemnae. The Sabines came en masse, with their wives and children. They were hospitably received in different houses, and when they had viewed the layout of the city with its walls and numerous structures they marveled that Roman power had increased so rapidly.

The time came for the show, and when all eyes and minds were centered upon it, a preconcerted tumult arose and young Romans darted this way and that to carry the girls off. . . . The performance broke off in a panic, and the parents of the girls fled in grief, charging that the laws of hospitality had been trampled upon and invoking the god to whose festival they had been lured by the pretense of religion and good faith. Nor were the kidnaped girls any more hopeful or less indignant. But Romulus went about personally and explained that the fault was their fathers' pride in refusing marriage rights to neighbors. "However, you shall be joined in wedlock," he said, "and share your husbands' prosperity, citizenship, and dearest of all to the human heart, children. So soften your anger, and bestow your affections where chance has bestowed your persons. Often has injury made way for kindness; you will find your husbands the more considerate because each of us will endeavor not only to be a good husband but as far as he can to make up for the parents and country you have lost." This plea was seconded by the cajoling husbands, who excused their act on the ground of passion and love, the most efficacious of all pleas to a woman's heart.

10. The brides were soon quite reconciled, but their parents donned mourning and kept agitating their communities with tears and lamentations. *The Caeninenses, who were the first to attack, were defeated by Romulus, who instituted the dedication of* spolia opima, *which were thereafter always to be offered when a Roman slew an enemy general in action. 11. Next Romulus defeated the Antemnates.* The last attack and the most serious was the Sabine. The Sabine aggression was not a matter of anger and greed, nor did they advertise their intentions, but used cunning as well as prudence. Spurius Tarpeius, who was in command of the Roman citadel, had a daughter who was a Vestal. When she went outside the wall to fetch water for the ritual, Tatius bribed her with gold to admit armed men into the citadel. Once inside, they killed her by heaping shields upon her, whether to give the impression that the citadel had been stormed, or to enforce the lesson that engagements to traitors are not binding. An alterna-

tive legend declares that Tarpeia bargained for what the
Sabines had on their left arms—upon which they wore
heavy golden bangles and richly jeweled rings—and that
they "gave" her the shields instead of the baubles. Some
say that she actually demanded the shields, by the terms
of her bargain, and that the Sabines kept the bargain, when
they saw the trick, by crushing her with the shields.

12. In any case the Sabines were in possession of the
citadel. . . . *The next day the Romans dislodged them
by a heroic charge, and the two armies confronted one
another at the site of the Forum.* 13. At this crisis the Sabine women, whose seizure was the source of hostility,
with hair disheveled and dresses torn, female shyness
crushed by disaster, boldly threw themselves amidst the
flying missiles. Charging in from the flank they parted
the hostile lines in their furious contention, and implored
their fathers on this side and their husbands on that.
Fathers-in-law and sons-in-law, they pleaded, must not
stain themselves with impious bloodshed nor brand their
children, their fathers' grandsons, their husbands' sons,
with the infamy of parricide. "If you disdain the relation-
ship," they said, "if you regret the marriage tie, it is upon
us you must direct your fury: we are the cause of wounds
and slaughter to husbands and parents. Better we perish
than lose either of you and be widowed or orphaned."
Men and officers alike were touched; silence fell, there
was a sudden hush. The leaders step forward to make
terms; they not only conclude peace but combine the two
states into one.

14. *Romulus next defeated nearby Fidenae and* 15.
*concluded an indecisive war with Veii by a hundred-year
truce.* 16. Such were Romulus' immortal achievements.
While he was conducting a review of the army in the Campus Martius near the marsh of Capra suddenly a storm of
crashing thunder arose and enveloped the king in so thick

a cloud that he could not be seen by the assemblage. Thereafter Romulus was not on earth. The panic of the Roman soldiery was allayed when the tempest gave way to clear and untroubled sunlight. The empty throne the senators who had stood near it explained by saying that Romulus had been rapt aloft by a blast; the soldiers believed the tale, but kept a gloomy silence, as if struck by fear of orphanhood. But then when a few had taken the initiative all hailed Romulus as god born of a god, king and father of Rome. They implored his favor and prayed he would always preserve their progeny with gracious benevolence. Even at that date I believe there were some who secretly maintained that the king had been dismembered by the senators; such a rumor has trickled down, but in very veiled terms. Admiration for the hero and active terror have legitimized the other version. Credit is also said to have been conferred upon it by the shrewdness of one man. When the city was distressed by the loss of their king and bitter against the senators, Proculus Julius, who is reported to have possessed sufficient prestige to carry any matter, stepped forward in the assembly and declared: "Fellow citizens, this day at dawn Romulus, the father of this city, glided down from heaven and presented himself before me. As I stood before him awestruck and abashed and prayed it might be lawful for me to look directly at him he said, 'Go proclaim to the Romans it is heaven's will that my Rome shall be capital of the world; accordingly they must cherish soldierliness, and they must be assured, and transmit to posterity the assurance, that no human power can withstand Roman arms.' So saying," Proculus concluded, "he departed on high." It is remarkable how that gentleman's tale was credited and how longing for Romulus on the part of the commons and the army was allayed by the belief in his immortality.

17. But the senators were agitated by rival ambitions

for kingship. It was not yet a question of individuals, for in a people so new none had reached outstanding eminence; the contest was between the Roman and Sabine factions. Men of Sabine stock wished a king chosen of their number because they had had none since the death of Tatius and feared that with equalized status they might lose a share in rule. The old Romans disdained the notion of an alien king. But with preferences at odds all were at one in wishing kingly rule, for they had not experienced the sweets of liberty. The senators were apprehensive that some aggression on the part of the disaffected states nearby might find the state without a government and the army without a leader. That there must be a head all men were agreed, but no one could bring himself to yield to his neighbor. And so the hundred senators shared authority by dividing themselves into ten decuries, with an individual from each decury to preside. The ten who thus ruled rotated in office; only one at a time had the insignia of office and lictors, and his term was limited to five days. The gap in kingship lasted for a year; the interval was called "interregnum," a term still in use.

But then the commoners began to complain that their bondage was multiplied: now there were a hundred masters instead of one. It was plain that they would tolerate only a monarch, and one of their own choice. When the senators sensed the popular temper they resolved to offer voluntarily what they must in any case lose; by granting the people power they won their good will, but the prerogatives they yielded were no greater than those they retained. Their decree provided that when the people had designated a king the act would become effective only if the senators ratified it. The same practice is followed to this day in balloting for laws and magistrates, but it is emptied of force; now the senators ratify an election when the people go to vote, before the results are determined. On this occasion the interrex convoked an assembly and said: "Be it good, prosperous, and blessed! Citizens, choose your king; such is the pleasure of the senators. Then, if he is worthy to be named successor to Romulus, the senators will ratify your choice." The commoners were highly gratified, and to match this generosity they confirmed a resolution that the senate should decide who would bear rule at Rome.

18. At that time Numa Pompilius, who lived in the Sabine town of Cures, was celebrated for justice and piety. So far as it was possible to be in that age, Numa was expert in all law, sacred and profane. It is falsely stated, because no other name is on record, that Pythagoras of Samos was the source of all his learning. But it was in the reign of Servius Tullius, more than a century later, that Pythagoras foregathered with his devoted students, and in the extreme south of Italy, in the region of Metapontum, Heraclea, and Croton. From places so remote, how could his reputation penetrate to the Sabines even if he had been a contemporary? Or in what common tongue could he have communicated the incentive to study? Or what protection could enable him to make his solitary way through so many peoples of different speech and habits? It was Numa's own gifts, in my judgment, that produced his virtuous character; and it was not imported doctrine that shaped him but the stern and puritanical ethic of the old-fashioned Sabines, than whom no people was ever freer of corruption. Upon hearing Numa named the Roman senators apprehended that a king of their number would give the Sabines an advantage; still, no one made bold to prefer his own or his faction's or indeed any senator or citizen's name to Numa's, and so they voted unanimously to bestow the kingship upon him.

19. When Numa had become king in this manner, he set about giving the new city, which had been founded by

force of arms, a new foundation in constitution and enactments and procedures. To accustom men to these principles in the midst of war, which renders spirits savage, was impossible; in the belief that tempers could be softened by disuse of arms, he built the temple of Janus at the foot of the Argiletum, to indicate, when it was open, that the state was at peace, and when it was shut that all the peoples round about were pacified. Twice after Numa's reign has the temple been closed, once in the consulship of Titus Manlius, when the First Punic War was finished, and again in our own day when the gods vouchsafed us the spectacle after the Emperor Caesar Augustus had ensured peace on land and sea after the Battle of Actium. Numa closed the temple after he had secured the good will of neighboring states by alliances and treaties.

Heretofore military discipline and fear of foreign enemies had kept the people under restraint, but with the apprehension of danger from abroad removed it was likely that idleness would unbridle their temper; Numa therefore made it his first business to imbue them with fear of gods, a most effective device for an ignorant and as yet uncivilized populace. And because he could not impress them deeply enough without some miraculous fiction, he pretended that he held nocturnal conferences with the goddess Egeria and that it was by her instruction that he instituted rites most acceptable to the gods and appointed appropriate priests for each of them.

His first undertaking was to divide the year into twelve months, corresponding to the revolutions of the moon. However, inasmuch as the moon's revolution does not take thirty days for each month, and the lunar year is shorter by six days than the complete year which is prescribed by the solar revolution, he systematically introduced intercalary months to ensure that every twentieth year the same dates should coincide with the same positions of the sun as when the cycle began. In addition, he appointed holidays on which all public business was forbidden, realizing that it would sometimes be expedient for no business to come before the people.

20. Next he addressed himself to the establishment of priesthoods. He himself performed many priestly offices, especially those now belonging to the chief priest of Jupiter; but he realized that in a warlike country there would be more kings like Romulus than like Numa, who would themselves go to war and neglect the king's religious functions. Accordingly he created a permanent priest of Jupiter whom he provided with a dress symbolic of his majesty, as well as the royal curule chair. He also appointed two additional priests, one for Mars and one for Quirinus, and selected virgins to be priestesses to Vesta. This institution had its origin in Alba and belonged to the race of that city's founder. He established for them a stipend from the public treasury so that they might devote their full time to the duties of the temple, and by the rule of chastity and other sacred conventions endowed them with a particular sanctity. . . . Next he created the office of Pontifex Maximus and appointed to it Numa Marcius, the son of Marcus, one of the senators. He committed to the keeping of the Pontifex all religious regulations, written out and authenticated by his seal. . . . In addition he placed under his jurisdiction the regulation of all religious rites, both public and private, so that the people would have some authority to consult.

21. The organization and establishment of these institutions gave the people a new interest and diverted their thoughts from warfare. Their constant attention to the gods, since heaven now seemed to them to be concerned with human affairs, had imbued all their hearts with piety; respect for covenants and oaths rather than fear of the laws and punishment became the sanction for discipline in

the community. And as the people fashioned their characters in emulation of the singular example of their king, the neighboring peoples ceased to consider their city an armed camp placed in their midst for the purpose of disturbing the peace of all. Indeed, they came to esteem the Romans so highly that they considered it sacrilege to wrong a people so dedicated to the worship of the gods.

There was a grove watered by a perennial spring which flowed out of a dark cave; there Numa often retired alone, ostensibly to meet with the nymph Egeria. On the ground that his colloquies with his spouse took place in that grove, he dedicated it to the Muses. He also instituted an annual festival to the goddess Faith. . . . The greatest of all his benefits was that throughout his reign he watched over peace as carefully as over his throne. Thus two successive kings contributed to the prosperity of the state—one through peace, the other through war. Romulus ruled thirty-seven years, Numa forty-three.

22. The death of Numa [672 B.C.] was followed by an interregnum. Subsequently Tullus Hostilius [672-640] was chosen king by the people and confirmed by the senate. . . . 24. War was declared between Rome and its neighbor and rival, Alba, in the reign of Tullus. When the two armies were about to come to grips it was decided to settle the dispute in the manner described below.

It happened that there was a set of triplet brothers in each army, the two sets being very nearly equal in age and strength. No event in ancient history is more famous, and there is general agreement that their names were Horatius and Curiatius; but widely known as the tradition is, there is still a point of uncertainty, for it is not clear whether it was the Horatii or the Curiatii who were Romans. Each view has its supporters, but I find that the majority of authors hold that the Horatii were the Romans, and so I am disposed to adopt this version.—It was proposed to these brothers by their respective kings that they fight, each set on behalf of its country, and that sovereignty would accrue to the country of the victors. They agreed readily, and time and place were decided upon. Before the contest took place a compact was made between Alba and Rome that the state whose champions proved victorious would receive unequivocal dominion over the other.

25. After the treaty was concluded, the three brothers on each side armed themselves as had been agreed. On either side their countrymen exhorted them to remember that the gods of their fathers, their fatherland, their parents, and all their fellow-citizens at home and in the army were spectators of their prowess. Filled with their native courage and aroused by the shouts of their countrymen, they stepped into the open space between the two lines of battle. The two armies were planted each in front of its own camp, free for the moment of danger, but not of apprehension, for upon the courage and fortune of these few men rested the decision of sovereignty. Anxious and intent, they gazed upon a spectacle anything but pleasing. The signal was given. With swords drawn the triplets rushed to the charge as if they were complete armies and displayed the courage of mighty hosts. Neither side considered its own danger; their sole anxiety was for the supremacy or subjugation destined for their people and for the future of their country which their own hands must forge.

As the shields first rang and the swords glittered the spectators thrilled with horror; then, as the battle hung in uncertainty, they were seized with a breathless silence. As the fighting grew furious it became more than a spectacle of physical agility and of proficiency with sword and shield; now there were wounds and blood for the onlookers to see. All three Albans were wounded, and two Romans fell dying one upon the other. As they fell the Alban army cried out with joy; the Roman legions abandoned all hope, but anxiously awaited the fate of their sole champion, now surrounded by the three Curiatii.

As it happened he was unwounded, and though he was no match for all three, he was able to confront them individually with confidence. In order to separate them he took to his heels, thinking that each would follow at a different rate of speed, in the degree of their wounds. After running some distance he looked back to see his three opponents following at long intervals, the nearest now quite near. He turned with a furious rush and cut him down; and while the Alban army cried to the others to aid their brother, Horatius was already rushing victoriously upon his second adversary. With the jubilation of men who applaud an unexpected success the Romans began cheering their champion on as he rushed to complete his victory. Before the third, who was not far away, was able to reach the scene, the Roman had killed the second Curiatius. In numbers the struggle was now even, but not so in morale and strength. One pressed forward confidently, flushed with double victory and still unwounded. The other, demoralized by the slaying of his brothers before his very eyes, could only drag his exhausted body to offer his victorious enemy. That was not a battle. "Two of you," said Horatius triumphantly, "I have sacrificed to the spirits of my brothers, the third I will offer to the cause of this battle—the sovereignty of the Roman over the Alban." With that he plunged his sword down into the throat of his opponent, who could scarcely still hold his shield, then stripped the body of its spoils where it lay on the ground. Horatius was welcomed by the Romans with joy; their previous despair made their exultation all the greater. Both armies then turned to burial of their dead, but with feelings very different; one was elated at its new sovereignty, the other subjected to foreign domination. The tombs are to be seen where each man fell; the two Romans are buried in one place nearer Alba, the three Albans nearer Rome, but at intervals, where they fell.

26. Horatius marched at the head of the army displaying the spoils of the three brothers. Before the Porta Capena he was met by his sister, who had been betrothed to one of the Curiatii. Recognizing a cloak draped over her brother's shoulders as one she had made for her betrothed, she loosened her hair and tearfully called upon her lover by name. Horatius was outraged at the sight of his sister's mourning at a time of such great public jubilation and of his own triumph; drawing his sword, he plunged it into her breast. "Go," he cried, "to your lover with your ill-timed love, since you are so unconcerned for your dead brothers, for the one who lives, and for your country. Thus may any Roman woman die who laments the death of an enemy." Although his recent service was thought to compensate for his guilt, both the patricians and the plebs were appalled at this monstrous atrocity, and Horatius was taken to the king for judgment. [Horatius was duly condemned, and appealed his case to the people.]

In making their decision the people were most influenced by the father, Publius Horatius; he proclaimed that in his opinion his daughter had been killed justifiably. If that were not the case, said he, he would have exercised his paternal authority to punish his son. He then begged them not to leave him childless, a man recently blessed with such a noble progeny. With these words he embraced his son, and pointing toward the spoils of the Curiatii, which were hung at the spot now called the Pila Horatia, he said; "A little while ago, Roman citizens, you saw this man marching in triumph, arrayed with the spoils of his foes. Can you now bear to see him whipped and tortured while bound to a yoke? Not even the Albans could bear so

grotesque a spectacle. Go, lictor, and bind these hands—
hands which just now brought sovereignty to the Roman
people. Go, veil the head—of the liberator of this city.
Hang him to an accursed tree. Scourge him within the city
—so that you do it in the midst of the weapons and spoils
of the enemy; or outside the city—so that it be among
their tombs. To what place can you take him which will
not testify his glory and redeem him from such a shameful
punishment?"

The people were proof against neither the tears of the
father nor the unwavering courage of the prisoner himself. They freed him more out of respect for his courage
than because of the righteousness of his cause. In order
that the guilt for such a flagrant murder might be expiated
by some means, the father was ordered to make atonement for his son, but at public expense. After first per-
forming certain expiatory sacrifices, which thereafter were
traditionally maintained by the Horatian family, he
erected a beam across the street. As a token of abasement
and absolution the young man was made to pass, as it
were, under the yoke, with his head covered. This beam,
called the "Sister's Beam," still stands today, kept under
repair at public expense. A tomb of hewn stone was built
for Horatius' sister at the spot where she fell.

27. The peace with Alba was not of long duration.
The Albans grumbled at the dictator for staking the future of their state on three soldiers, and their dissatisfaction subverted his already unstable character. Since honest devices had proven unprofitable, he resorted to deceitful schemes to reconcile the people. In time of war he
had been anxious for peace, but now in peace he yearned
for war. Since he saw that his people had more daring
than power, he provoked other states openly to declare
war on Rome; he allotted to his countrymen the task of
betrayal while ostensibly remaining allies of Rome. With

the promise that Alba would desert to them, he persuaded Fidenae, a Roman colony, along with Veii, to declare war. When Fidenae had openly revolted, Tullus sent for Mettius and his army, and with them marched against the enemy. He crossed the Anio and established a camp where this river runs into the Tiber. The army from Veii had crossed the Tiber between this point and Fidenae. When the battle began they occupied the right wing, nearest the river; on the left stood the army of Fidenae flanked by the mountains. Tullus drew up his own forces opposite those of Veii, and established the Albans opposite the army of Fidenae. Mettius had no more courage than honesty. He dared neither to stand firm nor openly to turn on the Romans, but instead retreated gradually toward the mountains. Finally, when he thought that he had withdrawn far enough, he halted and busied himself with marshaling his troops. Being unsure what he should do, he resolved to wait and to throw in his lot with whichever side fortune favored. When the Romans nearest the Albans saw their allies withdrawing and leaving their flank unprotected they were astonished. A rider was sent at full gallop to tell the king of the Alban's desertion. In alarm at this crisis Tullus vowed to establish a college of twelve Salian priests as well as temples to Pallor and Terror. In a voice loud enough for the enemy to hear he rebuked the horseman, telling him to return to battle: there was nothing to be afraid of. The Alban army had withdrawn at his order, he said, in order to flank the enemy and attack their exposed rear. At the same time he gave orders for the cavalry to raise their spears so that the defection of the Alban army was concealed from much of the infantry. Those who had seen it believed what the king had said, and fought all the more fiercely. Now it was the enemy who panicked; they also had heard the king, for since Roman colonists had been settled in Fidenae a large num-

ber of them understood Latin. Fearing that the Albans
would attack suddenly from the hills and cut them off
from the town in the rear, they broke and fled. With that
wing routed, Tullus turned more fiercely upon the Veientines. They were infected with their allies' panic, and
could not resist his onset, but the river at their backs prevented a headlong retreat. When it arrested their flight
some threw down their arms and dashed blindly into the
water; others stopped short at the bank and were cut
down as they hesitated whether to fight or flee. The Romans had never before fought a bloodier battle.

28. The Alban army, which had passively been watch-
ing, now marched back down to the field. Mettius congrat-
ulated Tullus on his defeat of the enemy. Tullus, in his
turn, greeted Mettius cordially. He instructed the Albans to
pitch camp next to the Romans, and prepared a sacrifice of
purification for the next day. At dawn all the customary
preparations for the sacrifice were made and the king gave
orders for both armies to assemble. The heralds began at
the farther end of the camp, summoning the Albans first.
They were fascinated by the novelty of the affair and gathered close around the Roman king to hear him speak. As
they had previously been instructed, the Romans armed
themselves and gathered around them. The centurions had
been charged to carry out any instructions without delay.
Tullus then began to speak:

"Romans, if there ever was a time in any war when
you should give thanks to the immortal gods, as well as
to your own courage, it is now. For yesterday while fighting against the enemy you fought a much more perilous
battle with your faithless and treacherous allies. Do not
be deceived—the Albans did not withdraw to the mountains at my order. The command to the messenger which
you heard was not genuine; it was only a device so that
you should not panic at being deserted, and so that the

enemy should flee in terror at being outflanked. Not all the Albans are guilty of this treachery which I am disclosing to you. They followed their commander, just as you would have done if I had ordered you to withdraw from the battle. Mettius led that withdrawal; Mettius was architect of the war; Mettius broke the treaty between Roman and Alba. Let others dare to commit such crimes if I do not make him an example which men will never forget."

Armed centurions stepped forward and surrounded Mettius, as the king continued: "What I intend to do I am sure will be in your best interests as well as Rome's and mine, men of Alba. I am going to transfer the Alban people to Rome, to grant citizenship to your people, to enroll your leaders in the senate, to make one city and one people. Just as Alba once was divided into two cities, let it now again become one." The Alban soldiers heard these words with mixed feelings; but being unarmed and surrounded, they were compelled by fear to remain silent.

"Mettius Fufetius," Tullus continued, "if it were possible for you to keep your word and observe treaties I should let you live and attempt to teach you. But your state of mind is incurable. Die then, and by your death teach mankind to reverence the things which you have besmirched. Just as yesterday your mind was torn between Fidenae and Rome, today you shall have your body pulled asunder."

Two chariots were driven forward, and Mettius was stretched lengthwise and tied between them. Simultaneously the horses were driven in opposite directions; each chariot carried part of his severed body, dragged along by the chains in the rear. Everyone turned away from this horrible sight. Among the Romans this was the first and the last such punishment so blind to the laws of humanity. In every other instance we may justly boast that no other race has been satisfied with more moderate punishments.

29. Meanwhile horsemen were sent ahead to transfer the population to Rome, and then the legions marched in to demolish the city. When they entered the gates there was not the rioting and panic customary in captured cities, when gates have been smashed, walls leveled with battering rams, citadels stormed, when the yells of the enemy and the rush of armed men through the streets confound everything with steel and flame. A funereal hush, a speechless grief so froze all hearts that they were too dismayed to think what they should leave behind or carry with them. Now they would stand at their stoops asking one another's advice, now they would roam aimlessly through their houses for a last look. But when the shouts of the horsemen bidding them march became insistent, when the crash of razed buildings could be heard from the outskirts of the city and dust rising in a cloud from separate quarters had covered everything, then everyone snatched up what he could and departed, leaving behind his *lares* and *penates* and the house in which he had been born and brought up. An unbroken line of refugees filled the streets, and their mutual commiseration, when they encountered others, brought fresh tears. Pitiful cries could be heard, especially women's, when they passed revered temples beset by armed men and left their gods, as it were, prisoner. When the Albans evacuated their city the Romans leveled all buildings, public and private, to the ground; a single hour gave over to destruction and desolation the toil of four hundred years during which Alba had stood. The temples of the gods, as the king had decreed, were spared.

30. The destruction of Alba increased the size of Rome. The number of citizens was doubled and the Caelian Mount was added to the city. Tullus himself chose this section of the city for a palace in order to induce more people

to settle there. The leaders of the Albans he appointed to the senate, so that the strength of this division of government might also be increased; among the families granted senatorial status were the Julii, the Servilii, the Quinctii, the Geganii, the Curiatii, and the Cloelii. After increasing the size of this order Tullus also built for it a senate house as a consecrated meeting place. This building retained the name Curia Hostilia even within the memory of our fathers. And in order to make certain that every order should receive new strength from the annexation of Alba, he appointed ten squadrons of Albans as knights. From this number he enlarged the old legions to their full complement and established new ones.

Confident in these new numbers, Tullus then declared war on the Sabines, which was at that time the largest and most powerful nation next to the Etruscans. Each side had inflicted injuries upon the other and refused all claims for reparation. . . . Soon both sides were bending all their efforts toward war preparations. When it became apparent that the advantage would go to the nation which should assume the offensive, Tullus forestalled the Sabines by crossing into their territory. There a fierce battle was fought near the Silva Malitiosa. Partly the strength of their infantry, but mainly the recent additions to their cavalry accounted for Roman superiority. A sudden charge of horse threw the Sabine line into such disorder that they could neither stand and fight without being slaughtered nor escape by fleeing.

31. The victory over the Sabines greatly enhanced the prestige of Tullus and the whole Roman state and added to their power. Soon, however, the king and the senate were informed that a rain of stones had occurred on the Alban Mount. This seemed scarcely credible, but men were sent to investigate the prodigy. Before the eyes of these

emissaries a deluge of stones came falling from the sky as thick as hail stones driven by the wind. From the grove at the mountain top they seemed to hear a great voice bidding the Albans observe their ancestral rites. These rites they had consigned to oblivion just as if they had turned away from their gods when they had left their native city. Subsequently they either had adopted Roman rituals or had abandoned religious observance altogether in anger at their bad fortune. Because of this prodigy the Romans also celebrated a public festival of nine days. Perhaps this too was prescribed by the voice or perhaps, as some authorities say, by soothsayers. At any rate the custom was established of observing this nine-day celebration whenever the same portent was reported.

Soon after, an epidemic spread through Rome. Although this made men disinclined to go to war, the warlike king thought that they would be healthier in the field than at home, and would allow them no peace. Finally, however, he himself was seized by a lingering disease which subdued his ferocious spirit. Previously he had considered nothing less befitting a king than excessive concern for questions of religion; but suddenly he became addicted to all sorts of superstitions, great and small, and filled the people with religious zeal. In general men felt a need for the religious climate which had prevailed under Numa and believed that their one remaining hope against the disease was to make peace with heaven and to seek the mercy of the gods. It is said that the king was reading the memoranda of Numa when he found directions for certain occult sacrifices to Jupiter Elicius. He performed these sacrifices in secret, but failed to begin or to complete them properly. Consequently, not only was he denied a vision from heaven, but Jupiter, in anger at the perversion of his ritual, struck him down with his thunderbolt and burned his house down on top of him. Tullus ruled for thirty-two years, winning great distinction for his prowess in war.

32. With the death of Tullus, the Roman government, following custom, reverted to the senate, which appointed an interrex to hold an election. Ancus Marcius, whose maternal grandfather was the late king Numa Pompilius, was elected king by the people and confirmed by the senate. He was mindful of his grandfather's renown and was of the opinion that the previous reign, which had been otherwise so beneficial, had failed in one respect—the proper observance and performance of religious obligations. Considering it of greatest importance to observe the public rites just as they had been instituted by Numa, he ordered all those in Numa's records to be inscribed on a white tablet by the Pontifex Maximus and displayed for public view. The citizens of Rome and the neighboring peoples were desirous of peace, and Ancus' conduct gave them hope that he would return to the customs and policies of his grandfather.

A treaty had been made with the Latins during the reign of Tullus, but the behavior of the new king encouraged them to take heart and to make an incursion into Roman territory. When Rome demanded restitution they arrogantly refused, thinking that the unwarlike Roman king would content himself with his shrines and altars. However, Ancus modeled his character after Romulus as well as Numa. During the reign of his grandfather, he believed, peace was essential, for the nation was young and predisposed to aggression; moreover, whereas in Numa's reign peace had gone unchallenged, Ancus was sure that it would not be easy for him to maintain it. His patience was being tested, and if it remained unruffled, he would be despised. The times, he realized, demanded a king like Tullus, not like Numa. As Numa had established religious usages for peace, therefore, Ancus determined to adopt ceremonies for war, so that war should be declared as well as waged in accordance with some established usage. The same ritual for demanding satisfaction which is used by the fetial priests [the diplomatic college] even today, he borrowed from the ancient clan of the Aequicoli.

According to this rite, when the envoy reaches the boundaries of the nation from whom restitution is sought he binds his head with a fillet of wool and utters the following formula: "Hear, Jupiter, hear, you boundaries of —naming the nation to whom they belong—hear, O Justice. I am the official messenger of the Roman people and I come righteously and lawfully; give credence to my words." He then enumerates his demands, appealing to Jupiter to witness: "If it is impious or unjust for me to demand that these men and these things be surrendered to me, may you never allow me to see my country again." This formula, with a few changes in the phraseology, he repeats as he steps over the boundary, again to the first person he meets thereafter, once more as he approaches the city gate, and once again after entering the forum. If his demands are not satisfied within thirty days, the period established by custom, he declares war in the following manner: "Hear, O Jupiter, and you, Janus Quirinus, and all you gods of heaven, the earth, and the world below. I call you to witness that this nation (which he names) has acted unjustly and has not given just reparation. But with regard to these matters we shall consult the elders of my country in what way we should obtain our rights." The envoy then returns to Rome. It was customary for the king immediately to address the senate in approximately these words: "Concerning the demands, the disputes, and the claims which the *pater patratus* (the fetial priest) of Rome has announced to the *pater patratus*

of the Ancient Latins, which demands they have not fulfilled as it was fitting for them to do, say (he addresses
the man whose opinion he asks first) what you think
should be done." That person answers, "It is my opinion
that those demands should be exacted through a just and
pious war, and so I approve and I affirm." Then the question was asked of the others in order. When the majority
of those present had given the same opinion, war was
officially approved. Then, according to custom, the fetial priest would carry a bloody spear, either tipped with
iron or burned at the end, to the boundaries of the country involved, and there, in the presence of at least three
adults, would declare: "Whereas the nations and the people of the Ancient Latins have acted unjustly toward the
Roman people; and whereas the Roman people have decreed that war be made against the Ancient Latins, and
the senate of the Roman people has approved and af-
firmed this war; on behalf of the Roman people I hereby
declare and make war upon the Ancient Latins." With
these words, he would throw the spear into enemy territory. In this fashion reparation was sought from the Latins and war declared, and the custom was retained by
posterity.

33. After the levy of a new army, Ancus entrusted the
care of the sacred rites to the priests and set out for the
Latin city of Politorium, which he took by assault. After
the example of previous kings, who had increased the
size of Rome by adopting enemy peoples into citizenship,
he led the whole population back to Rome. . . . Shortly
after, with the capture of Tellenae and Ficana, more new
citizens were added. . . . In the end . . . many thousands of Latins were made citizens. In order to connect
the Aventine with the Palatine these people were assigned land in the vicinity of the altar of Venus Murcia.
The city limits also were extended to prevent its ever be-

coming a stronghold for the enemy. For the sake of convenience this hill was connected with the city by the Sublician bridge as well as by a wall. This bridge was the first built across the Tiber. The Moat of the Quirites, an important defense in the areas where the approach to the city was level, also was the work of King Ancus.

In the huge impersonal population which resulted from the large additions to the city the distinction between right and wrong came to be disregarded, and misdeeds were committed by stealth. In order to intimidate such offenders and deter this growing crime wave a prison also was built adjoining the forum.

34. While Ancus was king a wealthy and enterprising man named Lucumo moved to Rome in the hope of attaining high office. This was impossible at Tarquinii, where he was born, since he was of foreign stock. He was the son of Demaratus, a Corinthian, who had been exiled from his homeland on a charge of sedition. This Demaratus had settled by chance at Tarquinii, and there had married a wife who bore him two sons, Lucumo and Arruns. Lucumo survived his father and inherited all his wealth, since Arruns had died before. Although Arruns left behind a wife with child, the father did not long survive his son and died without knowing of his future grandchild, so that he failed to mention him in his will. As a result the boy received no share of the inheritance and was given the name Egerius, which means "needy." Lucumo, on the other hand, was inspired with ambition by his new-found wealth, and his marriage to Tanaquil increased his aspirations. Tanaquil was a woman of very high birth and was not at all content for her station to be lowered by her marriage. When the Etruscans looked down upon Lucumo, she could not bear this indignity. Forgetting her inborn love of her native land in her desire to see her husband honored, she decided to emigrate from Tarquinii.

For her purposes, Rome seemed to her the most promising city. In a new nation, where all nobility was of recent origin and was based upon personal ability, there would be a place for a brave and energetic man. Tatius, who was a Sabine, had held the throne; Numa had been called from the town of Cures to become king; Ancus was born of a Sabine mother, and his only antecedent of noble rank had been Numa. She easily persuaded her husband, who was ambitious of honors and whose only connection with Tarquinii was through his mother. Thus they moved to Rome with all their property.

They had reached the Janiculum and Lucumo was sitting in his wagon with his wife beside him when suddenly an eagle gently glided down and seized his cap. Then, just as if sent by the gods for this purpose, it swooped down again with a loud beat of its wings and replaced the cap adroitly on his head and soared back into the sky. It was common among Etruscan women to be learned in interpreting omens, and Tanaquil shared this skill. Joyously she embraced her husband and told him to hope for a great future. This happy destiny was portended by the kind of bird, by the part of the sky from which he came, and by the god who sent him. In addition, the focus of the prodigy had been the highest part of his person: the eagle had removed an article of adornment placed upon a human head and had returned it at the bidding of heaven. Bearing with them such thoughts and expectations as these, they entered the city, where they provided themselves with a house; Lucumo adopted the name of Lucius Tarquinius Priscus. This rich stranger easily attracted attention among the Romans, and he devoted his efforts to furthering his fortune. By courteous language, generous hospitality, and acts of kindness he made friends of everyone he could, until word of his character reached even to the palace. Because of his generosity and tact his acquaintance with the king quickly developed into a fast friendship, and soon he was taking part in deliberations concerning both public and private affairs, civil as well as military. Finally, after testing Tarquin in every capacity the king in his will appointed him guardian of his children.

35. Ancus reigned twenty-four years. In military and administrative ability and in personal renown he was unequaled by any of his predecessors. At the time of his death his sons were almost full-grown. This fact made Tarquinius especially concerned that the election of king should be held as soon as possible, and just before the date set for it he sent the boys away on a hunting trip. He is said to have been the first man to campaign for the throne and to make a speech calculated to win the good will of the plebs. "It is nothing unprecedented I am seeking," he said. "You need not wonder or object. For I am not the first, but the third foreigner to aspire to the throne at Rome. Tatius was not only a foreigner, but an enemy when he was made king. Numa was not even acquainted with the city; he did not seek the throne but you invited him of your own accord. As for myself, as soon as I became legally responsible I moved to Rome with my wife and all I possessed. I have spent at Rome the greater part of the time of life during which men participate in civil affairs. I have learned the laws and the sacred rites of Rome from king Ancus himself—a master not to be despised. I have contended with everyone in loyalty and service toward the king, and with the king himself in kindness toward others."

What he said was true enough, and he was unanimously elected king by the people. Although in all other respects an admirable man, as king he retained the same ambition which had driven him to seek the throne, and he was no less concerned with reinforcing his own position than with increasing the power of Rome. He enrolled one hundred new members into the senate, who afterwards were called senators of the "Lesser Families." These constituted a faction in the senate of unswerving loyalty to the king since to him they owed their new status.

The first war he waged was with the Latins; in this he took the town of Apiolae by assault. After returning with a larger amount of booty than had been expected from such an inconsequential war, he sponsored a series of public games which were more expensive and more elaborate than any given by the previous kings. At this time the site was first marked off for what is now called the Circus Maximus. Places were apportioned among the senators and the knights where they each might build seats for themselves. These seats, which were called *fori,* were bleachers built about twelve feet off the ground. The sports consisted of horse racing and boxing; most of the contestants were brought from Etruria. The games continued as an annual festival and were called indifferently the "Roman" or "Great" Games. This same king allotted to private individuals building sites around the forum where arcades and small shops were erected.

36. Tarquinius was preparing to build a stone wall around the city when war with the Sabines intervened. . . . Tarquinius did not think his cavalry strong enough and decided to add more centuries to the three established by Romulus—the Ramnenses, Titienses, and Luceres—and to designate them by his own name. But Romulus had first consulted the auspices, and Attus Navius, a famous augur of the time, declared that no change or innovation could be made without the confirmation of augury. This so angered the king, it is reported, that he ridiculed the augur's art. "Come now, O divine," he said, "foretell for me whether that which I am picturing in my mind can possibly occur." Attus tried the auspices and replied that it could. "Well," said Tarquinius, "I was im-

agining you splitting a whetstone with a razor. Take the
things and do what your birds say can be done." In answer to his words, it is said, the augur split the stone without further ado. A statue of Attus with his head veiled
used to stand where the deed was done, in the comitium
on the steps to the left of the senate house. They say that
the whetstone, too, was placed at the same spot as a
reminder of this miracle for posterity. At any rate, such
great honor was accorded to augury and augurs that at
home and at war nothing was done without first consulting them. Meetings of the *comitia tributa,* of the *comitia
centuriata*—even the most important matters—were
postponed when the birds failed to sanction them.

*After several encounters the Sabines sued for peace,
and the town of Collatia was surrendered as an indemnity.
Tarquin then turned to the Latin peoples, and by attacking their towns separately, one after the other, succeeded
in conquering all of Latium.*

38. The king now set about works of peace with even
greater spirit than he had devoted to war, and the people
were allowed no more serenity at home than during the
previous military campaigns. When Tarquin first had undertaken to build a stone wall around the city he had
been prevented by the war. Now he was able to encircle
the areas of the city which had not yet been fortified. He
also constructed conduits leading down to the Tiber which
drained the lowest areas of the city and the valleys between the hills, where the drainage was poor. Finally,
he turned his attention to the temple of Jupiter, which he
had vowed during the Sabine war. On the Capitoline he
built a foundation for this building, the size of which indicates that he foresaw the future grandeur of the place.

39. At about that time there occurred in the palace a
portent which was miraculous in appearance and which

proved to bode a remarkable issue. The story is that many people saw a flame blazing from the head of a boy named Servius Tullius as he lay asleep. The hubbub which arose at this extraordinary event awakened the royal family, who came to see the sight. When one of the servants brought water to extinguish the flames, Tanaquil, the queen, stopped him. She quieted the uproar and forbade anyone to disturb the boy before he should awaken of his own accord. Then leading her husband aside, she said to him: "Do you see this boy whom we are rearing in such a lowly fashion? Some day he will be a light to us in our confusion and a guardian for our beleaguered house. Let us therefore bestow every care and attention upon one who is destined to bring great glory to ourselves and the state." Thereafter they treated the boy as their own child, and educated him in those accomplishments which incite men to strive for high station. What the gods will, comes to pass without effort. The young man proved to be of a character so princely that the king betrothed his daughter to him. None among the Roman youth was found comparable to Servius in any respect when the king began to cast about for a son-in-law. This great honor, for whatever reason it was bestowed, forbids us to believe that Servius was the son of a slave or had himself been a slave in childhood.

40. When Tarquin had been ruling for some thirty-eight years, Servius Tullius had come to be held in the highest regard, not only by the king but by senators and plebeians as well. The two sons of Ancus had always considered themselves defrauded of their father's throne by their guardian, and were extremely resentful that a foreigner, who was not even of Italian, to say nothing of Roman, origin, was ruler of the city. They considered it a still greater outrage that after Tarquinius, instead of reverting to them, the throne would fall into the hands of

a slave born of a slave—that throne which a hundred years before Romulus the son of a god and himself a god had occupied while he was on earth. For the throne to be accessible not merely to foreigners but even to slaves while there were living male descendants of Ancus seemed to them a disgrace to the Roman people in general and to their own house in particular.

This indignity they resolved to prevent by the sword. But they made their objective not Servius' life but the king's. In the first place they were more resentful of Tarquin than of Servius; secondly, the king would be able to exact severer vengeance if he should survive than a private individual could do; and finally, if Servius should be killed Tarquin might well choose another son-in-law who would inherit the throne. To perpetrate the assassination two cutthroat shepherds were hired. These men, armed with the iron implements of their trade, took their stand in the vestibule of the palace. They attracted the attention of the royal guards by feigning a boisterous quarrel, and then began to appeal to the king. When he heard their cries the king summoned them into the palace. At first each tried to outshout the other, whereupon a lictor quieted them and ordered them to speak in turn. They ceased brawling, and in accordance with their prearranged plan, one explained their case to the king. While the king was giving the speaker his full attention, the other raised his ax and struck the king in the head. Then both shepherds rushed out, leaving the weapon in the wound.

41. Bystanders lifted the dying Tarquin and lictors apprehended the fleeing assassins. An uproar arose and people came running to see what was the matter. Amid the confusion Tanaquil ordered the palace closed and all witnesses ejected. She carefully prepared medicines to treat the wound, as if there were reason for hope; but at

the same time she took other precautions, as if the case were hopeless. She sent for Servius and showed him her dying husband; then she took his right hand and begged him not to allow his father-in-law to die unavenged nor his mother-in-law to become an object of mockery to her enemies. "The throne is yours, Servius," she said, "if you are a man. It must not fall to those who perpetrated this foul deed by the hands of others. Follow the guidance of the gods who once prophesied glory for this head of yours by wreathing it in flame. Now let that divine flame arouse you, now wake in truth! We have held the throne though we were foreigners; you too must remember what you are, not whence sprung. If this sudden crisis has paralyzed your faculties, follow my counsels."

When the shouting and press of the mob outside could hardly be restrained, Tanaquil addressed the populace from an upper story of the palace. She stood at a window which faced onto the Via Nova (the palace was near the temple of Jupiter Stator), and bade the people not lose hope; the king had been stunned by the sudden blow, but the weapon had not penetrated far. The blood had been cleaned away and the wound examined, and all the symptoms seemed favorable. Already the king had recovered consciousness, and she was confident that they would soon see him again. Meanwhile he had enjoined the people to obey the bidding of Servius Tullius, who would administer justice and perform the other duties of the king. Servius then appeared in a robe of state, attended by lictors, and seated himself on the king's throne. There he sat in judgment, rendering decisions in some cases, and in others pretending he would consult the king. Thus, under the pretense of discharging duties for another Servius strengthened his own position. Tarquin had in fact already died, but his death was concealed for several days. Finally, cries of mourning heard from within the palace made the fact known to the public. Servius protected himself with a strong bodyguard; he ruled with consent of the senate, but without ratification by the people. When the sons of Ancus heard that their hirelings had been apprehended and that the king had survived and Servius was in a strong position, they retired into exile at Suessa Pometia.

42. Servius took both public and private measures to strengthen his position. In order that Tarquin's children might not feel the enmity toward him which the sons of Ancus had felt toward Tarquin, he married his two daughters to the king's sons, Lucius and Arruns Tarquinius. But human precautions could not forestall the destiny which fate had in store. Envy of his sovereignty created hostility everywhere—even among his own family.

Soon war again broke out with Veii—for the truce had now elapsed—and with other Etruscan states. This foreign threat was very opportune for maintaining the peaceful state of affairs at home. In this war Servius proved himself both courageous and fortunate. After routing a great enemy army he returned firmly established as king in the eyes of the senators as well as the plebs.

He now turned to what was by far his greatest peacetime work. Just as Numa was the author of divine law, Servius is credited by posterity with being the founder of the classes of society which establish the differences of rank and dignity among the citizens. He inaugurated the census—a very beneficial institution in a state which was destined to grow so large. This allotted civil and military duties in accordance with a property qualification rather than indiscriminately to every citizen as before. Servius divided the classes and centuries according to the following arrangement, which was applicable in time of peace as well as in war.

43. Of those whose possessions were valued at eighty

thousand *asses* or more, Servius composed eighty centuries, forty of "seniors," men over the age of forty-six, and forty of "juniors," men under that age. These were known as the first class. The duty of the seniors was to guard the city, of the juniors to do military service abroad. These men were required to furnish their own armor, consisting of helmet, a round shield, greaves, and corselet, all of bronze. Their offensive weapons were a spear and a sword. Attached to the centuries of this class were two centuries of artisans who were not required to provide arms or serve in the field. Their function was to construct siege works.

The second class consisted of those whose property was valued at between one hundred thousand and seventy-five thousand *asses*. From these, both juniors and seniors, twenty centuries were formed. Their armor was like that of the first class except that they carried a long rectangular shield of hides instead of a round bronze one, and they wore no corselet. The third class was comprised of those whose property amounted to more than fifty thousand *asses*. These were divided into the same number of centuries with the same age classification. Their equipment was the same as that of the third class except that they had no greaves. The property requirement of the fourth class was twenty-five thousand *asses*. These again were divided into the same number of centuries, but their equipment was different, consisting only of a spear and a javelin. Thirty centuries were formed of the fifth class, which was larger. They were equipped only with slings and stones. Reckoned with these were the hornblowers and trumpeters who were arranged in two centuries. Their property amounted to at least eleven thousand *asses*. The rest of the population, whose property was valued at less than this, constituted a single group which was not liable to military service.

After the infantry had been equipped and classified, Servius enrolled the leading citizens into twelve centuries of knights. In addition, he organized six other centuries of cavalry, attaching to them the name of the three (Ramnenses, Titienses, and Luceres) which had been established by Romulus. The knights were allotted ten thousand *asses* each from the public treasury for the purchase of horses, and for their upkeep two thousand *asses* were assessed annually from certain unmarried women. The tendency of these measures was to shift burdens from the poor to the rich.

The matter of class prestige was also provided for. The former kings had maintained the practice, which had originated with Romulus, of granting equal suffrage to all male citizens. The census created a new system of precedence whereby power was in the hands of the leading citizens, although ostensibly no one was excluded from the suffrage. First the knights were summoned to vote, then the eighty centuries of infantry of the first class. If the vote still was indecisive—which rarely occurred—the centuries of the second class were called. The voting almost never continued until it reached the lowest class.

44. Servius hastened the completion of the census by the enactment of a law prescribing imprisonment or death for all who did not register. When it was finished, he published an edict that all citizens, knights and foot soldiers, should assemble at dawn on the Campus Martius. There he purified the whole army with lustral sacrifices consisting of a swine, a sheep, and a bull. This was called the "completion of the lustrum," since it made an end to the census. It is said that eighty thousand citizens were enrolled in that first census. The most ancient authority, Quintus Fabius Pictor, declares that that was the total of all citizens bearing arms.

To accommodate this population it was plain that the

city would have to be enlarged. Servius annexed two more hills, the Quirinal and the Viminal, and subsequently added the Esquiline also. To make the new area respectable he moved there himself. He enclosed the city with a rampart of trenches and a wall, and so enlarged the *pomerium*. This word is taken to mean "the area behind the wall" by those who look to its derivation; actually it means "the area around the wall." Such an area, precisely delimited, the Etruscans used to consecrate with solemn auguries for the purpose of eventually building a wall, when they were founding cities. The object was that no buildings should adjoin the inside of the wall, as they commonly do today, and that there should be a space outside the wall left free of cultivation. The consecrated area it was sacrilege to inhabit or cultivate, and the Romans called it *pomerium* both because it was behind the wall and the wall behind it. As the city grew, the boundaries of the *pomerium* were extended as were the actual walls.

45. After enlarging the city and preparing it in every way to meet the demands of peace as well as war, Servius turned to international affairs. He deprecated the constant use of force to increase the city's power and tried diplomacy instead; at the same time he might add to the city's beauty. The temple of the Ephesian Diana, which was already famous at that time, was supposed to have been built by the states of Asia in common. In the presence of the leaders of the Latin peoples, with whom he had purposely established relations of hospitality and friendship, Servius extravagantly praised this spirit of concord and religious unanimity. By often repeating these sentiments he finally persuaded the Latin tribes to build a temple to Diana at Rome in common with the Roman people. This, of course, was a tacit recognition of the supremacy of Rome, with whom they had fought so often.

It seemed that, after many futile attempts at war, the Latins now had abandoned all thought of challenging Rome's superiority.

One of the Sabines, however, thought he saw an opportunity of recovering the supremacy through his own individual efforts. A heifer of remarkable size and beauty had been born in the Sabine country; for many generations its horns were mounted in the vestibule of the temple of Diana as substantiation of this miracle. This heifer was considered a portent, and prophets foretold that if any person should sacrifice it to Diana the state of which he was a citizen would be supreme in Italy. This prophecy reached the ears of the priest of the temple of Diana. On the first day on which sacrifice was permitted, the Sabine drove the heifer to Rome and stood her before the altar of the temple. When the priest recognized the celebrated beast from its great size, remembering the prophecy, he said to the Sabine, "What are you about to do, stranger? Do you intend to sacrifice to Diana without purifying yourself? First you must bathe in flowing water. Yonder is the Tiber flowing through the lowest part of the valley." The stranger was anxious to do everything according to ritual, and this made him apprehensive. He went down to the Tiber at once, and meanwhile the Roman sacrificed the heifer. This greatly pleased the king and all the people.

46. Long possession had now given Servius indisputable title to the throne; still he received reports that the young Tarquin was spreading accusations that he had seized power without the confirmation of the people. First, then, he obtained the good will of the plebeians by distributing the land he had taken from the enemy to individual citizens, and then introduced the question of his ratification. He was confirmed with greater unanimity than any previous king had enjoyed. Nevertheless, this fact did not diminish Tarquin's hopes of obtaining

the crown. On the contrary he had observed that the distribution of land to the plebeians had displeased the patricians, and was confident that this presented him an opportunity of denouncing Servius and increasing his own influence in the senate. In his own right, he was a person of volatile temperament, and he had a wife, Tullia, who goaded on this restless disposition. Accordingly the royal house of Rome itself produced a scene of atrocity for the tragic stage. The abomination of kings which resulted made the people ready for liberty more quickly, and this tyranny gained by crime proved to be the last in Rome. . . .

The two daughters of Servius, as I have said before, had been married to the brothers, Lucius and Arruns Tarquinius. These girls (like the Tarquins) were of very different dispositions, and it happened that the two of violent disposition were not mated—owing, I am sure, to the good fortune of Rome. For as a result Servius was allowed a longer rule and the reformed constitution became firmly established. It greatly vexed the strong-willed Tullia that her husband, Arruns, had no proclivity either toward daring or toward greed. Thus, she turned all her attention to his brother. She soon inspired the young man with her own temerity, and by almost simultaneous murders they removed the obstacles to their marriage. Soon they were joined in a match which Servius did not prevent but did not approve.

47. Thereafter the old age of Servius became more vexed each day, as his crown became more insecure. After one crime the woman only anticipated the next. She allowed her husband peace neither by night nor by day, for fear that the previous murders would go for nought. She did not want a husband for the sake of being called a wife, she said, or with whom she might acquiesce to servitude. She wanted a husband who considered him-

self worthy of a crown, who remembered he was the son of Tarquinius Priscus, who would rather have than hope for a throne. "If you are the man I thought I was marrying, I call you husband and king; if not, my condition has changed for the worse, since in you there is guilt as well as cowardice."

With tirades of this sort she constantly goaded him. She could not rest for the thought that Tanaquil, who was of foreign birth, had possessed such spirit that she could obtain the throne twice in succession, once for her husband and then her son-in-law; but she herself, she thought, though the daughter of a king was to have no influence in either giving rule or taking it away. Instigated by his wife's raging ambition Tarquin began to solicit the support of the patricians—chiefly those of the newer families which had been raised by his father to patrician status. He reminded them of this benefaction and asked that they repay the favor. He also attracted the younger men through gifts, and by enormous promises and accusations against the king increased his influence among all classes.

One day when the time seemed ripe for action, he burst into the forum surrounded by armed men. While everyone was still paralyzed with fear he seated himself on the royal throne in the senate house and ordered a herald to summon the senators to "King Tarquin." They assembled immediately, since some were prepared for this beforehand, while the others were afraid it might prove dangerous to refuse. They were stunned by the suddenness of this unheard of proceeding and were sure Servius was finished. Tarquin then began to malign Servius, beginning with his very origin: After the ignominious death of Tarquin's father, this son of a slave woman had usurped the throne. There had been no interregnum as before, no election by the people or ratification by the

senate; the throne was the gift of a woman. After such
an origin and such a usurpation he had become patron
of the lowest classes, his brothers; out of envy of noble
blood he had wrested land from the aristocracy and distributed it to society's scum. He had laid upon the upper
classes the burdens which had once been shared by all.
He had instituted the census in order to reveal the wealth
of the rich and expose it to jealousy, thus making it available for appropriation when he wished to bribe the
needy.

48. Summoned by a trembling messenger, Servius arrived in the middle of this speech. As he set foot on the
vestibule he called out loudly, "What is this, Tarquin?
How dare you convene the senate and sit on my throne
while I am still alive?" Tarquin answered violently that
he was sitting on his father's throne, that as the son of
the king he had much better title to it than a slave;
Servius had mocked and insulted his natural masters long
enough. With this the partisans of both sides raised a
clamor and people rushed into the senate house. It became apparent that this battle would decide the question
of sovereignty. These critical circumstances forced Tarquin
to dare the ultimate step. Being a younger and stronger
man he seized Servius around the waist, carried him out,
and threw him down the steps of the senate house. Then,
going back in, he reconvened the senate. Servius' lictors
and attendants fled, and he was feebly dragging himself
home alone, when men sent by Tarquin overtook him
and killed him. It is believed—since it is not inconsistent
with her brutal conduct—that the assassination was ordered by Tullia. It is certain at least that she rode in her
carriage to the Forum where, before the crowd of people,
she brazenly called her husband from the senate and
was first to hail him king. He ordered her to leave the uproar. As she was returning home . . . her driver stopped

and pointed with horror to the butchered body of Servius. There it is said that a brutal and inhuman crime took place, in memory of which the locale is called Wicked Street. Maddened by the avenging Furies of her sister and her husband, she drove the carriage over her father's body; stained and spattered with her father's gore, she carried remains of her bloody deed into her own and her husband's hearth. The wrath of the household gods caused this evil reign to end as it had begun.

Servius Tullius so ruled for forty-four years that it would have been difficult for even a good and moderate successor to rival him: the circumstance that with him just and lawful monarchy perished enhanced his glory. Yet lenient and temperate as his rule was, there are authorities who say that he intended to abdicate because sovereignty was vested in his one person, but that his design to free his country was frustrated by the wickedness of his own family.

49. Then [532 B.C.] began the reign of Lucius Tarquinius, whose conduct earned him the surname "Proud." He denied burial rites to his father-in-law, alleging as an excuse that Romulus too had perished without burial. The leading patricians, whom he believed to be partisans of Servius, he executed; and realizing that others might turn his example against him and attempt to seize the throne illegally, he surrounded himself with an armed bodyguard. Indeed, his only right to the throne was that of forcible possession, since he held it without an election of the people or an endorsement of the senate. And besides, since he could not rely on popular favor, it was necessary for him to safeguard his throne by intimidation. In order to be more feared he took into his own hands trials in capital cases, depending upon no advisers; in this way he was able to execute, to exile and to confiscate the property of not only those whom he suspected

or hated but many whom he only wished to plunder. The number of senators, especially, was reduced in this manner, and he decided to appoint no one to fill these vacancies; thus he hoped to diminish their prestige along with their numbers and to remove the threat of their resentment at the usurpation of their prerogatives. For he was the first of the kings to abandon the traditional practice of consulting the senate in all matters. He governed the state solely on the advice of his own friends, and made war, peace, treaties, alliances, on his own authority, without the confirmation of the people or the senate.

Tarquin undertook to insure his safety at home by strengthening his influence abroad. He made efforts to conciliate the Latin people in particular, and established not only relations of hospitality but marriage connections with their leaders. To Octavius Mamilius of Tusculum he gave his daughter in marriage. This man, if we are to believe the legend, was by far the most distinguished of the Latin race—a descendant of Ulysses and the goddess Circe. Through this marriage Tarquinius established friendships with many of Mamilius' friends and relatives.

50. After Tarquin had become very influential among the leaders of the Latins he appointed a certain day for them to meet together at the grove of Ferentina. He wished to confer with them, he said, about certain matters which concerned them all. Everyone arrived at daybreak except Tarquin, who delayed his arrival until a little before sunset. Meanwhile, throughout the day many matters were brought up and varying opinions expressed. A certain Turnus Herdonius, an Arician, bitterly inveighed against the absent Tarquin. . . . This Turnus himself was a scoundrel who had won his own position by the very practices for which he was attacking Tarquinius. While he was speaking Tarquinius arrived. This ended the speech, as everyone turned around to greet him. Those standing

nearest warned him to apologize for being so late. When everyone was silent he said that he had been chosen to settle a dispute between a father and his son. He had been delayed by his efforts to reconcile them, and since this had consumed the whole day he would introduce his proposals on the next. Turnus did not accept even this in silence. He remarked that no dispute could be shorter than that between a father and son. It could be concluded in a few words: If the son did not obey his father it was his misfortune.

51. With these angry words the Arician left the council. This angered Tarquin more than he revealed, and he immediately began plotting Turnus' death. He intended him to serve as an example to intimidate the Latins just as he had intimidated his fellow citizens at home. Since he had no authority to execute him officially he accused him of a crime of which he was innocent. Through certain members of a faction in Aricia opposed to Turnus, he bribed one of Turnus' slaves to allow a large number of swords to be hidden in his lodging. This was accomplished in one night. A little before dawn Tarquin summoned the Latin leaders to his tent and, making a great show of being agitated, declared that his late arrival of the previous day had been caused by providence; it had been the salvation of them all. For he had received reports that Turnus was preparing to assassinate him and all the leaders and to seize sole power for himself. Turnus had intended to attack the previous day in the council but had been delayed because his primary target, the man who had called the council, had not been present. This disappointment was the reason for his attack on Tarquin in his absence. If his information was correct, he had no doubt that when the council was convened at dawn Turnus would arrive accompanied by a band of armed conspirators. It had been reported to him that a

large number of swords had been delivered to the Arician. It was possible to know at once whether this was true or false, and he requested them to accompany him to make a search of Turnus' quarters.

Turnus' violent character and his speech of the previous day gave them grounds for suspicion, and Tarquin's late arrival was a reasonable motive for Turnus' delay. Thus, the Latins were inclined to believe what Tarquin said, but determined to reserve judgment until the swords actually were discovered. When they arrived at Turnus' dwelling they awoke him and surrounded him with guards. His slaves, who were loyal to their master and were preparing to use force, were then apprehended, and swords were found hidden everywhere in the lodging. This seemed to prove the charge, and Turnus was thrown into chains. Amid a great uproar the council was convened. When the swords were displayed indignation was so fierce that Turnus was executed immediately without a trial. He died a monstrous death, being cast into the fountainhead of the Ferentina river and drowned under a wicker basket weighted with stones.

52. After this the council was reconvened and Tarquin praised the Latins for punishing Turnus as his murderous attempt at insurrection deserved. He then spoke to this effect: "I may be permitted to act by a right of long standing; for since all Latins attribute their origin to the city of Alba, they are bound by the treaty made by Tullus according to which all of Alba with her colonies were ceded to Rome. But I think it is to the best interests of all to confirm that treaty in order for the Latins to share in the benefits of Rome's good fortune. This is better than always to be fearing or suffering the destruction of your cities and the devastation of your fields, which first Ancus and then my father inflicted upon you." It was not hard to persuade the Latins, even though the treaty

recognized Roman supremacy. For they saw that their
leaders sided with the king, and the fate of Turnus provided each with a recent example of the danger which
opposition involved. Thus the treaty was confirmed, and
in accordance with it all the men of military age were
ordered to assemble at the grove of Ferentina on an
appointed day. When they assembled in obedience to
this edict, the king amalgamated the Roman and Latin
companies, by uniting half of one with half of the other.
Over these mixed companies he then appointed centurions. This he did so that the Latins would not have their
own leader, or a separate command, or their own special
standards.

53. Although in peace Tarquin was an unjust king, he
was no mean general in time of war. Indeed, he would
have been unsurpassed by other kings in this field if his
depravity in other respects had not detracted from this
virtue also. He first began the war with the Volscians,
which continued more than two hundred years after his
death, and captured from them the city of Suessa Pometia. He had conceived the idea of building a temple
which would be worthy of the king of gods and men, of
the Roman empire, and of the grandeur of Rome itself.
Thus when he had accumulated forty talents of silver from
the sale of booty he set aside this money for construction
of a great temple to Jupiter.

Next he began a war with Gabii, a town nearby. After
a futile attempt to take it by storm, efforts to besiege the
city also were frustrated, and the war proved to be unexpectedly long. For when the Romans attempted to in-
vest the city, they were driven away from the walls.
Finally Tarquinius pursued his attack by trickery and de-
ceit—tactics least befitting a Roman. As if he had lost all
interest in the war, he pretended to be completely absorbed in laying the foundation of the temple and in other

urban projects. Then, by agreement, his youngest son Sextus fled to Gabii, complaining bitterly of his father's harsh treatment. His father's cruelty toward others had now directed itself upon his own family, he said. He had wearied even of the company of his own children; he was determined to make his own home as empty as he had made the senate house, and not to leave a single descendant or a single heir. He himself had escaped from the very points of his father's swords and he believed himself safe only among Tarquin's enemies. And they should make no mistake: even though Tarquin had pretended to abandon the war, he would attack them unawares at the first opportunity. But if they had no place for suppliants he would travel through all Latium, then would petition the Volscians and Aequi and Hernici until he found someone willing to protect a son from the cruelty and persecution of his father. Perhaps he would even find some nation eager to take up arms against a brutal tyrant and a savage people.

The Gabinians, thinking that if they hesitated Sextus would take offense and leave, received him graciously. It was no wonder, they said, if a man like Tarquin came to treat his children in the same way that he had treated his allies and his own people. Eventually he would persecute even himself, when no one else was left. They welcomed his arrival, they told him, and with his help the fighting would soon move from the gates of Gabii to the walls of Rome.

54. Subsequently Sextus was admitted into their public councils. There he tacitly assented to the recommendations of the Gabinian elders in all matters in which he said that they were more experienced. But again and again he advised them to resume the war and claimed that in this matter his judgment was superior; he was familiar with the strength of both nations, and knew that the tyranny of the king was so hated by the people that not even

his children were able to endure it. As he gradually won over the leaders of the Gabinians, he began to lead the bravest of the young men on war parties and plundering raids. His deceitful words and actions bolstered their misplaced trust more and more until finally he was chosen general. He fought several small battles in which Gabii was generally successful. In their ignorance, the Gabinians from the highest to the lowest all eagerly agreed that Sextus Tarquinius had been sent as a gift of the gods. His willingness to share dangers and hardship with the rest and his generosity in distributing booty made him so popular among the soldiers that Tarquin had no more power at Rome than his son at Gabii.

When Sextus thought he had enough power to accomplish anything he attempted, he sent one of his companions to Rome to tell his father that the gods had made him all-powerful at Gabii and to ask what he wished him to do. Tarquin gave this messenger no reply—probably because he was suspicious of him. Instead the king stalked out of the house seemingly lost in thought, with the messenger following behind. There it is said that he paced back and forth silently, knocking off the heads of the tallest poppies with his staff. Finally the messenger grew tired of waiting for an answer and returned to Gabii thinking his errand unsuccessful. He reported to Sextus what he had said and had seen, and informed him that either out of anger or hatred or his own ingrained arrogance his father had refused to speak. But soon Sextus deduced what his father's obscure charade meant, and he proceeded to destroy the leading men in the state. Some he accused before the people; others, because of their bad reputation, were already susceptible to attack. Some were killed openly; others were assassinated secretly, since no accusations against them would have seemed plausible. Some were allowed to flee or were driven into exile. The property of all those slain and exiled was confiscated. This was distributed as booty to the people, whose relish for personal gain benumbed all concern for the harm suffered by the state. Finally, when Gabii was stripped of all its prudence and strength it was delivered into the hands of the Roman king without a fight.

55. After the surrender of Gabii, Tarquin made peace with the Aequi and renewed his treaty with the Etruscans. Then he turned his attention to urban affairs. His first concern was to build a temple of Jupiter on the Tarpeian Mount as a monument to his reign and his name. He wished posterity to remember that of the two Tarquins who had reigned the father had vowed the temple and the son had completed it. In order that worship of other gods might be restricted from this area and the temple built there might belong wholly to Jupiter, he decided to nullify the consecration of several shrines and chapels built there. These had been vowed by Tatius during his critical battle with Romulus and had been consecrated afterwards.

It is said that as the great work was begun the gods sent signs foretelling the destined greatness of the empire: although the birds of augury permitted the de-consecration of all the other shrines, at the shrine of Terminus they refused. This omen was interpreted in the following way: Since the home of Terminus could not be moved and he alone of all the gods could not be summoned away from the precinct consecrated to him, this meant that all Rome would be stable and enduring. After this portent of lasting stability, followed another omen foretelling the empire's vast extent. It is reported that when they were digging for the foundations of the temple a human head in a state of perfect preservation was found. This was a manifest prophecy that Rome would be the bulwark of the empire and the capital of the world. Such was the interpretation of both the prophets in the city and those whom were called for consultation from Etruria. This encouraged the king to spend even more, so that the money from the booty of Suessa Pometia, which had been intended to complete the whole work, was scarcely sufficient even for the foundations. Because of this (aside from the fact that he is the earlier authority) I prefer to believe Fabius rather than Piso. The former states that the original sum was only forty talents, while the latter says forty pounds of silver—an amount which could never be expected from the booty of a single city of that time, and which would be excessive for the foundations of any building even today.

56. Among Tarquinius Superbus' accomplishments was the building of the temple to Jupiter Capitolinus, of seats in the Circus, and of the Cloaca Maxima, the main artery of the sewage system of Rome. . . . In the midst of these operations a terrible portent was seen. A snake slid out from a wooden column, creating a great panic and disturbance in the palace. This did not so terrify the king as it filled him with anxious premonitions. Only Etruscan soothsayers were consulted to interpret prodigies for the state; but, being thoroughly frightened by this portent, which seemed to concern him only, he decided to consult the oracle at Delphi, the most renowned in the world. Since he dared trust no one else with the oracle's answers, he sent into Greece his two sons, through lands little known at that time and seas stranger still.

Titus and Arruns set out, and with them as a companion went the son of the king's sister, Lucius Junius Brutus, a young man of an intelligence far greater than that which he feigned. He had heard how the leading men of the state, among them his brother, had been put to death by Tarquin, and he resolved to give the king nothing to fear in his own temper nor to covet in his fortune; since the laws offered no protection he would find security in contempt. Therefore he deliberately accustomed himself to feign stupidity, and allowed the king to do what he wished with himself and his fortune. Not even at the sobriquet "Brutus" (Dullard) did he take offense; under the veil of this name the mind which was to free Rome might bide its time in secret.

This man, then, was taken to Delphi by Tarquin's sons, more as a butt for their amusement than as a companion. It is said that he carried with him and offered to Apollo a golden staff enclosed in a shaft of cornel wood as a symbolic representation of his own character. After they had arrived and had carried out their father's mission the young men conceived a desire to learn who would succeed to the throne. It is said that a voice answered from the innermost depth of the cave: "Whichever of you shall be first to kiss his mother shall receive the sovereignty of Rome." The Tarquins gave strict orders that this prophecy be kept secret in order that Sextus, who had been left at home, might not learn of it and might thus be deprived of a share of the throne. They drew lots to decide which one first should kiss his mother when they returned. But Brutus thought the oracle had a different significance; he pretended to trip, and as he fell he touched his lips to the earth, which is the common mother of all mankind.

57. [During the siege of Ardea] the young princes passed their idle hours dining and drinking together. Once when they were drinking at the quarters of Sextus Tarquinius where Collatinus Tarquinius too was dining, they fell to talking of their wives. Each praised his own in extravagant terms, and when rivalry grew warm Collatinus declared there was no need for words when a few hours would show them how far his own Lucretia surpassed the others. "Why don't we take horse, if we have energy and enterprise, and inspect our wives' characters in person? The best proof is what a man sees when he comes unex-

pected." They were all flushed with wine. "Come on,
then," they cried, and galloped off to Rome, where they
arrived as darkness was beginning to fall. From Rome they
went to Collatia, where they found Lucretia very differently employed from the princes' wives. These they had
seen whiling their time away in luxurious banqueting
with their friends, but Lucretia was sitting in her parlor,
late in the evening, busy with her wool, surrounded by
maids working by lamplight. The award for womanliness
went to Lucretia. She received the Tarquins and her husband graciously, and the victorious husband courteously
invited the princes into his home. It was then that Sextus
Tarquin conceived a villainous desire to force Lucretia's
virtue; not her beauty alone but her proven chastity
pricked him on. But for the present they concluded their
nocturnal escapade by returning to the camp.

58. A few days later, unbeknownst to Collatinus, Sextus Tarquin went to Collatia with a single attendant. His
design was not suspected, and he was graciously received and after dinner brought to a guest room. When
everything seemed safe and everyone asleep, fired with
passion and with sword drawn he approached sleeping
Lucretia. Holding her down with his left hand on her
bosom, he said: "Silence, Lucretia! I am Sextus Tarquin.
My sword is in my hand. You will die if you utter a sound."
Frightened out of her sleep, the woman saw there was no
help but only imminent death. Then Tarquin declared his
love, begged, mingled threats with prayers, brought to
bear all the arguments that could sway a woman. When
he saw she was obdurate, that not even fear of death
would move her, he compounded that fear with scandal:
by her corpse, he declared, he would place the dead
body of a slave he would murder, so that it would be said
she had been killed for foul adultery. With this awful prospect victorious lust downed stubborn modesty as if by

violence, and Tarquin departed, exulting in his ruthless assault on a woman's honor. Downcast at her disaster, Lucretia sent the same message to her father at Rome and her husband at Ardea: "Come with a single trusted friend; you must do this and do it quickly; a horrible thing has happened."

Lucretius brought Valerius, Volesus' son, and Collatinus brought Junius Brutus, with whom he chanced to be going to Rome when his wife's messenger encountered him. Lucretia they found sitting downcast in her room, and when her husband asked, "Is all well?" she answered, "All ill. What can be well for a woman when she has lost her chastity? The print of a strange man is on your bed, Collatinus. But only my body has been violated. My spirit is guiltless. Death shall be my witness. But pledge your honor with your right hands that the adulterer shall not go unpunished. Sextus Tarquin is the man who last night returned hostility for hospitality and by force of arms won the pleasure that is my bane, and his too if you are men." They took the pledge in due order, they consoled the sick-hearted woman by turning the guilt from the helpless victim to the sinning agent: "It is the mind that sins, not the body; where there is no intention, there is no blame." "What he must pay," said she, "is for you to determine; as for me, though I absolve myself of sin, I do not free myself of punishment. Never shall unchaste woman cite Lucretia's example as a plea for life." She had hidden a razor under her dress; this she plunged into her heart, and fell dying upon her wound. Husband and father raised the death wail.

59. The others were paralyzed with grief, but Brutus drew the dagger from the wound and held it before him, dripping with blood. "I swear by this blood," he said, "so chaste before tyrannical brutality—and I call you, gods, to witness: By fire, by sword, by whatever force I can com-

mand I will banish Tarquin the Proud with his accursed wife and all his children; and never will I allow him or anyone else to rule over Rome." He then handed the knife to Collatinus, then to Lucretius and Valerius as they stared in amazement at the miraculous change in Brutus' character. As he directed they took an oath; their grief began to change to anger, and together they followed Brutus' lead as he called upon them to overthrow the tyranny at once.

They carried Lucretia's body from her house into the forum where a crowd collected, astonished at the unheard-of outrage. Each man had his own complaint to make of the violence and depravity of the tyrant's family, and they were moved by the father's sadness. However, Brutus rebuked them for their tears and idle complaints and incited them to take up arms, as befitted men and Romans, against those who engineered this persecution. The bravest of the young men volunteered their arms immediately and the rest followed suit. Lucretia's father was left to hold Collatia; guards were posted to prevent the news of the rebellion from reaching the king, while the rest set out for Rome under Brutus' leadership.

When they arrived there, the sight of this large number of armed men created panic and confusion wherever they went; but when people saw that the force was led by the most prominent men in the city, they were assured that there was good reason for it. The news of the terrible incident affected the people at Rome just as it had at Collatia. They rushed from everywhere into the Forum. As soon as they arrived a herald summoned the people to hear the Tribune of the Celeres, an office which Brutus happened at the time to be holding. The speech which he gave revealed none of the character which he had previously feigned. He spoke of the lust and violence of Sextus Tarquinius, of the unspeakable violation of Lucretia and

her miserable death. . . . Of these and of more outrageous incidents, which the present grievance suggested
but which it is difficult for the historian to enumerate, he
reminded his listeners as he inspired the enraged multitude to depose the king and to banish Tarquin, his wife
and children. Then, collecting a force of young men who
gave their names as volunteers, he set out for the camp at
Ardea to stir the army against the king. The city he left
in charge of Lucretius, the prefect of the city appointed
by the king. During the disturbance Tullia fled from her
house pursued wherever she went by the curses of men
and women appealing to the Furies, the avengers of parents.

60. When news of this reached the camp the king was
alarmed at the uprising and set out at once for Rome to
quell the disturbance. Brutus, however, was informed of
the king's approach and took a different route in order to
avoid meeting him; he arrived in Ardea at almost the
same time as Tarquin reached Rome. There Tarquin
found the gates closed and a decree published ordering
his exile. Brutus was received as a liberator in the
jubilant camp and the sons of the king were expelled. Two
of them followed their father, who went into exile at Caere,
in Etruria. Sextus departed for Gabii, considering it almost as his own kingdom; but there he was murdered in
revenge for old hatreds which he had inspired by murder
and rapacity.

Lucius Tarquinius ruled for twenty-five years [534-
510 B.C.]; the Roman monarchy, from the founding of the
city to its liberation, lasted 244 years. Then, in accordance with the regulations of Servius Tullius, two consuls
were elected by the Comitia Centuriata with the prefect
of the city presiding. They were Lucius Junius Brutus and
Lucius Tarquinius Collatinus.

Book 2
509-468 B C

1. From this point my subject will be the history of a
free people—its deeds in peace and war, its magistrates
now elected annually, and the rule of laws more powerful than men.

The despotism of the last king added to the general
enthusiasm for this freedom. The prior kings had so ruled
that they might well be counted founders of the city, at
least of parts of it; for each added new sections to house
the population which their efforts had made larger.
Brutus earned much glory from the expulsion of the
tyrant; but undoubtedly even he would have acted very
much to the detriment of the people if he had ambi-
tiously wrested the throne from any of the prior kings before the time was ripe for liberty. The plebeians were a
miscellany of shepherds and vagabonds, fugitives from
their own countries, who had obtained liberty, or rather
escape from punishment, under the protection of the sanctuary at Rome. What would have happened if such men
had been freed from the threat of royal power? What if
they had been stirred by the violent harangues of tribunes
and had begun to pick quarrels with the patricians while
they were still strangers to the city? A sense of common responsibility comes only with family ties and a
slowly maturing love of the soil; the young state would
have been destroyed by dissension. Actually, the moderate
guidance and domination of the kings nurtured the state

until it matured and was able to produce a rich harvest of liberty.

The origin of this new liberty should not be attributed to any reduction in the authority possessed by the kings but to the limitation of the consular term of office to a single year. The earliest consuls retained all the prerogatives of kings and all the symbols of their authority; but in order to prevent the impression that one tyrant had simply been exchanged for two, one consul only was allowed the *fasces* (the symbols of absolute power). Brutus, with the consent of his colleague, was the first to hold the fasces. He was as zealous in guarding liberty as he had been in obtaining it. First of all he feared that entreaties and bribes of a king might later win over the people; so while they were still jealous of their new liberty he bound them by an oath to allow no man to assume royal power. Then, since many of the senatorial order had been killed during Tarquin's reign of terror, he increased the power of the senate by filling the vacancies. Selecting some of the leading men of equestrian rank, he increased the number of senators to three hundred; from this it is said the custom arose of calling the senators "Patres Conscripti"— or "The Fathers and the Enrolled." This measure did much to promote harmony among the citizens and sympathy between the patricians and the plebs. 2. Brutus then devoted his attention to religious matters.

3. No one doubted that war with the Tarquins was imminent, but it came later than anyone expected. Moreover, liberty was almost lost through subversion and treason, which the Romans least expected.

There were certain young men of high birth in Rome who were contemporaries and friends of the younger Tarquins and had been accustomed to living like princes. Under the monarchy they had been free to do as they pleased, and now that all were equal before the law, they wished to recover that license. They complained among themselves that the liberty of the others had been bought by their own servitude. The king, they said, was human and from him favors could be obtained, whether justified or otherwise; with him favoritism and partiality had their place; he could be severe, but could also be lenient, and he could distinguish between friends and enemies. The law, on the other hand, was an inanimate thing, deaf and inexorable, more advantageous to the weak than the powerful; it knew neither indulgence nor leniency for those who transgressed; and in view of human error, it was dangerous to rely upon innocence alone for security. Such reflections had already made them discontented when ambassadors arrived in Rome from the royal party. . . . The ambassadors were ostensibly seeking the return of the king's property but they secretly undertook a plot for the restoration of the monarchy. While pretending to solicit favor of the young nobles for their official requests, they were sounding their inclinations toward the monarchy. To those who seemed favorably disposed toward them they gave written messages from the Tarquins and with them made plans to admit the royal party secretly into the city by night.

5. The plot was discovered and reported by a slave, and the conspirators, among whom were the two sons of Brutus, were apprehended.

. . . After the property of the royal family had been plundered by the people the traitors were condemned and executed. This sentence was especially dramatic, since the office of consul imposed upon a father the duty of inflicting punishment upon his own children; the one man who should have been spared the sight of the execution had been appointed by fate to carry it out. The young men who stood tied to the stake were all of high birth, but the others were ignored as if they were unknown, and the eyes of all were upon the sons of the consul. Men did not pity them more for their punishment than for the crime which made it necessary. For in that year above all, they had persuaded themselves to betray their newly liberated country, their father its deliverer, the consulship which had its origin with their own family, the patricians, the plebs, all the men and gods of Rome, to a once tyrannical king who now was exiled as a public enemy.

The consuls took their seats upon the tribunal, and the lictors were ordered to carry out the sentence: The culprits were stripped and scourged, then beheaded. All the while the natural anguish of a father was apparent on Brutus' face as he performed his duty as public executioner.

After the Etruscan cities of Veii and Tarquinii had taken up the cause of the Tarquins and had been defeated by Rome, the former king appealed to King Porsinna of Clusium for aid. Porsinna marched upon Rome and would have taken the city without a siege but for the heroism of Horatius Cocles.

9. Porsinna believed it would promote Etruscan security for Rome to be ruled by a king, and Etruscan dignity for that king to be an Etruscan, and so marched to war against Rome. Never before was the senate so terrified; Clusium was very powerful, and Porsinna's reputation formidable. They feared not only the enemy but also their own citizenry; the plebs might receive kings into the city in a panic, and accept servitude as the price of peace. Many concessions were therefore granted to the plebeians by the senate at this time. The food supply received special attention, and agents were dispatched to the Volscii and to Cumae to buy grain. The monopoly of salt, which was very dear, was taken from private individuals and assumed by the government. The plebeians were relieved of imposts and taxes, and the burden shifted to the

rich who could bear it: the poor contributed enough if
they reared children. This indulgence of the senate produced such harmony in the state, despite the hardships
of blockade and famine, that nobles and commons alike
abhorred the name of king. Demagoguery, in later years,
never made a man so popular as good administration then
made the whole senate.

As the enemy drew near, everyone from the surrounding countryside fled into the city, which was then encircled
with guards. Some areas of the city seemed well protected
by the city walls and by the barrier of the Tiber river; but
the Sublician Bridge would have afforded the enemy access to the city if not for one man, Horatius Cocles. His
strength was the final rampart which fortune provided the
city. He happened to be stationed on guard at the bridge
when he saw the Janiculum suddenly taken by attack and
the enemy rush down from it at full speed. His own
men, when they saw this, threw down their arms and fled
from their posts in panic and confusion. Seizing one
after another, he tried to stop them, crying to them and
swearing by the faith of the gods that they were deserting
their posts in vain. If they crossed the bridge and
abandoned it, there would soon be more of the enemy
on the Palatine and Capitol than were now on Janiculum.
He admonished them to destroy the bridge with their
swords or with fire, or any way possible, while he withstood the enemy's attack, as long as he was able, alone.
With that he marched resolutely to the head of the bridge.

There he stood with his sword in his hand, a stirring
sight among the fugitives who had turned their backs upon
the fight. When the enemy caught sight of him, they were
astounded at his audacity. Two men were shamed into
remaining with him, Spurius Larcius and Titus Herminius,
both men of high birth and great personal reputation.
With their help Horatius repulsed the first and most vio-

lent assault; but he ordered them to retreat when only a small part of the bridge remained and those who were cutting it down shouted to them to go back. Then, looking round at the Etruscan leaders with fierce and menacing eyes, he challenged each one. He taunted them all with being slaves of tyrants and with attacking the liberty of others while being unconcerned for their own. For a moment they hesitated, each looking to the others to begin the battle; but at length, shame compelled them to attack. Raising the battle cry, from all sides they threw their spears at their single opponent. But all of them stuck in his shield, and Horatius remained unmoved, with feet firmly planted at the head of the bridge. They were about to dislodge him with a concerted charge, when the loud crash of the falling bridge and the Romans' shout of exultation announced that their work was completed. As the Etruscans hesitated in dismay, Horatius cried, "Father Tiber, I beseech you to receive these arms and this soldier in safety in your stream." With that, still wearing his armor, he dived into the river and with missiles falling all around swam safely to the shore. He had dared a deed which posterity has cherished in memory better than it has believed. In gratitude for such bravery a statue of Horatius was erected in the comitium, and he was given as much land as he could plow a furrow around in one day. In addition to these public honors the citizens individually showed their gratitude to Horatius: In spite of the great scarcity, they contributed to Horatius a share of their own supplies, each in proportion to his means.

11. After being repulsed in this first attempt, Porsinna decided to take the city by siege rather than by storm. He first established a garrison on the Janiculum and pitched camp on the plain by the banks of the Tiber. Then he set about collecting boats to guard the river and prevent grain from being transported across to Rome and also to

carry his own troops across to plunder whenever the occasion presented itself. Soon he made the area around Rome so unsafe that even the cattle were shut up in the city and no one dared to drive them out to graze. The Romans permitted the Etruscans to move about with such impunity as a stratagem rather than because of fear. The consul, Valerius, intended to wait for the opportunity to attack a large number unexpectedly when they were widely scattered; he disregarded small raids, resolving to revenge himself on a larger scale. In order to attract plunderers, he gave orders for a large number of his men to drive a herd of cattle on the next day out of the Esquiline Gate, which was farthest from the enemy camp. He was sure the enemy would get wind of this since many slaves were deserting because of the siege and famine. Just as he thought, they learned of it through a deserter, and a larger number than ever before crossed the river in hope of seizing the whole herd. Valerius ordered Titus Herminius to take a small number of troops and wait in ambush two miles away on the Via Gabina. He ordered Spurius Larcius with light-armed troops to take a post at the Colline gate until the enemy passed, then to cut off their retreat to the river. At the enemies' approach the other consul, Titus Lucretius, marched out to the Naevian gate with several companies, while Valerius himself charged from the Caelian hill with a group of picked men; these were the first whom the enemy saw. When Herminius heard the sounds of battle he rose from his ambush and attacked the enemy rear, driving them toward Lucretius. Answering shouts were heard on right and on the left, from both the Naevian and Colline gates. The plunderers were caught in the middle, surrounded by a larger force, but unable to retreat, and were cut to pieces. Thereafter the Etruscans ceased to venture so far from their own lines.

12. But the blockade remained as tight as ever. Grain grew more and more scarce and expensive, and Porsinna was confident of capturing the city, simply by refusing to move. Gaius Mucius, a young noble, thought it disgraceful for the Romans, now that they were free, to be blockaded within their city by an Etruscan enemy whom they had often routed; while in bondage to the king, the Romans had never been besieged by any foe. Thinking that this indignity should be avenged by some magnificent and daring deed, at first he decided to slip into the enemy camp without asking permission of the senate. But then it occurred to him that if he should go without permission of the consuls and without anyone's knowledge he might be captured by Roman pickets and brought back as a deserter—a reasonable suspicion in the city's present state. Therefore he went before the senate and addressed it: "I wish to cross the Tiber, Senators, and enter the enemy camp, not for booty nor merely to avenge their forays. With the help of the gods, I have in mind a greater deed." The senate gave its approval, and, concealing a sword under his tunic, he set out. It happened to be the Etruscan soldiers' payday, and when he reached the camp he mingled with the large crowd standing around the royal tribunal. The soldiers were receiving their pay from a scribe, dressed almost as grandly as the king, who was sitting on the tribunal beside him. Mucius could not ask which was Porsinna without betraying himself by his ignorance. Blindly trusting to fortune, he stabbed the scribe instead of the king. Turning, he rushed through the frightened crowd, clearing a way with his bloody sword; but at the uproar, men came running from every direction, and he was seized and dragged back by the king's bodyguard. Standing solitary before the tribunal, even in such dire jeopardy, he inspired more awe than he felt. "I am a Roman citizen," he said. "My name is Gaius Mucius. I

wished to slay you, as my enemy, and I am no more afraid to die than I was to kill. It is the Roman custom to act with daring and to suffer with resignation. I am not alone in harboring this design against you; there is a long line behind me seeking this glory. Make up your mind for a struggle in which you must risk your life each hour and always have an enemy in arms at your door. This is the war we Romans declare on you. You will have to fear no army marshaled against you in battle. The battle will be a single combat against you alone."

The king was both outraged and terrified. He threatened to burn Mucius at the stake unless he immediately revealed what kind of plot he was boasting of so ambiguously. To this Mucius answered, "See how important the body is to those who see glory before them." He plunged his right hand into a sacrificial brazier, and held it there resolutely, as if he did not feel the pain. The king jumped up in astonishment and ordered his guards to pull Mucius away from the altar. "You may go in safety," he said. "You have harmed yourself more than you tried to harm me. I would praise you for your courage, if it were dedicated to the good of my country. I absolve you from the penalty justified in warfare and release you untouched and unharmed." Mucius answered in acknowledgement of this kindness, "Since you honor bravery I shall grant you the information which you could not elicit by intimidation. Three hundred young Romans have taken an oath to attack you in this way. My lot was drawn first; the rest, as the lot of each man falls, will come in turn until someday fortune exposes you to attack."

13. Mucius later came to be called Scaevola because of the loss of his right hand. Upon his release, ambassadors from Porsinna followed him to Rome. This experience had so perturbed the king that he offered terms of peace to the Romans. Nothing had saved him but the

mistake of the assassin, and he realized that he might be exposed to the same peril as many times as there were conspirators. Among his proposals Porsinna introduced the question of restoring the Tarquins to the throne. He did this because he could not renege on his promise to the Tarquins, but he realized very well that the Romans would refuse. He also demanded that the territory taken from Veii be restored and that the Romans give hostages as a condition for withdrawing his garrison from the Janiculum. On these terms a treaty was compacted; Porsinna withdrew his army from the Janiculum and out of Roman territory. To Mucius, in reward for his valor, the Senate voted a grant of land across the Tiber. This tract later became known as the Mucian meadows.

With virtue thus so well rewarded, even women were inspired to seek public honor. Cloelia, one of the girls given as hostages, eluded her guards and escaped to the Tiber, whose banks were not far from the Etruscan camp. Leading the rest of the maidens, she swam across the river with spears falling all around and restored them all safely to their relatives in Rome. When this was announced to the king, at first he was incensed. He did not think the others important, but sent emissaries to Rome to demand Cloelia's return. Soon, however, his anger turned into admiration, and he declared that hers was a greater deed than those of Horatius and Mucius. He sent word that if she were not returned as a hostage he would consider the treaty broken; but if she was returned he would restore her to her parents unharmed. Both sides abided by their agreement. The Romans surrendered her as a guarantee of peace in accordance with the terms of the treaty; in the hands of the Etruscan king she was not only safe but honored for her courage. After praising the girl he announced that he would give her half of the hostages, whom she should choose. When the hostages were brought forward, she chose the adolescents. This was consistent with maidenly modesty and was approved by all the hostages, who felt that they should first be freed who were of the age most liable to abuse. When peace was restored, the Romans rewarded this newly discovered feminine heroism with a new kind of honor—an equestrian statue: A figure of a maiden seated on a horse was erected at the highest point on the Via Sacra.

Eight other Latin towns formed an alliance intended to challenge Rome's claims to dominance in Latium. The rivalry which resulted led to open warfare at the battle of Lake Regillus in 499 B.C.

19. Latin war which had been threatening for several years could no longer be avoided. Aulus Postumius, the dictator, and Titus Aebutius, the cavalry commander, proceeded with a large force of both cavalry and infantry to Lake Regillus near Tusculum, where they came upon the enemy. Word had come that the Tarquins were with the Latins, and the angry army could not be restrained from an immediate attack. Because of this the battle was exceptionally fierce and bloody. The commanders did not confine themselves to directing maneuvers; they personally took part in the fighting; almost none of the officers on either side, except for the Roman dictator, left the battle unwounded. Tarquinius Superbus was now infirm with age; but when he saw Postumius in the front line encouraging and marshaling his troops, he charged straight against him. He was wounded in the side, but was rescued by his own men who quickly rushed to his aid and carried him back to a place of safety. On the other wing the cavalry commander, Aebutius, charged upon Octavius Mamilius. The Tusculan commander caught sight of him coming, however, and spurred his horse forward toward him. They met with such violence that Aebutius'

arm was pierced through, and Mamilius was wounded in the breast. Mamilius fell back into the Latin second line; Aebutius could not hold a spear with his wounded arm and retreated from the battle. The Latin general was undeterred by his wound and continued to urge on his forces. When he saw his own men being beaten back he summoned a company of Roman exiles commanded by one of Tarquin's sons. The resentment of these Romans at the loss of their country and wealth inspired them with fury and for a short time they restored the battle.

20. As the Romans began to retreat in that area, Marcus Valerius, the brother of Publicola, caught sight of the young Tarquin fighting ferociously at the head of the exiles. Since his house had been responsible for expelling the tyrants, he was inspired to add to its glory the claim that it had destroyed them as well. Pointing his javelin at Tarquin, he spurred his horse and charged; but his quarry eluded him by withdrawing into his own line. As Valerius rushed recklessly into the exiles' line he was struck in the side. The wound of his rider did not check the horse, but Valerius slipped dying to the ground with his armor falling upon him. When the dictator saw this brave man dying, the exiles swiftly pressing forward, and his own forces falling back, he ordered his personal guard of picked troops to attack whomever they saw fleeing. Under this new pressure from the rear, the Romans who had panicked turned back toward the enemy and once again battle was restored. The company of the dictator also entered the battle for the first time, attacking the exiles; being fresh and eager, they easily cut to pieces their exhausted enemy. Here another duel between two officers took place. When the Latin general saw the company of exiles almost surrounded by the dictator and his troops, he hurried forward toward the front line with a small body of reserves.

Titus Herminius, a lieutenant, caught sight of the reserves advancing and recognized Mamilius by his dress and armor. With even greater fury than the cavalry commander had shown a short time before, he charged upon the enemy general and pierced him through the side with one blow. But as he was stripping the body he himself was struck by an enemy javelin; he was carried back to the camp, but died before they finished treating the wound. The dictator now rode quickly to his cavalry and urged them to dismount and aid the exhausted infantry. Immediately they leapt from their horses and rushed to the front, where they fought in the first rank with only their small shields for protection. The foot soldiers recovered their courage at once when they saw the young nobles fighting side by side with them, sharing their danger. At last the Latins were overcome and began to flee. The horses of the cavalry were brought forward so that they could pursue the enemy. The infantry followed behind.

In this critical battle the dictator overlooked no aid, divine or human. It is said that he vowed a temple to Castor and also proclaimed prizes to the first and second men entering the camp of the enemy. So great was the Romans' eagerness that they routed the enemy and overran their camp with the same charge. This was the battle of Lake Regillus. The dictator and cavalry commander returned in triumph to the city.

21. . . . Four years later [495 B.C.] the important news arrived of Tarquin's death. He died at Cumae, where he had sought asylum with the tyrant Aristodemus after the dissolution of Latin power. Both patricians and plebeians were elated at this announcement. But they were immoderately triumphant; and the plebs, who until this time had been treated with great consideration, soon found themselves exploited by their leaders.

The successive wars following the overthrow of the monarchy caused the common people particular hardship, and this economic stress was multiplied by the severity of the Roman law against debtors. This law, which bound the debtor to his creditor virtually as a slave, was not changed until 326 B.C. But discontent with it brought about the first secession of the plebeians, which was ended only by the institution of the plebeian tribunate in 494 B.C.

23. . . . . Meanwhile the state was torn with internal dissension. New animosity broke out between the patricians and the plebeians, chiefly because of the requirement of servitude for debtors. The plebeians complained loudly that after fighting foreign wars for liberty and empire, at home they were oppressed and made prisoners by their own fellow citizens; and that the freedom of the plebs was more secure in war among the enemy than among their own countrymen. This discontent already was growing spontaneously; but the sight of one man's cruel hardships brought it to a head.

An old man whose appearance gave evidence of great suffering suddenly entered the forum. His clothing was covered with filth, and the pale and emaciated condition of his body was even more shocking. His long unkempt beard and hair made his appearance almost bestial. In spite of his grotesque appearance he was recognized; some said that he had been a centurion, and recounted other military honors he had attained. He himself bared his breast and exhibited scars which bore witness to his honorable conduct in many battles. When he was asked the cause of his wretched condition he declared to all that while he had been fighting in the Sabine War all his property had been burned, the crops in his fields devastated, his flocks driven off; and when a special emergency tax was exacted at this difficult time he was driven into debt. As this debt had accumulated with excessive interest rates, it had first deprived him of the farm which had belonged to his father and grandfather, then of the rest of his belongings, and finally had spread like a disease to his own person. He had been dragged by his creditor not just into slavery, but into a place of punishment and torture. With these words he showed his back, bearing the welts of recent beatings.

When the crowd, which had grown to the size of a public assembly, saw and heard all this, an indignant clamor arose. Soon the pandemonium was no longer confined to the Forum, but had spread through the whole city. Men involved in debt—both those in chains and those still free—rushed into the streets from everywhere, imploring the protection of the Roman citizens; everywhere appeared people eager to join the insurrection; through every street ran shouting mobs of rioters to the Forum.

Only the prestige of the consuls was able to quell the fury of the mob, and the discontent causing it continued unabated. When news arrived that a Volscian army was marching against Rome, only an edict that any citizen might escape servitude by joining the army prevented the complete disaffection of the plebs. And after two further wars, when peace finally was established, again the problem of domestic concord presented itself.

32. The senators now were afraid that there would be a recurrence of cabals and intrigues if the army should be dismissed. Therefore, on the pretext of a renewal of hostilities with the Aequi the senate ordered the army to march out of the city; for although the dictator (now resigned) had recruited the army, the soldiers had taken their oath before the consuls, and the senators considered

them still bound by this oath of allegiance. However, this step only precipitated open sedition.

It is said that at first the plebeians talked of assassinating the consuls. But when they were told that a religious obligation could not be nullified by criminal action, they decided to adopt the suggestion of a certain Sicinius, and withdrew from the city to the Sacred Mount, which is beyond the River Anio about three miles from the city.

This is a more common version than that given by Piso, that they established themselves upon the Aventine. There, with no supplies but the bare essentials and no commander, they fortified a camp where they remained several days offering no provocation and receiving none.

The city was gripped with panic and paralyzed by mutual suspicion. The plebeians left in the city feared injury from the patricians; they, in turn fearing the plebeians, were unsure whether to want them to leave the city or to remain. How long, they wondered, would the crowd which had seceded keep the peace? What would happen if some foreign enemy should declare war in the meantime? Their only remaining hope, they thought, was to effect a reconciliation among the citizens by fair means or foul. They decided to send as the advocate Menenius Agrippa, an eloquent orator who was popular among the plebians, since he himself was of plebeian origin. It is said that when he was admitted into the camp, he merely told the following fable in the unpolished old-fashioned style:

"Once when a man's parts did not, as now, agree together but each had its own program and style, the other parts were indignant that their worry and trouble and diligence procured everything for the belly, which remained idle in the middle of the body and only enjoyed what the others provided. Accordingly they conspired that the hands should not carry food to the mouth, nor the mouth accept it, nor the teeth chew it. But while they angrily tried to subdue the belly by starvation, the members themselves and the whole body became dangerously emaciated. Hence it became evident that the belly's service was no sinecure, that it nourished the rest as well as itself, supplying the whole body with the source of life and energy by turning food into blood and distributing it through the veins." By thus showing that the plebeians' anger was like internal sedition in a body he swayed the men's minds.

33. After this, negotiations for a reconciliation were undertaken. The concession was made to the plebs that they should have their own special magistrate. Those elected to this office, which could not be held by a patrician, were to be sacrosanct and were to have the power of affording protection to any citizen against the consuls. Two men, Gaius Licinius and Lucius Albinus, were elected tribunes of the plebs [493 B.C.] and they chose three others as colleagues. One of these was the Sicinius who originally had suggested the withdrawal from the city, but the names of the others are uncertain.

Gnaeus Marcius, surnamed Coriolanus, a patrician who was forced into exile because of his opposition to popular reform, allied himself with the Volscian army and in 488 B.C. stood with an army before the walls of Rome.

40. A large number of matrons gathered about Venturia, the mother of Coriolanus, and Volumnia, his wife. It is uncertain whether this was inspired by the women's fear or was contrived by government officials; in any case, they succeeded in obtaining the assistance of mother and wife. Venturia, then a very aged woman, and Volumnia, carrying her two small sons, accompanied them into the enemy camp. With tears and prayers the women defended the city which the arms of men could not protect.

When they reached the camp it was reported to Coriolanus that a large number of women were present. Previously the majesty of the state, personified in its envoys, had failed to move him, as well as the religious awe which the sight of its priests had inspired. Now he resolved to be even more inflexible against women's tears. However, the excessive grief of Volumnia, who stood weeping between her daughter-in-law and her grandsons, soon attracted the attention of one of his friends, who said to him, "Unless my eyes deceive me your mother and wife and children are here." Coriolanus sprang from his seat like a madman and tried to embrace his mother; but she, abandoning her tears for words of anger, said, "Tell me before I suffer your embrace: Have I come to see my son or an enemy? Am I a captive in your camp or your mother? Is it for this that I have struggled through a long life and an unhappy old age—in order to see my son first an exile, then an enemy? Could you really devastate this land which gave you birth and nurtured you? However hostile and vengeful your coming, did not your anger subside when you crossed your country's borders? When you came in sight of Rome, did not this thought occur to you, 'Within those walls are my home and the gods of my family, my mother, wife and children?' But for me, Rome would not be besieged: If I had never had a son I should have died a free woman in a free country. I am able now to suffer no greater misery, and you no greater disgrace. But, miserable as I am I shall not be for long: It is these you must consider; for if you continue, only an untimely death or long slavery remains for them."

With these words his wife and children embraced him; at the same time a great wail arose from the crowd of women lamenting their own fate and that of their country.

At last he relented; after embracing his family he sent them away, and withdrew his army from before the city.

In the year 477 B.C. an army under the consul Titus Virginius was almost destroyed by a foray from the Etruscan city of Veii. Since wars with several other nations seemed imminent and it was apparent that Veii would continue its incursion, the Fabian clan offered to carry on this relatively minor campaign alone. Although later they were ambushed and annihilated, their noteworthy patriotism exemplifies the spirit which ultimately made Rome dominant in Italy and throughout the world.

48. . . . With affairs in this state the consul, Gaius Fabius, went before the senate and addressed it on behalf of his clan: "As you know, Senators," said he, "a large force is unnecessary for the war with Veii, but a garrison must constantly be maintained. Therefore, give the Fabian clan the responsibility for Veii and devote all your attention to our other campaigns. We will warrant that Roman sovereignty will be safe on that front. We propose to carry on this war as a private war, at our own expense, and it will be unnecessary for the state to provide either troops or money." A vote of thanks was enthusiastically approved. The consul then left the senate house and returned home escorted by the Fabii, who had stood in the vestibule awaiting the decision of the senate. After ordering them to assemble in arms the next day in front of his house, he dismissed them to go home.

49. The news spread throughout the city, and the Fabii were praised to the skies for assuming from the state all the burden and all the responsibility for the war with Veii. "If two other clans of the same strength should come forward and request responsibility for the Volscian and Aequian campaigns," the people said, "it would be pos-

sible to subdue all the neighboring states while the Roman people as a whole enjoyed the benefits of peace."

On the next day, the Fabii armed themselves and assembled as ordered. The consul, dressed in military attire, emerged from his house to see all his family drawn up in marching order in his courtyard. Taking his place in their midst, he gave the order to advance. Never has a smaller army marched through the city, or one more praised and admired by its fellow citizens. Three hundred six soldiers went by, all patricians, all of one family; any one of them might have been a worthy general, and together they might have made an excellent senate. With the resources of a single family they threatened destruction for the whole Veientine nation. A great crowd followed them excitedly: some, who were friends and relatives, were filled at once with boundless hope and unlimited fear; others, inspired by concern for their country, were transported with admiration and enthusiasm. "May you be as fortunate as you are brave," they shouted, "and may your venture end as happily as it has begun. From us you may expect consulships, triumphs, and all other rewards when you return." As they passed the Capitol and the citadel and other temples the people prayed to every god whom they saw or who occurred to their memory that they might be sending the Fabii to an auspicious destiny, and that soon they might safely restore them to their parents and their country. Their prayers were in vain. The Fabii passed through the right arch of the Carmental Gate and proceeded on their unhappy journey to the river Cremera. Here there was a position which seemed strategic for a fortified garrison.

In 483 B.C. an agrarian law was passed authorizing the appointment of a commission to distribute to the plebs a portion of the public land. This law was allowed to remain a dead letter until 474 B.C. when a tribune indicted

the consuls Lucius Furius and Gaius Manlius for not en-
forcing it.

54. The indicted Furius and Manlius went around in mourning among the younger senators as well as among the plebs. They warned them insistently to avoid public offices and the administration of public affairs. For the consular *fasces,* the *toga praetexta,* and the curule chair should be regarded as nothing more than funereal splendor. They were doomed to death by these symbols of renown just as much as the sacrificial victim by the fillet on its head. But if they still were attracted to the consulship they should recognize that it had been shackled and made impotent by the power of the tribunes. It had become necessary for the consul, like a subordinate, to do everything at the tribune's beck and call. But if a consul should act on his own initiative or show considera- tion for the patricians—if he should imagine that the state consisted of others besides the plebs, he should re- member the exile of Gnaeus Marcius and the condemna- tion of Menenius.

The senators soon were aroused by these words and began to hold private rather than public sessions, which were open only to a few. As a result, they found agree- ment upon this one point—that they must resort to any expedient to save the defendants. Moreover, the most vi- olent method seemed the most acceptable, and volunteers were available for the most daring crime. Thus, on the day of the trial, as time passed, the plebeians who at first were waiting with great expectation in the Forum began to wonder when the tribune did not come. Then, as the delay became more suspicious, they believed that he had been intimidated by the patricians and began to complain that the public interest had been betrayed. Finally, how- ever, the news arrived that the tribune had been found dead in his house. As this news spread through the as-

sembled crowd it scattered in every direction like an army
routed after the death of its general. The tribunes especially were terrified. They considered the death of their
colleague a warning that the laws regarding their inviolability were absolutely powerless to protect them. The patricians, on the other hand, were highly elated; so far
were they from regretting the crime, that even the innocent wished to be considered its perpetrators, and it was
openly asserted that the power of the tribunes could be
curbed by violence.

Book 3
4 6 7 - 4 4 6   B C

*In 458 B.C. when a Roman army was surrounded by
the Aequi and held under siege, Lucius Quinctius Cincinnatus was appointed dictator. While the incident itself,
in view of late Roman history, seems an unimportant one,
Cincinnatus was enlarged by tradition into the Roman
version of the homespun hero.*

26. For those who are disdainful of all human values except riches and who think that high position and
excellence are impossible without great wealth, it is worth-
while to listen to the following story.

The one hope of the people and the empire of Rome,
Lucius Quinctius, cultivated a farm of four acres on the
other side of the Tiber. It was directly across from the
spot where the dockyard now is situated and to this day
is called the Quinctian meadows. There he was found by

the deputation from the senate, either bent over his spade as he dug a ditch or plowing—at any rate, as historians agree, occupied with the work of his farm. After greetings had been exchanged, they expressed the wish that "it might turn out well for both him and his country" and requested that he put on his toga and hear the mandate of the senate. Crying out in surprise, "Is everything all right?" he called to his wife to hurry and bring the toga from the cottage. There, after wiping off the dust and sweat, he put it on and came forward to the deputation, who hailed him dictator and summoned him into the city. When they had explained the army's alarming situation he crossed over the Tiber in a boat provided by the state. On the other side he was greeted by his three sons, who had come out to meet him, followed by other friends and relatives, and by most of the senators. Accompanied by this gathering he was conducted to his house by the lictors. A great crowd of plebeians also collected, not at all overjoyed to see Cincinnatus' selection; they considered the office too powerful and the man himself even more relentless and uncompromising. For that night no precautions were taken, aside from posting a watch in the city.

27. The next morning Cincinnatus arose and went into the Forum before daybreak, where he named Lucius Tarquitius as master of horse. This man was a patrician by birth, although he had been forced by poverty to serve in the infantry, and was considered the finest soldier in Rome. Accompanied by Tarquitius, the dictator went into the assembly of the people, where he proclaimed a suspension of all civic affairs, ordered shops to be closed throughout the city, and forbade the transaction of all private business. He then issued an order that everyone of military age should report in arms at the Campus Martius before sunset, carrying rations for five

days and twelve stakes for palisades. Those too old for
military duty he ordered to prepare rations for their
neighbors serving in the army while these were preparing their arms and looking for stakes. Immediately the
young men ran to collect stakes, taking the first they
came to, with no one stopping them, since everyone was
eager to carry out the orders of the dictator. At the appointed time the line was drawn up in an order adapted
for battle as well as marching, in the event that the occasion should arise; the dictator led the infantry in person,
with Tarquitius at the head of the cavalry.

*Cincinnatus surprised the enemy at night and the
Aequi soon were reduced from besiegers into besieged.*

28. . . . Beset now by a double attack, the Aequi
abandoned their resistance for supplication, begging first
the commander of one army, then the other, not to make
their victory a slaughter. The consul ordered them to go
to the dictator. Cincinnatus, wishing to humiliate them
in defeat, angrily ordered that their general Gracchus
Cloelius and their other officers be brought to him in
chains, and the town of Corbio be evacuated. He did not
want the blood of the Aequi, he said; they could go if
they would confess that they were conquered and pass
under the yoke. A yoke was made of three spears and
under it were marched the Aequi.

33. In the 302nd year after the founding of Rome
[451 B.C.] its form of government was changed for a
second time. The sovereignty now passed from consul
to decemvirs, just as previously the consuls had received
it from the kings. This change was temporary, however,
and of short duration; for although this government flour-
ished in the beginning, it soon grew to great excess. Because of this it withered and fell more quickly, and the
practice was reinstituted of investing two men with the
consular power and title.

Those chosen as decemvirs were Appius Claudius, T. Genucius, P. Sectius, L. Veturius, C. Julius, A. Manlius, P. Sulpicius, P. Curiatus, T. Romilius, and Spurius Postumius. The position was conferred upon Claudius and Genucius, who were consuls-elect for that year, in compensation for the office of which they were deprived. To Sestius, one of the consuls in the previous year, it was given because he had proposed the change to the senate against the wishes of his colleague. The next three were the envoys who had gone to Athens; they were selected as a reward for their long expedition and because it was thought that their knowledge of foreign laws would be useful in formulating a new constitution. It is said that for the last four positions old men were chosen who would not present vigorous opposition to the measures proposed by the others. Because of his popularity among the plebeians the direction of this commission was accorded to Appius; he had abandoned his former role as a harsh and relentless persecuter of the plebs, and suddenly emerged in a new character, becoming a friend of the people and a suitor for their favor. Each of these men administered justice in turn every tenth day; on that day he was accompanied by ten lictors, while only one attended each of his colleagues.

In spite of an exceptional unanimity among them (a thing which often proves harmful to private citizens) they exhibited the greatest equity toward others. One instance will serve to illustrate their moderation: The right of judgment without appeal was entrusted to this office. However, when a corpse was found buried in the house of a patrician, P. Sestius, and was brought into the assembly, the decemvir in charge, C. Julius, limited himself to indicting Sestius. In this case of obvious guilt he appeared before the assembly as a prosecutor of a man whom he could legally have judged, and relinquished his own prerogative in order to increase the rights of the people.

34. Thus, even while the decemvirs were occupied with the framing of laws, the highest and lowest citizens alike received this prompt execution of justice, as impartial as if pronounced by an oracle. At length they called an assembly and exhibited to the people the ten tablets so eagerly awaited by all. Then, with a prayer that their work might prove beneficial to the commonwealth, themselves, and their children, they directed the people to go and read the laws proposed. They had, they said, to the best of their judgment, provided equality before the law for high and low alike; however, the wisdom and understanding of many men would be more reliable than that of ten alone. They requested the people to reflect upon and discuss each detail and to bring before the assembly whatever in each article was over-emphasized or slighted. In this way the Roman people would be governed by laws which they had not only ratified but had themselves unanimously proposed. When it appeared that each article of the code had been amended sufficiently in accordance with the opinions expressed about them, the ten tables were introduced before the Comitia Centuriata and approved. These same statutes, even in the profusion of laws of the present day, remain the basis of all public and private jurisprudence.

Later the opinion came generally to be expressed that two tables were still needed in order to complete, so to speak, the whole corpus of Roman law. As the day of election approached, the prospect of this caused the people to wish to appoint decemvirs for a second term. For, besides hating the name of consul as much as that of king, the plebeians now no longer required even the aid of the tribunes, since the decemvirs recognized the right of appeal from one to the other.

35. But after it was announced that the election of decemvirs would be held on the third market day, a great flurry of electioneering arose. Prominent men in the city began to solicit votes shamelessly, inspired, of course, by fear that if they did not seek the office it might fall into improper hands. They now sought election to an office which they had vigorously opposed, servilely beseeching the votes of the plebeians with whom they had fought. Appius Claudius was prompted to feverish activity by the fear that, at his time of life, after holding positions of great importance, he was in danger of losing this one. It was difficult to know whether to consider him a decemvir or a candidate; he seemed more like a person ambitious for an office than one who already held it. He slandered candidates of high rank, praised the humblest and basest, bustled about the Forum with tribunes like Duillius and Icilius, using their influence to obtain the votes of the plebeians.

Up to that time his colleagues had been especially devoted to him, but now they looked upon him in amazement, wondering what he meant. They were sure that he was insincere, and that this new-found affability was not disinterested. They became convinced that this self-abasement and association with private citizens were symptoms not of haste to be rid of an office, but of anxiety to prolong it by any means possible. But since they did not dare to oppose his efforts openly, they tried to moderate his violent activity by feigning compliance with his wishes. They agreed to appoint him, as the youngest of their group, to preside over the elections. This stratagem was designed to prevent his election, for no one had ever certified his own election except for tribunes of the plebs—and even this had the poorest of precedents. Nevertheless, he declared that he would hold the election, and he turned this impediment into an opportunity. He conspired to bring about the defeat of the two Quinctii, Capitolinus and Cincinnatus, of his own uncle, C. Claudius, a steadfast supporter of the nobility, and of other citizens of this rank; he certified the election of men who were far from their equals, while announcing his own name among the first. This act was disapproved all the more by good citizens because no one had ever thought he would dare it. With him were elected M. Cornelius Maluginensis, M. Sergius, L. Minucius, Q. Fabius Vibulanus, Q. Poetelius, T. Antonius Merenda, K. Duillius, Spurius Oppius Cornicen, and Manius Rabuleius.

36. Now Appius abandoned his impersonation. He began to live according to his natural disposition and to mold his colleagues according to his own pattern before they succeeded to office. Each day they held private conferences, where they secretly elaborated plans for tyranny; confident in these plans, they no longer concealed their arrogance, but became difficult to approach, and uncivil to those who spoke to them. Affairs continued in this atmosphere until May 15, at that time the usual date for entering office.

From its first day their term of office was distinguished by an exhibition which caused great apprehension. The previous decemvirs had observed a rule that only one at a time should be accompanied by *fasces,* and had rotated this emblem of sovereignty among themselves; but now all ten suddenly appeared in public accompanied by lictors. 120 lictors filled the Forum, holding before them axes bound up in rods. They asserted that there was no reason to take the *fasces* away, since by their office the decemvirs were granted absolute power of life or death. In them the people saw ten kings instead of one, and terror multiplied among both nobles and commoners. They were sure that they were only seeking a pretext for instituting a reign of terror; that if anyone in the senate or among the people should raise his voice in remembrance of liberty immediately the axes would fall so as to intimidate the rest. The previous decemvirs had permitted their decrees to be revoked by appeal to a colleague, and had even referred to the popular assembly matters within their own jurisdiction. But these men abolished the protection of appeal to the people and by agreement repudiated repeal to each other.

For some time the terror was universal, but soon the decemvirs began to direct their oppressive measures toward the plebs. They avoided offending the patricians, but conspired cruelly and arbitrarily against men of the lower classes. In judgment they considered only personalities, not the facts of the case; with them interest supplanted justice. They pronounced their decisions in the Forum, but made them in their homes. If anyone appealed, he went away regretting that he had not abided by the decision of the first decemvir. The rumor even spread that the suffering which they had contrived was not temporary; that they had sworn an oath to hold no more elections and to retain their power, now that it was obtained, by making their office permanent.

The decemvirs began to suffer serious reverses. When no elections were called the following May the plebs were despondent, and criticism even from the patricians could no longer be ignored. Danger from the enemy forced the levy of an army, but the disaffected Roman soldiers suffered several defeats.

43. To the disasters suffered at the hands of the enemy the decemvirs added two unspeakable crimes. Lucius Siccius, seeing their hatred of the decemvirs, began secretly to disseminate among the common soldiers ideas about electing tribunes and of seceding. He was therefore sent to select a place for a camp site and with him were

sent soldiers under orders to assassinate him in some suitable spot. He did not die unavenged, however, for he was a man of great strength, and even though surrounded defended himself courageously. Several of the assassins fell around him and the survivors reported in the camp that Siccius, along with some of the soldiers, had fallen into an ambush and died fighting bravely. At first they were believed; but soon a cohort, with the permission of the decemvirs, was dispatched to bury the victims. They discovered that none of the bodies had been plundered, that Siccius was lying in the middle of the others who lay facing him, and that there were no enemy bodies to be found or any traces of the enemy withdrawal. When they brought back the report to the camp that Siccius had evidently been killed by his own men the army was enraged; it was decided to take Siccius' body straight back to Rome. However, the decemvirs thwarted this by hastily giving Siccius a military funeral at public expense. He was buried amid great mourning on the part of the soldiers, and the gravest suspicions against the decemvirs.

44. In the city a second atrocity took place—this one inspired by lust. Its outcome was equally as disgraceful as the violation and death of Lucretia, which had caused the expulsion of the Tarquins; thus the decemvirate suffered not only the same end as the monarchy, but for the same reason.

Appius Claudius was seized with passion for a certain plebeian maiden whose father, a courageous soldier and a worthy citizen, was serving as a centurion in the army at Mount Algidus. His wife was a person of equally high character, and their children were being educated to these same principles of conduct. His daughter, a mature young woman of remarkable beauty, was betrothed to Lucius Icilius, a former tribune who was an energetic and courageous defender of the plebeian cause. Appius passionately tried to seduce her both by money and by promises, but, finding her modesty proof against all approaches, vengefully resolved to use force. He instructed one of his clients, Marcus Claudius, to claim the girl as his slave and not to yield to demands that she be freed pending trial. He was sure that in her father's absence his audacity would be successful. As the girl entered the Forum, where the grammar schools then were located, the decemvir's procurer laid his hand on the girl, calling her a slave and the daughter of his slave; he ordered her to follow him or be dragged away by force. The girl stood petrified with fear but the shrieks of her nurse imploring "the protection of the Roman citizens" attracted a crowd. The names of her father Verginius and her fiancé Icilius were well known, and their popularity as well as the anger at this outrageous action won over the crowd. Thus she was saved from violence.

The claimant protested that he wished to proceed legally, not by force, and that there was no need to rouse a mob. He summoned the girl into court and her supporters advised her to follow. They went to the tribunal of Appius, where the claimant recited a tale already known by the judge, since he had composed its plot. The girl, he said, was born secretly in his own house, clandestinely taken to the house of Verginius, and falsely represented to him as his child; he had sufficient evidence of this to convince even Verginius, who actually was more wronged than he; but in the meantime it was right for her master to have custody of the girl. The girl's supporters said that Verginius was away in the service of his country but could be present in two days if he was notified of the matter; it was unjust for a suit to be tried involving a man's children in his absence. They demanded that Appius adjourn the case until the father's arrival; that he bind her over to her supporters in accordance with the law which he himself had enacted, and not allow the reputation of a maiden to be endangered even before her liberty was threatened.

45. Appius prefaced his decision with the remark that the very law which the friends of Verginia pleaded was proof that he loved liberty. But liberty would find security in the law only if it was uniform for all persons and causes. In the case of one who was in servitude this right existed, since anyone might file suit on his behalf. But in the case of a girl still in the care of her father there was no one to whom her master was obliged to yield her custody. He decreed therefore, that the father should be sent for, and that the claimant should not be deprived of his rights, but should take possession of the girl and guarantee her appearance upon the arrival of her father.

Everyone murmured against this outrageous decree, but no one dared to speak out against it until Publius Numitorius, the girl's grandfather, and her fiancé Icilius arrived. The crowd thought that Icilius, if anyone, could resist Appius. But when they made way to let him pass a lictor declared that the decision had been made and, when Lucius loudly protested, undertook to eject him. This outrageous treatment would have infuriated even a placid temperament. Icilius cried out, "You will have to eject me with a sword, Appius, in order to succeed in hushing this up. I am going to marry this maiden and I intend to have an innocent bride. Call all your colleagues and lictors: Prepare the rods and axes for execution, but the betrothed of Icilius shall not remain in any house but her father's. Even if you have deprived us of the protection of the tribunes and the right of appeal to the people, the two bulwarks of our liberty, our wives and children are not subject to your lust. Flog and behead us! But let feminine virtue at least be safe. If she suffers any violence, I on behalf of my betrothed will appeal to these citizens, Verginius on behalf of his daughter to the soldiers, and all of us will implore the help of gods and men; you will only carry out your decision by killing us first. I beg you Appius, consider where this will end. Let Verginius when he comes determine what should be done about his daughter; but if he yields to this man's claims he must assuredly find another match for her. But I will die protecting my betrothed rather than desert her."

46. The crowd was aroused and a fight seemed imminent. Lictors had surrounded Icilius, but the dispute had gone no further than threats when Appius yielded. Icilius, he said, did not wish to protect Verginia, but was an ambitious man who was eager to reinstate the tribunate; he was looking for an opportunity to stir up rebellion. However, he would provide him no chance that day. In order to make plain that the concession was made not to his temper but to the absent Verginius, to the name of father, and to liberty, he would postpone his decision, asking Marcus Claudius to relinquish his right and allow the girl to go free until the following day. But if her father had not arrived by then, he warned Icilius and his ilk that as the author of the law he would uphold it, and as decemvir enforce it with firmness. And he would not call on the lictors of his colleagues to repress rabble-rousers; his own were quite sufficient.

Now that the threat of injury had been postponed, the girl's supporters withdrew to deliberate their next move. They decided that the brother of Icilius and the son of Numitorius should start at once and summon Verginius from the camp as quickly as possible; for the girl's safety depended upon his being present on time to protect her. These two started immediately and rode at full speed for Verginius' camp. Meanwhile the claimant pressed Icilius, insisting that he present bail for the girl's freedom; but

Icilius continued to delay in order for the messengers to get to the camp, saying the matter was being attended to. Everywhere people in the crowd raised their hands, to indicate their readiness to serve as his security. "Thank you," he said, with tears in his eyes. "Tomorrow I may need your help, but now I have securities enough." So Verginia was freed on the security of her relatives.

Appius waited awhile in order to avoid the impression that he had convened his court for that case only. Soon, however, he found that concern was so great for this one case that no other plaintiffs were interested in appearing. Therefore he hurried home and wrote to his colleagues in the camp not to grant Verginius a furlough, but to arrest him instead. This shameful message arrived too late, as it deserved. Verginius obtained leave and set out at about the first watch, but the orders for his detention were not delivered until the next morning.

47. At dawn the next day the citizens excitedly gathered in the Forum. Verginius and his daughter, who was attended by several matrons, entered the Forum followed by a large crowd of supporters. Both were dressed in mourning. Verginius immediately began to go about taking people by the hand, begging them to help him not only as a favor but as a debt they owed him. Daily, he said, he stood in the battle line defending their wives and children, and no other man could boast of such heroic deeds in war. Yet what good did it do if with the city still safe, their children had to endure the worst calamities that could follow its capture? To one person after another he pleaded in this way. Icilius did the same, but the silent weeping of the women moved men more than any words.

Appius—who was smitten rather with madness than with love—was unmoved by all this. He mounted the tribunal, and the plaintiff began to say a few words, complaining that the decemvir's desire for popularity had deprived him of his rights the day before. But before he finished and before Verginius had a chance to answer, Appius interrupted. Perhaps the words with which he justified his decision have been authentically transmitted by some of the ancient authorities. But since I can find nothing which might justify such a perverse judgment, it seems best to relate only the naked fact, of which there is no doubt: He decreed that the girl was a slave.

Silence fell. The crowd stood aghast with wonder and disbelief. Then, as M. Claudius went to take the girl, the women around her began to wail. Verginius pointed at Appius and cried, "I have betrothed my daughter to Icilius, not to you, and I have trained her for marriage, not harlotry. Do you wish to satisfy your lusts at your whim as do cattle or wild beasts? I do not know whether the men present will tolerate this, but I hope that those who are armed will not." The claimant was pushed away by the circle of women and the girl's supporters, and finally a herald commanded silence.

48. The decemvir was beside himself with lust. "You yourselves," he told the crowd, "have witnessed Icilius' insolence yesterday and the violent behavior of Verginius today. Not only from these actions but from definite evidence which has been discovered I have ascertained that secret meetings were held throughout the night, plotting to foment an uprising. Being aware of the impending danger I have brought with me a band of armed men, not to harm any peaceable person, but to restrain those who wish to disturb the peace. It behooves you, therefore, to remain quiet," he said. "Go, lictor, disperse the mob and make way for the master to take possession of his slave."

When he wrathfully thundered these words the crowd separated spontaneously and the girl stood deserted and helpless. Verginius saw that there was no help left and he cried out, "I beg you, Appius, make allowance for a father's grief if I have been abusive. Let me question the girl and her nurse in order to find out the truth about this matter. If I am really not her father I can leave her with more peace of mind." When he was given permission to do this he led his daughter and the nurse aside, to the shops near the shrine of Venus Cloacina, now called the New Shops. There he suddenly seized a knife from a butcher and cried, "In this one way only can I set you free, my daughter." Plunging the knife in her breast and looking up toward the tribunal, "With this blood, Appius," he cried, "I consecrate your head to perdition!" Appius, frightened by the clamor which arose at this awful deed, ordered the lictors to arrest Verginius; but by clearing a path before him with the knife he succeeded in reaching the city gate under the protection of the crowd of people following. Icilius and Numitorius picked up the lifeless body and showed it to the people, lamenting Appius' brutality, the girl's unhappy beauty, and the necessity forced upon her father. Behind them followed the women who had attended her, weeping and crying words of the kind which arise out of woman's great sensitivity and make her grief more pitiful. "Must we bear children under these conditions?" they pleaded. But the men talked only of the loss of the tribunician power, the loss of the right of appeal to the public assembly, and of the wrongs suffered by the people.

Verginius returned to the army on Mount Vecilius and aroused the soldiers, who returned to Rome and encamped on the Aventine, and later on the Mons Sacer (Sacred Mountain). Encouraged by their example, the plebeian civilians also seceded for a second time and joined them, demanding restoration of the office of trib-

une and the right of appeal. These demands were
granted, and a series of measures (the Valerian-Horatian
laws) were passed which greatly increased plebeian
power (449 B.C.).

55. In the first place it was a disputed legal question
whether the patricians were to be bound by laws enacted
by the popular assembly. Therefore the consuls (Lucius
Valerius and Marcus Horatius) proposed to the Comitia
Centuriata a law that all measures of their tribal assembly
should be binding on the people as a whole. This law
gave the tribunes a potent weapon, since the tribune initiated legislation. Another consular law was passed concerning the right of appeal, an important safeguard to
liberty which the decemviral power had abolished. This
right they not only restored but also reinforced by enacting a second law that if anyone caused the appointment
of a magistrate from whom there was no right of appeal,
he might lawfully be killed; such a homicide was not to
be a capital offense. When thus they had provided sufficient protection for the plebs . . . they turned their attention to protecting the inviolability of the tribunes.
By reviving certain ancient religious ceremonies they
strengthened this principle of inviolability which had
been almost forgotten. And in order to make the tribunes
sacrosanct by law as well as religion they passed a law
that if anyone should harm a tribune, aedile, judge, or
decemvir his person should be devoted to Jupiter and his
property sold at the temple of Ceres, Liber and Li-
bera. . . .

These, then, were the laws introduced by the consuls.
These same consuls also enacted a regulation that decrees of the senate, which formerly had been suppressed
and altered at will by the consuls, should be deposited
with the plebeian aediles in the temple of Ceres. Marcus

Duillius, a tribune, introduced a bill which was passed by
the plebs that anyone responsible for a failure to elect
tribunes or anyone who should create a magistracy from
whom there was no appeal should be scourged and beheaded. All these measures the patricians disliked, but
did not oppose, since they had not yet been used against
any particular individual.

Book 4

4 4 5 - 4 0 4 B C

1. The consuls that succeeded [in 454 B.C.] were
Marcus Genucius and Gaius Curtius. The year was one
of strife, both at home and abroad. At its beginning a
plebeian tribune, Gaius Canuleius, introduced a bill le-
galizing marriage between patricians and plebeians. This
the patricians thought would contaminate their blood and
nullify the prerogatives of their clans. But then the tribunes began to suggest that one of the consuls should be
elected from among the plebeians. Support for this proposal, at first tentative, grew to the point that nine tribunes introduced a second bill to grant the people power
to elect consuls either patrician or plebeian at their discretion. This bill, the patricians believed, would if passed
not only make the supreme authority accessible to the
lowest classes, but deprive the nobles of it completely.

It was with pleasure, therefore, that the patricians received word that new foreign wars were threatening.
Ardea had defected in protest at a Roman judgment
which dispossessed them of part of their territory, Veii

was ravaging the Roman frontiers, and Volsci and Aequi
were vehement in their complaints at the fortification of
Verrugo. Even disastrous war seemed preferable to ignominious peace. The patricians were sure that the war
effort would silence the agitation of the tribunes, and so,
upon receipt of exaggerated reports of the danger, the
senate ordered an immediate levy and a speedy mobiliza-
tion. . . . At this Canuleius vehemently declared before
the senate that it was futile for the consuls to try to
divert the interest of the plebs from the recent proposal
by frightening them. While he was alive, he said, they
would never hold a levy until the plebs had voted on the
measures introduced by himself and his colleagues. Then
he immediately called an assembly of the people.

2. Simultaneously the consuls began to incite the senate against the tribune, and the tribune to stir up the people against the consuls. The consuls declared that the
demagoguery of the tribunes could no longer be endured;
they had now gone too far. "A greater struggle is being
fomented at home than abroad," they said. "This, of
course, is no more the fault of the plebeians than of the
patricians, or of the tribunes than of the consuls. In any
state the activities which reap the greatest rewards always
flourish. Incentives evoke merit both in peace and in war.
But in Rome the greatest prize is awarded to insurrection. This always has won honor for individuals as well as
classes. There will be no end to this so long as revolutionaries are honored for their success. What radical
changes is Gaius Canuleius embarking upon! He is attempting to mongrelize the clans, to throw the taking of
the auspices into disorder. As a result nothing will remain
pure and undefiled! All distinctions will be nullified until
no one can recognize himself or his family! What else will
indiscriminate marriages between the patricians and the
plebs lead to but promiscuous intercourse like that of wild

beasts? The offspring of such a union will not know whose
blood flows in his veins or what religious rites he may perform. Half patrician, half plebeian, he will not be at peace
even with himself. But it is too little for these demagogues
to make chaos of all religious and secular conventions:
now their target is the consulship. At first they only suggested that one consul be elected from the plebeians; but
now they propose that the consuls be elected from either
order without distinction. And you may be sure that the
plebeians will elect the greatest revolutionaries among
their ranks. Your consuls will be men of the caliber of Canuleius and Icilius. The consulship is a sovereign power
of truly royal dignity: God forbid that it should ever be so
degraded! We would die a thousand deaths to prevent
such a disgrace. Concessions do not make the plebs more
reasonable, but spur them on to progressively more extravagant demands. Our ancestors could not have fore-
seen this or they would have endured any amount of strife
rather than allow such law as they did to be imposed
upon them. Once they granted tribunes to the plebs they
were forced to allow further concessions. You should recall the dignity and grandeur of the senate as you inherited it from your fathers, reflect what it will be when
you hand it down to your sons, and consider how the plebs
will glory in their redoubled influence. There can be no
end to this as long as you have plebeian tribunes and
patricians in the same state. Either that office or the patrician order will have to be abolished. Their brazen insolence must be resisted, and better late than never. Are
they to be allowed first to foment discord and incite neighboring states against us, then to prohibit the state to arm
and defend itself? After practically inviting the enemy,
can they forbid us to levy an army against him? But
Canuleius has the audacity to declare in the senate that
he will forbid the levy unless the senate acknowledges

defeat and accepts his laws! What is he doing but threatening to betray his country, to permit it to be attacked by the enemy? What confidence these words must inspire, not among the Roman plebs, but among the Volscians, the Aequi, and the Veientines! Will they not hope, under Canuleius' leadership, to be able to scale the Capitol and the citadel? If the tribunes have not deprived the senators of their courage along with their authority and prestige, we, the consuls, are prepared to lead you against the lawlessness of the citizens, then against the arms of the enemy."

3. While this was taking place in the senate, Canuleius was speaking on behalf of his proposals and against the consuls: "Roman citizens, I have observed before now how the patricians contemn you, how unworthy they consider you to live in the same city with them. But their present violent reaction to our proposals makes it obvious. And what is the purpose of these bills but to remind them that we are their fellow citizens, and if we do not possess the same resources, we do live in the same country? In one proposal we seek the right of intermarriage—a right which is often granted to foreign peoples. Indeed, we have granted citizenship, which is more important than intermarriage, even to conquered enemies. In the other bill there is nothing new or strange; we are only demanding the fundamental right of the Roman people to confer offices upon whomever they wish. Why should they turn heaven and earth upside down? Why was I almost attacked in the senate just now? Why do they threaten to use violence and to cease to observe our inviolability? If the Roman people are granted the privilege of conferring the consulship upon whom they wish, and if a plebeian worthy of the highest office is not denied the hope of attaining it, will Rome cease to stand? Is a plebeian the same as a slave or a freedman that he is so unfit to become con-

sul? Do you realize in what contempt you are held? If they could they would deny you a share in the very light of day. They are indignant that you breathe, and speak, and have human form. So help me, they even say that it would be an offense to the *gods* for a plebeian to become consul.

"I ask you, even if we do not have access to the records of the priests, do we not know what every foreigner knows —that the consuls are successors to the kings and have no authority or privilege not previously vested in the kings? You would think that no one had ever heard that Numa Pompilius was not even a citizen, let alone a patrician. But the people, with approval of the senate, invited him from the Sabine country to succeed to the throne. Later Lucius Tarquinius was made king even though Ancus was survived by sons. Tarquin was not even an Italian! He was the son of Demaratus, a Corinthian, and was a native of Tarquinii! After him Servius Tullius, the illegitimate son of a slave-woman from Corniculum, attained the throne through his own virtue and ability. Is it necessary to mention Titus Tatius, a Sabine, whom Romulus, the founder of the city, chose as his co-ruler? So long as no man of ability was scorned because of his origin, Rome grew in power. Do you now disdain a plebeian consul, when our ancestors did not reject even foreigners as kings? Even after the expulsion of the kings the city was not closed to worthy foreigners. The Claudian clan was granted not only citizenship but even admittance into the patrician order. Can a foreigner become a patrician and then a consul while a Roman citizen is denied the consulship because he is a plebeian? Are we to believe that it is impossible for a plebeian to be a man of courage and capability? And if a man resembling Numa and Lucius Tarquinius and Servius Tullius should appear, shall we deny him the reins of government? Are we to prefer consuls like the decemvirs, the most loathsome of mortals, all of whom were patricians, to consuls like the best of the kings, who had never served in the senate?

4. " 'But, no consul has been elected from the plebs since the expulsion of the kings,' someone may object. So what? Should we never try anything new? Should we avoid everything unprecedented—and in a young nation there are very few precedents—even if it is beneficial? There were no pontiffs or augurs during the reign of Romulus; they were created by Numa. There was no census or division of the people into centuries and economic classes; this was begun by Servius Tullius. There had never been consuls; the office was created after the expulsion of the kings. There had never been a dictator; our fathers originated this office. We have not always had plebeian tribunes, aediles, and quaestors. And within the last ten years we instituted the office of decemvir for codifying the laws, and then abolished it. Is there any doubt that in a city destined to endure forever and to grow to immense power new sacred and secular offices as well as new laws will be established? Was not this very law, which is so unjust to the plebs and detrimental to the public at large, enacted by the decemvirs within the last few years?

"Is there any greater affront than to scorn intermarriage with a part of the citizen-body as if they were lepers? What is this but to be exiled and banished within the very walls? They are afraid that we might become their relatives, that our blood might be mixed with theirs. Why, most of you patricians are of Sabine and Alban origin and do not belong to that order by right of birth or blood. You were adopted into the patrician ranks by order of the kings or, after their expulsion, by order of the people. But if intermarriage would pollute that noble blood of yours, couldn't you keep it pure by private agreements

not to marry plebeians yourselves and not to allow
your daughters and sisters to do so? No plebeian would vio-
late a patrician maiden; lust of that sort is a patrician attribute. No one can force another to make a marriage con-
tract against his will. But it is the greatest insult to the
plebs for intermarriage to be prohibited by statute. Why
don't you pass a law forbidding marriage between the rich
and the poor? Marriage contracts have always been matters of individual discretion everywhere; but now you
wish to impose upon this right the restrictions of a tyrannical law, in order to divide the community and make two
states of one. Why don't you enact a law that a plebeian
may not live in the same neighborhood with a patrician,
or travel along the same road, or attend the same social
function or stand with him in the Forum? What difference
does it make if a patrician does marry a plebeian woman
or a plebeian a patrician? What loss of status does this
involve for you? Of course the children inherit the condition of the father. We seek nothing else than to be numbered in the ranks of men and citizens. You have no reason to oppose us unless it pleases you to humiliate us as
much as possible.

5. "Is the supreme authority vested in the Roman people or in you? With the expulsion of the kings did sovereignty devolve upon you or was equal liberty granted
to all? Should the Roman people not be allowed to pass a
law if they wish? Or whenever a bill is proposed will you
order a military levy as punishment? When I call the assembly to vote, will you, the consuls, force the young men
to take the military oath and lead them off to camp? Will
you threaten the plebs and their tribunes? Have you not
twice experienced how little effect such threats have on
the plebs when they unite? Of course you have abstained
from violence out of solicitude for us! Or is it because the
more moderate among you are in the majority? There

will be no strife today, Roman citizens; they will always test your determination, but never your strength.

"Therefore, Consuls, if you unify the citizen-body by restoring the right of intermarriage, the plebeians are prepared to fight those wars which you claim are imminent—whether they are real or imaginary. But they must first be allowed to become united with you through bonds of marriage. Opportunity must be given to energetic and able men to seek offices. They must be allowed to take part in the administration of the government and to govern and obey in turn; that is the essence of democracy. If anyone opposes these things, spread wild rumors about wars. No one will enroll in the army, nor take up arms for arrogant masters by whom they are deprived of a share in public offices as well as the personal right of intermarriage."

6. The consuls arrived in the assembly, and soon the oratory degenerated into open quarreling. The tribune asked why a plebeian should not be made consul. To this one of the consuls replied, "Because no plebeians may take the auspices. Because of this the decemvirs abolished right of intermarriage, for fear that men of uncertain origin might impair the auspices." This answer was probably a legitimate one but at that moment impolitic. It greatly incensed the plebs—to be denied the auspices as if they were hated by the immortal gods! They had found a very forcible leader in their tribune and they supported him resolutely; there was no end to the controversy until the senate agreed to legalize the right of intermarriage. The patricians were confident that the plebeians now would be mollified by this new concession and that the tribunes would discontinue their agitation for plebeian consuls, or at least would postpone it until after the war and would permit a levy.

But fired by the great popularity which Canuleius had

won from his victory over the senate, the other tribunes spared no effort in support of their own bill. As rumor of war grew day by day they continued to prohibit the levy. When the tribunes' veto had frustrated all action by the senate, the consuls held private consultations with the senate leaders. It became apparent that they would have to concede defeat either to the enemy or to their fellow citizens. Of the men of consular rank only Valerius and Horatius refused to take part in the deliberations. Gaius Claudius was for empowering the consuls to use force against the tribunes. However, Cincinnatus and Capitolinus Quinctius strongly disapproved the use of violence against officials whom their treaty with the plebs had recognized as inviolable.

In the end they decided to effect a compromise with the tribunes. The office of military tribune with consular power was to be created, to which patricians and plebs might be elected; but qualifications for the office of consul remained unchanged. With this adjustment both tribunes and plebs were content. An election was declared for the purpose of choosing consular tribunes. Immediately all the former agitators (especially the tribunes and ex-tribunes) busily began electioneering all over the Forum. Seeing the antagonism of the plebs, the patricians despaired of ever being elected and also were indignant at the thought of having men of that stripe as colleagues in the office. At last, however, they were compelled to seek office by their leaders, who feared that they might seem to have relinquished claim to any share in administration of the government. The result of the election proved how different men's attitudes are when they are struggling for freedom and status, and when their struggle is over and their judgment is no longer prejudiced. All the tribunes elected were patricians, and the people were content that it was now possible for plebeians to run for office. Where can you now find a single man so moderate, fair, and high-principled as was then this entire nation?

Book 5
403 - 390 B C

The Romans' first significant step toward the subjugation of the rest of Italy was the capture of Veii, a powerful Etruscan city located about twelve miles north of Rome. After a siege of ten years (405-396 B.C.) the Roman dictator Marcus Furius Camillus is said to have succeeded in building an underground tunnel leading into the citadel of the city. When his work was completed he informed the senate, who decreed that any citizen who wished to share in the plunder should go out to the Roman camp.

21. The great multitude of people who went out filled the Roman camp: After the dictator had taken the auspices and had ordered the soldiers to make ready for battle, he prayed, "O Pythian Apollo, under your leadership and inspired by your will I set forth to the destruction of the city of Veii; to you, then, do I pledge a tenth part of its spoils. And to you, too, Queen Juno, who now are protectress of the city of Veii, I pray after our victory that you may accompany us to that city which is ours and shall be yours; there shall you find a seat worthy of your majesty." When he had prayed, he put to use the overwhelming numbers who had come into the camp by assaulting the city from all sides in order to divert the inhabitants

from the disaster erupting out of the tunnel. The people of Veii had not the least apprehension that their walls had been undermined and that their citadel was now filled with the enemy. They were completely unaware that they were given up as lost by their own prophets as well as by foreign oracles; that some of the gods had been invited to share in the plunder of their city and that others, summoned in prayer to quit their city, were anticipating new homes in the temples of the enemy, and that they themselves were living their last day. Each took up arms and ran out to the walls wondering why the Romans, who for so many days had not stirred from their posts, now were rushing blindly toward the walls as if suddenly stricken by madness.

At this point the legend is told that as the king of Veii was sacrificing, Roman soldiers within the tunnel overheard a soothsayer foretell that the man who should cut up the entrails of the victim would be granted victory. At these words, it is said, the Romans opened the tunnel, seized the entrails, and carried them to the dictator. But in matters of such antiquity I should be content if only things which seem probable be counted as true. For stories such as this are more fit for display upon the stage, which relishes marvels, than for winning credence. It is worth-while neither to affirm nor refute them.

Suddenly, armed men, picked troops who filled the tunnel, burst forth into the temple of Juno, which was situated within the very citadel of Veii. Some attacked the enemy standing on the walls from the rear; others wrested the bars from the city gates; others began setting afire the houses, from the roofs of which women and slaves were throwing stones and tiles. The whole city echoed with the cries of terror and exultation and with the wails of women and children. In a moment the defenders had been hurled from all of the walls and the gates thrown open. Some of the Romans burst through them in battle array; others scaled the deserted walls; the city everywhere was filled with the enemy. Finally the fighting flagged, after great blood-shed, and the dictator ordered the heralds to signal for the unarmed to be spared. This ended the slaughter. Immediately the Veientians laid their arms down and began to surrender, and the dictator permitted the soldiers to scatter in search of spoil.

When this booty was brought before Camillus it was more valuable than had ever been expected. Seeing this, it is said that he lifted his hands to heaven and prayed that if his own good fortune and that of the Roman people seemed excessive to any god or man, their envy might be appeased with the smallest possible detriment to both. And as Camillus was turning during his prayer, it is reported that he slipped and fell down. To those later speculating upon what subsequently occurred this was thought to have been an omen foreboding the banishment of Camillus and the capture of Rome which occurred a few years later. Thus that day was spent in the slaughter of the enemy and the sack of a very wealthy city.

22. The next day Camillus sold the free inhabitants of the city into slavery. Although income from this sale alone was allotted to the public treasury, even this offended the plebs, and for the booty which they themselves had received they gave credit neither to the senate nor to their general. It seemed to them that in order to make the senate agents of his own stinginess Camillus had referred to it a matter within his authority. They felt indebted instead to the Licinian family; for the father had been author of that popular proposal and the son had brought it to a vote in the senate.

When the Veians and their goods had been removed

and disposed of, the Romans began to pull down the shrines of the gods and gods themselves, but in the posture of worshippers rather than pillagers. The office of transporting Juno to Rome was assigned to young men chosen out of the whole army; they purified their bodies, put on white raiment, and entered the shrine with reverence. According to Etruscan practice, only a priest of a certain family could touch the image, and so at first they scrupled to handle it, but then one of the youths, whether by divine inspiration or in playfulness, said, "Do you wish to go to Rome, Juno?"—and the others cried out that she had nodded assent. Later the tale was added that she had spoken her willingness. At any rate, we are informed that although her image was moved from its resting place by engines of little power, it was light and easy to convey, as if she followed willingly. Subsequently the image was deposited safely on the Aventine hill, Juno's eternal abode, to which the prayers of the Roman dictator had summoned her, and where later Camillus himself dedicated to her the temple he had vowed.

This, then, was the fall of Veii, the wealthiest city of the Etruscan people, whose very destruction testified its greatness. For after a continuous siege of ten summers and winters during which it had inflicted greater loss than it had suffered, at last, under the pressure of destiny, it was subdued by a stratagem, not by force.

23.8 Presently the question of the offering to Apollo presented itself. Camillus declared that he had pledged a tenth part of the spoils, and the priests concluded that the people must carry out that religious obligation. However, no means could be discovered of prevailing upon the people to return the booty so that the portion owed to the god might be set aside. Finally they resorted to the plan which seemed least objectionable. Proclamation was made that everyone who wished to absolve himself and his household of this obligation, should appraise his own share of the booty, and should contribute the value of one tenth of it to the public treasury; from this sum an offering of gold might be made which would be in keeping with the dignity of the Roman people and worthy of the grandeur of the temple and the power of the deity. This assessment further increased Camillus' unpopularity among the plebs.

Plebeian hostility towards Camillus was temporarily countered by his campaign against Falerii (394 B.C.), in the course of which he demonstrated the usefulness of his high principles.

27. At Falerii it was the custom to employ the same person as schoolteacher and companion, and many boys were entrusted to his sole care, as is done in Greece to this day. The nobles' children, as was natural, were taught by their most eminent scholar. In peacetime this man had instituted the practice of taking the boys out into the country for play and exercise, and during the war he continued it. He would entertain them in short or long walks with games and stories, until one day he managed to bring them to the enemy outposts, then into the Roman camp, and then to Camillus' headquarters. His infamous deed he topped with a more infamous speech, saying that he was putting Falerii in the power of the Romans by delivering to them the children of the most influential Faliscans. Upon hearing this Camillus replied: "Neither the people to whom you bring this blackguard's gift, you blackguard, nor their general is of your stripe. With the Faliscans we have no fellowship founded on men's covenants; but there is and there will continue to be between us the fellowship implanted by nature. War as well as peace has its laws, and we wage it with justice as well as vigor. Our arms we bear not against children, who are spared even when cities are stormed, but against men armed like our-

selves, who attacked our camp at Veii without provocation. You have conquered them, as you think, by a scoundrel's trick; I shall conquer them, as I did Veii, in the Roman way, by courage, effort, weapons." He stripped the fellow, tied his hands behind his back, and gave him to the boys to drive back to Falerii, putting rods in their hands to scourge him as he went. . . . At Falerii, senate and market place rang with Roman integrity and their commander's justice. Unanimously they dispatched emissaries to Camillus' camp, and then by his permission to the senate at Rome, to surrender Falerii. This is reported to be their speech when they were introduced into the senate: "Senators, a victory which neither god nor man could begrudge, you and your general have won over us. We surrender to you because we believe (and what could be more handsome for a victor?) that life will be better under your administration than under our own laws."

32.6 In that same year [391 B.C.] a plebeian, Marcus Caedicius, informed the tribunes that in the silence of the night he had heard a voice more powerful than that of any human which had instructed him to tell the magistrates that the Gauls were coming. This portent occurred on the Via Nova at a point above the temple of Vesta, where a shrine is now located. As so often happens, however, because of the lowliness of the informant and because the Gauls were a far distant and almost unknown people, the magistrates ignored this warning. As the inevitable drew nearer not only were the warnings of the gods ignored, but the only man who could help Rome, Marcus Furius Camillus, was banished from the city. Camillus, who in addition had recently been bereaved of his son, was indicted in the matter of the spoils of Veii by Lucius Apuleius, a tribune of the plebs. When this occurred, he summoned members of his tribe and his clients (who comprised a large proportion of the plebs) to his house, in order to learn their opinions with regard to the matter. They replied that they themselves would pay any fine which he incurred, but that it was impossible to get him acquitted. Therefore he went into exile, entreating the immortal gods, if he was innocent of wrong, to cause his ungrateful country to regret his banishment. In his absence he was fined the sum of 15,000 *asses*.

Beginning in the time of Tarquinius Priscus successive migration of the Gauls into Italy pushed progressively farther southward, leading to the eventual penetration of the Senones into central Italy.

35. It was the Senones, as I have determined, who came to Clusium and from there to Rome. But it is uncertain whether they were alone or were accompanied by allies from other tribes of Cisalpine Gaul.

The people of Clusium were terrified at this strange enemy, for they saw before them a great host of men of uncommon appearance and bearing unfamiliar weapons, and they heard that these men often had routed Etruscan armies on this side of the Po and beyond. Thus they were moved to send envoys to Rome to seek assistance from the senate. However, they could assert no claim to alliance or friendship with the Roman people (except that they had not defended their kinsmen at Veii against the Romans) and were unsuccessful so far as military aid was concerned. The Romans did send the three sons of Marcus Fabius Ambustus as ambassadors to negotiate with the Gauls. They were to caution them on behalf of the senate and the Roman people against attacking a people from whom they had received no injury and who were friends and allies of Rome; for in order to defend them, the Romans were prepared to resort to war if necessary. It seemed better however, to avoid war if possible, and it behooved the Gauls, as a race hitherto unknown, to become acquainted with the Romans in peace rather than in battle.

36. The effect of this embassy might have been conciliatory, if the envoys themselves had not been overimpetuous men, more like Gauls than Romans. When they had delivered their message in the council of the Gauls they received the following reply: "Although we have never before heard the name of Rome, we are sure that you are brave men, since the Clusini have sought your aid in this critical situation. And, since you prefer to protect your allies through negotiation rather than armed force, we do not reject your offer of peace. Our only demand is that the Clusini, who possess more land than they can cultivate, surrender part of their territory to the landless Gauls. Otherwise peace is impossible. We wish also to receive their reply while you are here, and if our demand is refused, to fight in your presence, so that you may inform your countrymen how far the Gauls excel all other men in valor."

The Romans responded by asking what right they had to demand land from its possessors and to threaten them with war, and what business the Gauls had in Etruria in the first place. The Gauls insolently replied that they bore their right in their swords and that everything belonged to brave men. Tempers flared on both sides, and they rushed to arms and joined battle. At this, the relentless destiny driving Rome to its doom prompted the Roman envoys to seize arms, contrary to international custom. And these three of the bravest and noblest of the Romans so distinguished themselves in the front line of the Etruscans that this fact could not be concealed. Indeed, when a Gallic chieftain rode straight at the Etruscan standards, Quintus Fabius rode out in front of the lines and ran him through with his spear. He was recognized by the Gauls as he stripped the body of spoils, and the word passed through their ranks that he was one of the Roman envoys. Immediately all their fury against the Clusini was forgotten and they sounded the retreat, roaring threats against Rome. Although there was sentiment among the Gauls for marching immediately against Rome, the older men persuaded them first to send ambassadors to make a protest and demand that the Fabii be surrendered for violating international law. When the Gallic ambassadors had presented their case the Roman senate was displeased with the conduct of the Fabii and the demands of the barbarians were considered just; but because of the influence of the Fabian clan, political considerations made it impossible to make the decision which seemed equitable. Therefore the senate referred the demands of the Gauls to the popular assembly for consideration so that they should not be blamed if a war with the Gauls proved disastrous. But there the wealth and prestige of the Fabii exerted such great influence that instead of debating their punishment the assembly appointed the three envoys military tribunes with consular power for the following year. At this the Gauls were quite properly outraged, and departed, openly threatening war against Rome. The men elected military tribunes along with the Fabii were Quintus Sulpicius Longus, Quintus Servilius (for the fourth time), and Publius Cornelius Maluginensis.

37. On many occasions in wars against such neighboring nations as Fidenae and Veii Rome had appointed a dictator as a last resort. Yet Fortune deludes the minds of men when she does not wish her impending calamity to be checked; now, in the face of such imminent disaster, when a strange and unknown enemy from the ocean and the remotest regions of the earth prepared war, no dictatorship nor any other special precaution was proposed.

The men whose rashness had precipitated the war were in command as tribunes, and they took no greater pains with the levy of troops than were usual for ordinary campaigns. Indeed they even belittled the rumored seriousness of the war.

In the meantime the Gauls had learned that honors had actually been conferred upon the Fabii after their violation of international law, and that their own embassy had been scorned. Blazing with fury—an emotion over which the race has no control—immediately they jerked up their standards and set out on their march. The long and widespread column covered an immense area. Wherever they went, frightened cities rushed to arms and farmers took to flight before the tumult of their hurried march; but to them the Gauls would only roar as they passed by that they were bound for Rome. Rumors of their approach and messages from Clusium and other cities along the way preceded them. The swiftness of their progress terrified the Romans. A hastily recruited army, more like a mob, met them barely eleven miles outside the city, not far above the point where the River Allia, a deep river flowing from the Crustuminian mountains, joins the Tiber. There they were faced by a great mass of enemy on all sides; the air was filled with the turbulent din and the raucous cries of the Gauls, to whom useless pandemonium is second nature.

38. There the tribunes at once drew up their battle line, without first securing a place for their camp or preparing fortifications to which they might retreat. And they had no more consideration for the gods than for their men: they neither took auspices nor made sacrifice before battle. For fear that they might be outflanked by the superior numbers of the enemy, their line was drawn up with the wings extended. However, it could not be made as long as the enemy front, although their center was so

thinned and weakened that it scarcely held together. There was a small hill to the right which they decided to occupy with the reserves. And although the troops there were the first to panic, this measure afforded the fugitives their single means of safety. For Brennus, chieftain of the Gauls, was sure that when the reserves were routed, victory on the open plain would be easy for his overwhelming numbers. Therefore he first turned his attack toward this elevation. Seeing the small numbers of the enemy he particularly feared some deception and thought that the Roman reserves were stationed on the hill to attack his flanks and rear as soon as his front was engaged by the regulars. Thus the barbarians were supported not only by Fortune but by their own tactical foresight. But in the other army neither the soldiers nor their leaders behaved like Romans. They were overcome with panic and were utterly distracted. Though the Tiber was in their way, more of them fled to the hostile city of Veii than retreated by the unobstructed path to Rome and their wives and children.

For a short time the reserves were protected by their location. As soon as the rest of the army heard the shouting at their flank and rear, they fled unharmed almost before seeing the enemy. Not even the enemy's battle cry was returned, much less his attack, and no losses were suffered in combat; those wounded were cut down from behind by their fellows in the press and confusion of flight. The whole left wing threw down their arms and fled toward the Tiber where many weak or unskillful swimmers were weighed down by corselets and other armor, and swallowed by the flood. However most escaped safely to Veii, from which they sent no assistance nor even any report of the disaster to Rome. Troops on the right wing, which was some distance from the river and near the foot of the mountain, fled for Rome and there took refuge in the citadel without even closing the city gates.

39. The Gauls themselves were stunned with the marvel of their sudden victory and stood rooted in amazement, as if unsure of what had happened. Then, fearing an ambush, they refused to give chase but delayed to collect the spoils of the dead and to erect mounds of the arms in accordance with their custom. Only then did they set out for Rome, when no sign of the enemy was to be seen anywhere, and arrived only a little before sunset. There horsemen who had ridden ahead reported back that the gates were not closed, no guard was on duty, nor troops stationed on the walls. At this, they were astonished as before and wavered in uncertainty. Since they were apprehensive of the darkness and their ignorance of the terrain of the city, they camped for the night between Rome and the river Anio. Meanwhile they sent scouts around the walls to the other gates to discover, if possible, what the plans of the enemy in this desperate situation could be.

At Rome the city was filled with lamentation, both for the living and for the dead. A greater number of troops had fled to Veii than to Rome, and no one suspected that there were any survivors besides those in the city. However, when it was reported that the enemy had arrived, personal grief gave way to fear for the city's perils. Soon the people heard the wild cries and discordant chanting of groups of barbarians wandering around the walls. From that time until dawn of the next day the people were in such constant suspense that every moment they expected an assault to be made: When the Gauls first arrived attack seemed imminent; for otherwise they would have remained at Allia and not approached so near. Near sunset, they were sure the Gauls would attack before night; later, that the attack was put off until darkness, in order to cause more panic. Finally, the approach of dawn struck them breathless, and their constant terror was justified: hostile standards were borne through the gates.

But never during that night or the following day did the nation bear any resemblance to that which had timorously fled near the Allia. Since there was no hope of defending the city with such a small number of soldiers left, it seemed best for the men of military age with their wives and children, along with the younger and abler senators, to take refuge in the citadel and the Capitol. Arms and supplies were carried into this fortified position and there they prepared to defend the gods, the race, and the name of Rome. The Flamen and the Vestal priestesses were to carry the objects sacred to the state religion far from the slaughter and burning. The sacred worship was not to be abandoned as long as any one survived to maintain it. If the citadel and the Capitol which was the home of the gods, the senate, which guided the state's policy, and the men of military age should survive the ruin threatening the city, then the loss of the old people, who were doomed to die anyway, meant little. In order to help the common people to resign themselves to their fate, even the older men who had held consular power and who had celebrated triumphs declared that they would die with them; they refused to overextend the already inadequate supplies of the fighting men with bodies which could not bear arms nor defend their country.

40. With words such as these the older men who were doomed to death sought to comfort one another. Then they turned with words of encouragement to the young men whom they were accompanying to the citadel. They commended to their courage and strength whatever fortune remained for the city which had been unconquered in 360 years of warfare. It was painful to see the separation of the young men from the old. One group

took with them all hope and possibility of safety while the other had decided not to survive the capture and destruction of the city. But the weeping and despair of the women filled the cup of human misery. Now they ran after their husbands, now their sons, asking again and again to what fate they were being abandoned. Many of them followed their sons into the citadel where they took refuge. No one asked them or prohibited them; it would have been useful to the besieged to reduce the number of noncombatants but this would have been too inhuman. For the rest of the crowd—mostly plebeians—there was no room on the small hill and not enough food in the short supply. They poured out of the city in one unbroken line toward the Janiculum; from there some scattered through the countryside while others made for neighboring cities. With no leader and no concerted plan, each sought safety through his own devices and despaired of united action.

Meanwhile the Flamen Quirinalis and the Vestal Virgins were considering the disposition of the sacred objects with no thought for their personal property. Since they did not have sufficient strength to carry them all it was necessary to choose which to take with them and to find a safe hiding place for the rest. They decided it was best to store the latter in jars and bury them in a shrine next to the house of the Flamen Quirinalis; at that place it is still considered a sacrilege to spit. They then divided the remaining burden between them and set out by the road which leads to the Janiculum over the Sublician Bridge. As they climbed the hill they were noticed by L. Albinius, a plebeian, who was carrying his wife and children in a cart. Even in the midst of the confused mob leaving the city he observed the distinction between the human and the divine. Albinius thought it irreverent to allow the priestesses and sacred objects of the Roman people to travel by foot while he and his family were seen in a cart. Therefore, ordering his wife and children to get out, he placed the Vestals and their burdens in his cart and carried them to Caere, their destination.

41. At Rome when sufficient preparation (considering the circumstances) had been made for the defense of the citadel, the older men returned home and awaited the coming of the enemy with their courage steeled for death. Those who had been curule magistrates resolved to die wearing the symbols of their former rank. Clothed in the magnificent dress which those wear who drive the carriages of the gods at the games or celebrate triumphs, they sat in ivory chairs in the middle of their houses. Some authorities state that the Pontifex Maximus, Marcus Folius, led them in a recital of a vow by which they devoted themselves to death on behalf of their country and the citizens of Rome.

After the interval of a night the Gauls lost their eagerness to fight, and had become calm. They had never been strenuously opposed during the battle, and since they were not forced to take the city by assault, they entered the city the next day without undue anger or excitement. Entering through the Porta Collina, which stood wide open, they advanced into the Forum, gazing about at the temples, and then at the citadel which alone displayed a warlike appearance. After posting a small guard to prevent any attack from the citadel, they dispersed and scattered at once through the deserted streets in search of plunder. Some rushed straight for the nearest houses; others made for the farthest, thinking these would be undisturbed and well filled with booty.

But soon they turned back again and crowded together in and around the citadel; they were apprehensive of an enemy stratagem to capture stragglers and intimidated by the very silence and loneliness. The dwellings of commoners were bolted shut, while the mansions of the nobles were open, but they scrupled more to enter the open buildings than the closed. With great reverence they gazed at the men sitting in the vestibules of their houses; and stood before them as if they were statues; in addition to their ornaments and dress, which were too splendid for mere mortals, they seemed very like gods in the majesty and dignity of their countenances. But when one of the Gauls stroked the luxuriant beard of Marcus Papirius (all beards were worn long in that day), Papirius struck him on the head with his ivory staff and enraged him. Papirius' death began the slaughter; the rest were cut down in their chairs. After this massacre no one was spared, the houses were ransacked, and then set afire.

42. Perhaps the rank and file of the Gauls were not eager to demolish the city completely; or perhaps their leaders had decided to intimidate the Romans by starting only a few fires, and not to burn all the buildings at once. Thus, they may have left part of the city standing as a lure, hoping that the besieged enemy would be induced to surrender by love of their homes. At any rate the burning was by no means so widespread or indiscriminate as is usual on the first day a city is captured.

In the citadel the Romans were unable to control their eyes and ears, much less their senses. They saw the city full of enemy running everywhere through the streets and new disasters constantly occurring throughout the city. From whatever directon they heard the shouts of the enemy, the cries of women and children, the crackling of flames or the crash of falling buildings they turned their eyes in anguish. Here they were placed by Fortune as spectators, so to speak, of the destruction of their city, able to defend nothing they owned except their persons. These men were to be pitied more than any others who had ever been besieged, for they were shut off from their city and saw all which had belonged to them in the hands of the enemy.

The night which followed was no more peaceful than the fearful day. At length it dawned into another day of horror, with no relief from the spectacle of constant disaster. The Romans now had seen their city leveled by fire and destruction. Nevertheless, in spite of their overwhelming disaster, these men never wavered in their determination to defend the small and inadequate hill which was their last stronghold of freedom. Finally, as the destruction continued daily, they inured themselves to anguish: heedless of the loss of all which had been dear, they looked only to their arms, and the swords in their right hands as their sole remaining hope.

43. After the Gauls had for several days waged a useless war on the buildings of the city, they saw that nothing remained from the burning and destruction of the captured city except their armed enemy. Realizing that the Romans were unintimidated by their misfortunes and were unlikely to surrender without compulsion, they decided as a last resort to try to storm the citadel. When the signal was given at daybreak the whole Gallic army drew up in the Forum. Then, raising the battle cry, they joined together their shields above their heads and advanced upon the citadel. The Romans prepared for the attack without agitation or confusion: after reinforcing their defenses at all approaches they concentrated their strength where they saw the attack would be made. Then, taking a stand at about the middle of the hill, they allowed the enemy to advance upward without opposition, knowing that the steeper the incline the easier it would be to drive the enemy back downhill. Then charging from their superior position, which almost in itself hurled them against the enemy, they routed the Gauls with such carnage that they never again attempted such

an assault. After this the Gauls lost all hope of taking the citadel by force, and undertook a siege for which they were unprepared. They had anticipated no such necessity and had burned all the grain in Rome with the rest of the city; and during the last few days all the grain had been carried off from the neighboring fields to Veii. Therefore they decided to divide their army and with part of it to besiege the city and with the other part plunder neighboring peoples in order to provide the besiegers with grain. It was unquestionably Fortune herself who led the Gauls to Ardea . . . where Camillus was in exile.

Camillus persuaded the people of Ardea to resist the Gallic incursions, and under his leadership they took the Gallic camp by surprise, inflicting heavy losses. Meanwhile, the Roman soldiers at Veii under the leadership of Caedicius, a centurion, surprised and routed two parties of Etruscans who were making forays into Roman territory.

46. At Rome the siege continued uneventfully. The Gauls were content simply to prevent the escape of any enemy through their lines, and neither side was attempting any active measures. Presently, however, the daring action of one of the Roman youths commanded the admiration of friend and foe alike. There was a certain sacrifice which was performed by the Fabian clan on the Quirinal hill. In order to fulfill this religious obligation Gaius Fabius Dorsuo arranged his toga in the ceremonial style of dress known as the "Gabinian cincture" and descended from the Capitoline. After proceeding with dignity through the middle of the Gallic lines, unmoved by their shouts and threats, he reached the Quirinal hill unharmed and performed all the sacrifice according to ritual. Then, confident that the gods, whose worship he had not abandoned even under fear of death, would protect

him, he returned to the Capitoline with the same calm face and steady step. Perhaps the Gauls were stupefied at his amazing audacity; or perhaps they were restrained by religious scruple, since they are themselves by no means irreligious.

In the meantime, the garrison at Veii was growing daily in military strength as well as in courage. In addition to the Romans who had gathered there after being routed in the disastrous battle and capture of the city, volunteers were collecting from Latium in hope of booty. Now, therefore, the time seemed ripe for recapturing their city from the hands of the enemy; but this strong body lacked a head. Veii itself reminded them of Camillus, and a large part of the soldiers had served with success under his leadership and guidance. Moreover, Caedicius declared that he would give no one an opportunity to put an end to his authority, but that on the contrary he was mindful of his low rank and would himself request a commander. Therefore everyone agreed that Camillus should be summoned from Ardea; but even in this desperate situation they were guided by a sense of propriety; it was decided first to obtain the consent of the senate at Rome, and to preserve the proper distinctions. The great risk of passing through the enemy lines was undertaken by an able young man named Pontius Cominus, who made his way into the city by floating down the Tiber on a piece of cork. Then he ascended the hill to the citadel at the point nearest the river, where the cliff was abrupt and therefore neglected by the enemy guard. After presenting the message from the army to the magistrates he received a decree from the senate that after being recalled from exile by the Comitia Centuriata Camillus should immediately be declared dictator by order of the people and receive command of the army which desired his return. The messenger then descended the hill in the same way and hurried back to Veii. Ambassadors were sent at once to bring Camillus back from Ardea. Or perhaps—as I should prefer to believe—Camillus did not set out from Ardea before the decree of the senate was passed and he was declared dictator *in absentia;* for he was not entitled to enter Roman territory except by order of the people nor could he legally assume command unless declared dictator.

47. While these things were happening at Veii, at Rome the citadel and the Capitol were threatened with great danger. The Gauls either had noticed the footprints of the messenger who had come from Veii, or had themselves noticed how easy it would be to ascend the cliff near the temple of Carmentis. The first moonlight night, they sent ahead an unarmed man to choose the route, while the rest followed, handing their arms to their fellows when the going was hard, and supporting and pulling each other up in turn until they reached the top. So silently did they climb that they not only escaped the notice of the guards, but did not rouse even the dogs, which are very sensitive animals to nocturnal sounds. The geese, however, they did not elude; these the Romans had refrained from eating in spite of the lack of food because they were sacred to Juno. This fact saved them. Marcus Manlius, an excellent soldier who had been consul three years before, was wakened by the honking of the geese and the flapping of their wings. He rushed forward, snatching up his arms and shouting to his comrades. Before the others had recovered from their bewilderment, he had knocked the first Gaul off the edge of the cliff with the boss of his shield. When the Gaul fell he overturned those directly behind him, and Manlius himself cut down others who fearfully dropped their weapons in order to cling to the rocks. By this time other Romans had come and were bombarding the enemy with

spears and stones so that the whole company of Gauls fell headlong with a crash.

When this tumult had subsided, the Romans still were extremely worried (for even the danger which had passed disturbed them), but they devoted the remainder of the night to whatever rest was possible. At daybreak the soldiers were called by a trumpet to a council with the tribunes. First of all Manlius was commended for his courage, not only by the tribunes but by all the soldiers; he was presented with a half pound of corn and a pint of wine from each man. . . . This may seem a small reward, but considering the current hardship it was a striking proof of the gratitude toward him; each man contributed this portion from his rations, disregarding his own physical needs. Then the sentinels were summoned who had been guarding the position where the enemy had succeeded in approaching unnoticed. The military tribune, Quintus Sulpicius announced that he would punish them all according to military law, but he refrained when all the soldiers shouted that only one man was to blame. The culprit, who manifestly was guilty, was flung from the cliff with the approval of everyone. After this the guards were more careful on both sides; for among the Gauls the rumor had spread that messengers were coming and going between Veii and Rome, and the Romans remembered their narrow escape.

48. More than all the other hardships of the siege, famine was tormenting both armies. In addition, the Gauls who were encamped on low ground lying between hills were attacked by an epidemic. This enclosed place was still smoldering from the burning of the city and full of smoke which carried dust and even ashes when there was any wind. The Gallic race, which was accustomed to dampness and cold, could not endure such conditions, and great numbers began to die of a fever and suffoca-

tion, which spread like a plague through a herd. Soon they became tired of burying the dead individually, and began to pile bodies in great heaps and to cremate them together; from this the location came to be known as the Gallic Tombs.

Eventually an armistice was concluded and the soldiers were permitted to talk together by their commanders. During these conversations the Gauls again and again taunted the Romans with their lack of food and called upon them to surrender. In order to discourage the impression that their circumstances were desperate, it is said that the Romans threw bread down upon the heads of the enemy sentries. But finally they could no longer bear their hunger, much less conceal it. The dictator was levying troops at Ardea; with those which his master of horse, Lucius Valerius, was bringing from Veii, he was preparing a sufficient force to fight the Gauls on equal terms. But the army on the Capitoline ordered its leaders either to surrender or to buy off the enemy on any terms possible. The Gauls were hinting strongly that they could be persuaded to abandon the blockade for no great sum; and the Roman soldiers were so exhausted from day and night sentry duty and weakened by hunger that as they marched to their posts they were hardly able to support the weight of their armor. After they had looked day after day in vain for help to arrive from the dictator, all hope disappeared along with their food supply. The senate was convened and the duty of bargaining for peace was assigned to the military tribunes. An agreement was reached between the tribune Quintus Sulpicius and Brennus the Gallic chieftain, and the ransom price of the nation destined soon to rule the world was fixed at a thousand pounds of gold. Insult was added to this penalty which in itself was so degrading: when the tribune objected that the Gauls had brought false weights a Gaul

derisively added his sword to the scale, with the words
so intolerable to Roman ears, "Woe to the conquered."

49. But gods and men allied to save Rome from the
stigma of having been ransomed. By some chance the dictator arrived before this shameful transaction was completed and the payments of gold (which had been delayed
because of the quarrel) had been made. He ordered
the gold to be taken away at once and the Gauls ejected.
They resisted, saying that the treaty had been concluded,
but Camillus answered that after his appointment as
dictator no agreement was binding which had been made
by a magistrate of an inferior order without his permission. He also warned them to prepare for battle. His own
soldiers he ordered to throw their packs into a pile, to put
on their armor, and to redeem their country with steel,
not with gold. Here before their eyes were the temples
of the gods, their wives and children, the soil of their native land, now wasted under the ravages of war, and
everything which it was their sacred duty to defend, to
regain, and to avenge. He then drew up his line in the best
formation that the naturally hilly terrain and the ruins of
the half-destroyed city permitted, and took all possible
precautions for the safety and success of his men in battle. The Gauls, who were frightened by the turn of events,
took up their arms and rushed with more fury than
method. But now Fortune had turned, and all divine aid
and human skill were on the side of the Romans. Thus,
with no greater effort than they themselves had conquered near Allia, the Gauls were now routed upon the
first charge. After they had regrouped about eight miles
from the city on the road to Gabii, a second battle was
fought on more even terms, and the Romans were victorious under the guidance and leadership of Camillus. Here,
the camp of the Gauls was taken, and annihilation of the

enemy was so complete that not even a witness of the carnage survived. The dictator, who had recovered his country from the hands of the enemy, then returned to the city in triumph; and amid the rude jokes of the soldiers, which are customarily made on such occasons, he also was called "a Romulus," "Father of His Country," and "Second Founder of the City"—words of praise which were not undeserved.

Book 6

3 8 9 - 3 6 7   B C

1. In the five preceding books I have set forth the history of the Roman people first under the kings, then under consuls, dictators, decemvirs and consular tribunes, from the founding of the city to its capture. These events, foreign wars and domestic dissensions alike, are matters shrouded by the obscurity of time, like objects far away which are hard to distinguish. In addition, at that time written documents, the only safe depository of the memory of the past, were meager and few; and the records which existed in the chronicles of the priests and other public and private archives almost all perished with the burning of the city. But henceforth, from the second founding of the city, I shall tell of events both at home and at war which are more clearly and definitely known, just as if the bare roots had put on a more vigorous and luxuriant second growth.

At first the city leaned on that same prop by which it had raised itself from ruin—Marcus Furius Camillus;

the people would not allow him to abdicate until the full year of his dictatorship was completed. It was decided by the Comitia not to elect consular tribunes for the following year, since the city had been captured during their administration, and so the state reverted to an interregnum. While the people were still occupied with the ceaseless task of rebuilding the city, Quintus Fabius' term of office ended. He was immediately indicted by the tribune Gnaeus Marcius for fighting against the Gauls in defiance of international law while he was serving as ambassador. However, he was saved from prosecution by a death so timely that most people believed it self-inflicted. In the beginning of the interregnum Publius Cornelius Scipio served as interrex, and following him, Marcus Furius Camillus. Under Camillus' leadership the following consular tribunes were elected: Lucius Valerius Publicola (for a second term), Publius Cornelius, Aulus Manlius, Lucius Aemilius, and Lucius Postumius.

The first measures these tribunes proposed to the senate, as soon as they assumed office, were concerned with religion. Their first decree was that all the treaties and laws which had not been destroyed be sought out. These included the Twelve Tables and certain laws enacted during the monarchy. Some of these were publicly circulated; but those which pertained to religious observances were kept secret by the pontiffs, chiefly in order to retain their religious influence over the people. They then turned to the selection of days of evil omen (on which it was sacrilege to sacrifice to the gods or begin any important undertaking).

Marcus Manlius Capitolinus, the patrician who wakened to save the Capitol during the Gallic invasion of 390 B.C., later antagonized men of his class by becoming a champion of the plebs in their struggles to relieve themselves of the oppressive burden of debt.

11. In the following year [385 B.C.] the consular tribunes were Aulus Manlius, Publius Cornelius, Titus and Lucius Quinctius Capitolinus, Lucius Papirius Cursor (for the second time), and Gaius Sergius (for the second time). During this year a serious foreign war broke out, and an even more serious internal conflict. The war, which was started by the Volsci, was complicated by defections of the Latins and the Hernici; the domestic struggle was set in motion by a man of whom it was least to be expected, a patrician of great renown, Marcus Manlius Capitolinus.

This man's excessive ambition made him disdainful of other prominent men, but envious of the one man distinguished above all in honors and ability. It galled him to see the unique position which Marcus Furius Camillus occupied in the administration of civil affairs as well as in the army. So preëminent was Camillus that, as Manlius thought, he treated the men who were elected to office with him not as colleagues but as servants. "If the matter were considered in the proper perspective," Manlius told himself, "Camillus could not have recovered the city from siege unless I myself had first saved the Capitol and the citadel. He attacked the Gauls while they were receiving ransom and were lulled off guard; I drove them back as they tried to take the citadel by force of arms. The greater part of his glory belongs to the soldiers who shared his victory; but no one on earth helped me gain my victory." His head was turned by ideas of this sort, and he was a violent and excitable man by nature. When he found his influence in the senate not as great as he thought he deserved, he became the first patrician to champion the popular cause.

Collaborating with the plebeian magistrates, he began to vilify the patricians and solicit the favor of the plebs. Soon he became carried away with popular acclaim

and came to prefer fame to honor. Not content with the
agrarian statutes, which had always furnished material for
plebeian insurrection, he began to denounce the laws of
credit as well. He realized that debt was a matter of
greater concern, since it not only carried with it poverty
and disgrace but threatened the free man with the bonds
of servitude. Many people lately had been drawn into
debt by building, an activity financially ruinous even to
the rich. Now the very serious Volscian war on top of the
defections of the Latins and Hernici offered the senate a
convenient pretext for the creation of a dictator; but the
real motivation was the revolutionary activity of Manlius. Aulus Cornelius Cossus was declared dictator and
appointed Titus Quinctius Capitolinus as his master of
horse.

*The dictator Cossus defeated the Volscian army and
captured their camp. He was preparing to continue his
campaign in the field against other peoples who had defected when suddenly he was summoned back to the
city.*

14. A more critical situation had developed at home
and made it necessary for the dictator to be called back
to Rome. Subversion was growing day by day, and it
was more than usually alarming because of its instigator.
For now the speeches of Manlius and even his actions,
which allegedly were liberal and progressive, actually had
become inflammatory when one considered their intent.
For instance, a centurion famous for his military exploits
was sentenced to bondage for debt. As the man was being
led away Manlius hurried up to him through the middle
of the Forum, followed by all his clients, and laid his
hand upon him. He complained loudly against the arrogance of the patricians, the high-handed cruelty of the
money lenders, the miseries of the plebs, and the misfor-

tunes of that courageous man. "Truly," he said, "I saved
the Capitol and the citadel in vain if I am forced to see a
comrade in arms seized and led away to slavery like a
prisoner of the Gauls." Then before the eyes of the
crowd he paid the creditor the sum of the man's debt,
and formally granted him his freedom. All the while the
debtor praised Manlius as his savior and the father of the
Roman plebs, calling upon gods and men to requite him.
Immediately he turned to the unruly crowd and began
to inflame them even more by displaying the scars which
he had received in wars against Veii, the Gauls, and
other successive enemies. While serving in the army, he
said, and rebuilding the home which had been destroyed
by the enemy, he had been ruined by usury; for although
he had paid the principal of his debt several times over,
this sum had been absorbed by interest. He now could
look upon the light, the Forum, the faces of his fellow citizens, by the grace of Marcus Manlius. He had received
from him all the generosity of a parent. He vowed to him
his zealous and devoted service for as long as he should
live. By all his obligations to his native land, he said, to
his private deities, and to those of his country he was
bound to one man.

The plebs already were aroused by these words and
had become passionately devoted to one individual, when
another incident occurred better calculated to increase the
general unrest. Manlius put up for auction a farm in the
district of Veii, which constituted the greater part of his
fortune, "In order, fellow citizens," he said, "that none of
you may be sentenced and led away to servitude as long
as I have a penny left." This so aroused the plebs that
they seemed likely to follow this defender of their liberty
to any excess.

Moreover, in his own house Manlius held meetings
where he thundered tirades full of slander against the

patricians. Without regard for what was true or false he charged that the patricians had hidden away a large cache of Gallic gold; they were not content with occupying public land, he said, but must appropriate public funds besides. If this fact were brought to light, this money would be adequate to free the plebeians completely of their burden of debt. When this story was circulated among the plebeians it was thought a shameful outrage. The money intended to ransom the city from the Gauls, they said, had been collected by a general taxation; but now that this money had been recovered from the enemy it had found its way into the hands of a few. At once they earnestly inquired where such a large sum could be concealed. Manlius, however, put them off with the answer that he would tell them in good time, and they forgot all other cares in their concern for this one thing. It was obvious that if this information were true their gratitude would be extreme—as would be their anger if it proved false.

Cossus, the dictator, ordered Manlius to name the men who were in possession of the Gallic treasure. When he refused he was imprisoned, but this so aroused public opinion that the senate soon released him.

18. Toward the end of the year the insurrection led by Manlius broke out anew. . . . Peace with all foreign powers was established at the beginning of this year, and this was beneficial to both the patricians and the plebs. Since the plebs were not being called away into military service and they now had a powerful leader, they had hopes of abolishing usury. The patricians were pleased that they were relieved of all worries about external threats and could devote themselves to clearing up domestic difficulties. Both sides were assuming much more aggressive attitudes, and conflict obviously was imminent.

Night and day in the secrecy of his house Manlius met with plebeian leaders laying plans for revolution. He was now much more bitter and determined than before. Being unaccustomed to slights, his recent humiliation rankled in his bosom. He grew bold with the thought that the dictator had not dared treat him as Quinctius Cincinnatus had treated Spurius Maelius; not only had the dictator abdicated in the face of the anger over his imprisonment, but not even the senate had been able to withstand it. He was both exhilarated and aggrieved by these thoughts, and now he set about arousing the already angered plebeians.

"How long," he asked, "will you be ignorant of your own strength? This knowledge nature has taught even dumb beasts. Come, count yourselves, then count your enemies. Each patrician will find as many of you his enemies as he now has clients following behind him. But even if you met them on equal terms, I believe that you would fight more fiercely for liberty than they for domination. Simply make a show of fighting and you will have peace. Let them see you prepared for war, and they will see fit to grant you your rights. We must face danger with unity or submit to injury separately. How long will you look to me to help you? Of course I shall never fail you; but you yourselves see to it that fortune may never fail me. I am your defender; but at our enemies' whim I was reduced to a cipher. I struck the chains from each of you. But you saw *me* led away in chains. What hope should I have if our enemies should attempt more drastic measures? Should I expect the fate of Cassius and Maelius? You may well recoil at such a thought. The gods will prevent such a thing, but they will never come down from the sky just for me. They must give you courage to prevent it, just as they inspired me to save you in peace and war, first from a barbarian enemy, then from your high-handed fellow citizens. Does this great nation have so little spirit that you always will be satisfied to be on the defensive—to be protected against your enemies by the tribunes' power? Is your only quarrel with the patricians how much you are to allow them to tyrannize you? This subservience is not implanted in you by nature; you have become slaves from habit. What makes you so confident against your foreign enemies that you presume to rule over them? Because with them you strive for empire, whereas with these you are accustomed to make half-hearted attempts to gain liberty rather than to maintain it.

"Nevertheless, in spite of the weakness of your leaders, in spite of your timidity, always either by force or by good fortune you have obtained whatever you sought. It is time to attempt greater things. Now try your own good fortune, and me, whom, I believe, you already have tested and not found lacking. You can impose a ruler upon the patricians with less effort than you imposed upon them tribunes to restrict their rule. The dictatorship and the consulship must be leveled to the ground in order for the Roman plebs to lift up their heads. Do not abandon me; forbid all judicial actions pertaining to money. I style myself the protector of the plebs; this title my diligence and fidelity have won for me. If you wish to designate your leader by some more august title, you will find me better able to obtain your desires." According to historians, this was the beginning of Manlius' efforts to obtain the throne; however we have no certain information concerning who his confederates were or how far his plot progressed.

19. Meanwhile, on the other side the senate was discussing the insurrection which was being fomented in a private house—a house which happened to be located in the citadel itself—and the danger threatening liberty. A large number asserted loudly that what was needed was a Servilius Ahala; he would not antagonize a public enemy

by ordering his imprisonment, but by the loss of one citizen would end this internal conflict. The result of this debate was a resolution couched in milder terms but having the same practical effect. It was resolved that the magistrates should see to it that the commonwealth should come to no harm because of the activities of Marcus Manlius.

The tribunes of the plebs saw that this danger to public freedom also threatened their own power, and they had placed themselves at the disposal of the senate. Accordingly, they and the consular tribunes met together to consider what measures were necessary. No one could propose any alternative to violence and bloodshed, but it was evident that this would result in great conflict. Finally the plebeian tribunes Marcus Menenius and Quintus Publilius arose and said, "Why do we make this a struggle between the patricians and the plebeians when it should be a dispute between the state and one dangerous citizen? Why do we attack the plebeians along with this citizen, when it is wiser to attack him with the help of the plebeians themselves? He will fall to ruin under the weight of his own power. We intend to indict him. Nothing is less popular than monarchy. The plebeians soon will see that you are not attacking them, that instead of advocates they are the judges, and that the accusers are plebeians, while the defendant is a patrician; and when they find that the charge is ambition for royal power they will favor no individual more than their own liberty."

20. Everyone agreed, and the tribunes indicted Manlius. At first this antagonized the plebeians, especially when they saw the defendant dressed in mourning and unaccompanied by any of the patricians. Indeed his relatives and relations by marriage, and even his own brothers, Aulus and Titus Manlius, had deserted him. Until that day never had a man's nearest kin failed to wear

mourning attire at such a time of crisis. When Appius
Claudius was thrown into prison the whole Claudian clan
—even Gaius Claudius, who hated him—had appeared
clad in crepe. Now, said the plebeians, there was a conspiracy to suppress this partisan of the people, because he
was the first of the patricians ever to voice opposition
against his class in favor of the plebs.

At length the day of the trial arrived. In none of my
sources do I find what accusations were made against the
defendant which related specifically to his indictment for
plotting to become king. The only charges mentioned are
the meetings of the plebs, Manlius' inflammatory remarks,
his public largesses, and his perjured statements. However, I do not doubt that the evidence was serious; for it
was not the strength of his case but rather the place of
trial which made the plebeians hesitant to condemn him.

The following facts should be noted in order for mankind to know how inordinate ambition for supreme power
made men depreciate and even detest the most illustrious deeds. It is said that Manlius brought forward almost
four hundred men to whom he had lent money without
interest and had rescued from the necessity of selling
their property or being bound into slavery. And he did
not simply recall his military exploits; he displayed the
spoils of some thirty enemies he had killed, and around
forty decorations which he had received from commanders, including two crowns for scaling the walls of enemy
cities and eight for saving the lives of comrades. In addition, he named all the citizens whom he had saved in battle; among these was Gaius Servilius, the master of horse,
who was not present. He recounted his military exploits
with an eloquence befitting their greatness, then bared
his breast, which was marked with the scars of battle.
Looking toward the Capitol, he called upon Jupiter and
the other gods to come to his aid, praying to them that in

his time of peril they should endow the Roman people with the same resolution which they had granted him when he had saved Rome by defending the citadel. With these words he begged each individual to look toward the Capitol and the citadel and to face the immortal gods while judging him.

The Comitia Centuriata was convened on the Campus Martius. But when the tribunes saw the defendant stretching forth his hands to the Capitol and addressing his entreaties not to the people but to the gods, they realized that they would have to remove the assembly from the scene of Manlius' great exploit; otherwise gratitude would never permit men to consider even the most valid accusation. They therefore adjourned the trial and called an assembly in the Peteline Grove outside the Flumentane Gate, where the Capitol could not be seen. There the charge was proven, and the people grimly rendered a terrible verdict, which was painful even to those approving it. Some sources say that he was condemned by two commissioners appointed to conduct trials for treason.

The tribunes threw him from Tarpeian rock; thus the spot which bore witness to this man's great valor became also the scene of his execution. Other marks of disgrace were added to his death. Since his house had stood where the temple of Juno and the mint now are located, a decree was passed by the assembly that thereafter no patrician might reside in the citadel or the Capitol. A rule was made by the Manlian clan that no one should be given the name Marcus Manlius. Thus died a man who would have been illustrious had he not been born in a free country. Now that he presented no danger, in a little while people remembered only his virtues and lamented his loss. Shortly afterward a terrible epidemic of disease broke out with no obvious cause; many attributed this to Manlius' execution. They said that the Capitol had been defiled by the blood of its savior, and that it had displeased the gods for the man who had saved their temples from the enemy to be punished almost before their eyes.

Chiefly because of the Gallic invasion and also because of numerous wars in which the plebeians had fought, the debt burden of the poor became heavier and heavier. In 377 B.C., the tribunes Gaius Licinius Stolo and Lucius Sextius introduced measures designed to bring relief to the plebeians. These measures proposed to reduce their debts, limit the amount of public land (held solely by the patricians) which one man might occupy, and grant representation in the consulship to the plebeians.

34. That year Rome enjoyed peace as a result of her successes in foreign wars. In the city, however, the power of the patricians and the misery of the plebeians grew in proportion to the tranquillity. The mere fact that immediate payment was compulsory made payment virtually impossible. When all a plebeian's personal property was gone he was brought into court and bound into slavery. He gave his person and reputation to satisfy his debtors, and punishment was substituted for payment. Not only the lower classes but even the plebeian leaders had sunk into such a state of hopeless apathy that the patricians seemed to have recovered forever the consular tribunate which the plebeians had merely appropriated for a few years. For there was not a man with sufficient courage to administrate or even to run for the plebeian offices, much less compete with the patricians for the consular tribunate, for the legal right to which they had fought so hard.

But, as is often the case, the patricians were denied excessive enjoyment of their victory by a trifling cause.

Marcus Fabius Ambustus was a man of great influence among the patricians as well as among the plebs, for they considered him a man who showed due regard for their interests. Fabius had two adult daughters—the elder married to Servius Sulpicius and the younger to Gaius Licinius Stolo, a man of considerable reputation, although a plebeian. The very fact that Fabius had not scorned this alliance gained him great popularity among the plebs. One day the younger sister happened to be visiting in the house of the elder when Sulpicius, a consular tribune, returned home. When one of his lictors in the customary manner rapped on the door with his rod, the younger sister, who was unfamiliar with this practice, started violently. Her sister laughed aloud in surprise at her ignorance, and at this she was mortified, for the merest trifle can vex a woman's feelings. Undoubtedly the crowd of attendants accompanying the tribune and asking his pleasure also made her feel her sister's marriage more fortunate. The foolish attitude which makes us unable to bear being surpassed by relatives caused her to regret her own choice.

While still smarting with this embarrassment she happened to meet her father. When he asked, "Is everything all right?" she tried to conceal her discomposure, thinking it unworthy of both her sister and her husband. However, under his kindly questioning she was persuaded to confess that she was hurt at being married to a person who was beneath her and into a family which could never attain either dignity or influence. Upon hearing this, Ambustus consoled his daughter, telling her to take heart, for soon she would see her own husband gain the same honors possessed by the husband of her sister. Subsequently he began to make plans with his son-in-law along with Lucius Sextius, another able young man whose plebeian birth was the only obstacle to his ambition.

35. The heavy indebtedness of the plebeians seemed to make it an opportune time for political and social reform. For the plebs' only hope of relief was to place men of their own order in positions of power. This was the goal toward which all their energies would have to be directed. In the past, by dint of vigorous efforts, the plebeians had made great strides; if they continued their exertions it was possible for them to reach an equal footing with the patricians in official distinctions as well as in personal character. For the present Licinius and Sextius determined to become tribunes of the plebs. From that office they might open for themselves a path to the remaining magistracies. As tribunes they proposed several bills, all of them detrimental to the interests of the patricians and favorable to those of the tribunes. One concerned the debt, that all money paid in interest be subtracted from the capital and the balance paid in three equal annual installments. A second limited holding of public land by an individual to five hundred acres. A third decreed that the office of consular tribune should be abolished and that at least one consul each year be elected from the ranks of the plebeians. These all were radical changes, which were destined to be effected only after great controversy.

Faced with the loss of all those things which men covet most—land, wealth, and political distinctions—the terrified patricians held many desperate public and private meetings. Their only weapon seemed to be the veto of the plebeian tribunes. This same weapon they had used in the past to settle many difficulties. Accordingly, they suborned other tribunes to oppose their colleagues' proposals. When the Comitia Tributa had been called to vote on the measures, these tribunes, protected by a bodyguard of patricians, refused to allow the proposals to be read or any other steps preparatory to passing the bills to

be taken. After the assembly had been called many times
to no avail and the bills were as good as rejected, Sextius
said, "Very well, since you have decided to make the
veto so powerful, we shall save the plebs with that very
weapon. Come, call the assembly for the election of consular tribunes, Senators. I'll see to it that you get your
fill of the words, 'I forbid,' which you so much enjoy hearing our colleagues chant." This was no idle threat. No
elections were held except for aediles and tribunes of the
plebs, since Licinius and Sextius were reëlected tribunes
and would allow no curule magistrates to be elected. With
the plebeians continually reëlecting these two tribunes,
and their colleagues preventing the election of consular
tribunes, the state was deprived of administrative officials
for five years.

36. Fortunately peace prevailed everywhere except
among the colonists of Velitrae whom tranquillity had
made arrogant. Knowing that there was no Roman army
they made several incursions into Roman territory and
even began to besiege Tusculum. When the people of
that city, who were ancient allies and recently had become Roman citizens, begged assistance, the plebeians as
well as the patricians felt a sense of obligation. The tribunes of the plebs yielded and allowed elections to be held
by an interrex. Lucius Furius, Aulus Manlius, Servius
Sulpicius, Servius Cornelius, and Publius and Gaius Valerius were elected consular tribunes. The plebeians
proved to be far less acquiescent to a conscription than
they had been to the election, and an army was enlisted
only after great controversy. Subsequently, however, this
army not only drove the enemy away from Tusculum but
pursued them to their own city, which they besieged
much more forcefully than the enemy had besieged Tusculum. Yet the tribunes who had begun the siege were
unable to take the city before time came for new tribunes

to be elected. These new tribunes were Quintus Servilius, Gaius Veturius, Aulus and Marcus Cornelius,
Quintus Quinctius, and Marcus Fabius. Even during the
term of these tribunes nothing occurred at Velitrae worth
recording.

Meanwhile at home a critical situation was developing.
In addition to Sextius and Licinius who had proposed the
controversial measures and were now serving their eighth
term as tribunes of the plebs, the consular tribune Fabius,
the father-in-law of Licinius, now was openly supporting
the program which he himself originally had formulated.
Moreover, originally there had been eight tribunes who
vetoed the proposals, while now there were only five, and
these, like most men who forsake their own party, were
unthinking puppets of the patricians. In defense of their
vetoes they could only repeat what others had privately
taught them to say: that a large part of the plebeians were
away serving in the army at Velitrae; elections therefore
should be postponed until the army returned in order
that every one of the plebs might vote on these matters
which were of interest to them all.

Many years' practice had made Sextius and Licinius
adept at working upon the minds of the plebs. With some
of their colleagues and the consular tribune Fabius they
would call up the patrician leaders and harass them with
questions about each of the bills which they had proposed to the people. "When only two acres of land are
apportioned to each plebeian, do you dare to demand
that each of you be allowed to hold more than five hundred acres? Do you believe that single individuals
should possess the land of almost three hundred citizens
when the allotment of the plebeian is hardly large enough
to admit a roof for his necessities and a spot for burial?
Or do you not wish the plebeians to be able to pay their
debts? Do you prefer for them to be ruined by usury? to

surrender their bodies to imprisonment and torment? to be bound over to creditors and led out of the Forum in throngs, and to fill the nobles' mansions with prisoners so that each patrician's house may become a private prison?"

37. Their audience, who had good reason to fear these deplorable circumstances which they described, were inspired with greater resentment than the speakers themselves felt. "Not," they continued, "until one of the consuls is elected from the people as a guardian of your liberty, will the patricians ever make an end to this usurpation of land and this murder of the plebs by usury. They now contemn the plebeian tribunes, since the source of our power, the veto, is destroying itself. There can be no such thing as equal rights as long as the patricians have power to command and we have only the right to intercede. Unless the plebeians are given a share of administrative authority we shall never have equal power in the government. Nor would it be sufficient, as some might think, for plebeians to be allowed to vote in consular elections. Unless it is made mandatory for one consul at least to be elected from the plebs, there shall be no more consular elections. Have you forgotten that once the office of consular tribunes was created to replace the consuls in order that the highest office might be available to plebeians? For forty-four years not a single plebeian was elected consular tribune! Who can believe that with only two positions each year available the patricians will voluntarily share the office of consul with the plebs? When consular tribunes are elected they are accustomed to occupy eight positions. And do you imagine that they will open wide the door to the consulship when you remember how long they blockaded the way to the tribuneship? We must obtain legally what they will not grant willingly, and one of the two consulships must be reserved

for the uncontested use of the plebs alone; for when there is a competition the prize inevitably goes to the more powerful. They no longer can make the claim which they used to make—that there are no plebeians capable of holding plebeian magistracies. Since Publius Licinius Calvus, who was the first plebeian elected consular tribune, held office has the administration of government been any more negligent or inept than it was when only patricians held the tribuneship? On the contrary, several patrician tribunes have been convicted for misconduct at the close of their terms of office, but never a plebeian. A few years ago we began electing quaestors also, like the consular tribunes, from among the plebs; and not one of them has given the Roman people cause for regret. But the consulship still remains; that is the citadel, the safeguard of liberty. When this is gained then the Roman people will truly believe that the kings have been banished from the city and their liberty made secure. Indeed, on that day everything will accrue to the plebs which distinguishes the patrician: power, honor, military glory, family distinction and nobility—great things for us to enjoy, but greater still for our children to inherit."

When they saw that the people were attentive to speeches of this kind, the tribunes introduced a new bill providing that the decemvirs in charge of the Sibylline books be replaced by a commission of ten men, half of whom would be patricians and half plebeians. They postponed a vote on all these measures until the return of the army besieging Velitrae.

38. The legions did not return until after the end of the year. Thus the problem of the new proposals, which had been deferred, devolved to new consular tribunes. The same tribunes of the plebs—or at least the two who had introduced the bills—were reëlected. At the very beginning of the new year [368 B.C.] came the final con-

test over the proposals. When the tribes were called the bills' proponents were thwarted by no veto from their colleagues, and the fearful patricians hastened to their last resource—the highest office, in the hands of the most eminent citizen: They decided to appoint a dictator. It is said that Marcus Furius Camillus was chosen and he selected Lucius Aemilius as his master of horse. Against these elaborate preparations of their adversaries the proponents of the laws fortified the cause of the plebeians with great zeal, and after announcing an assembly of the plebs called the tribes to a vote.

The dictator entered angry and menacing, escorted by a whole troop of patricians. When he had taken his seat the proceedings began in the usual way, with a controversy between tribunes introducing the proposal and those intervening to prevent a vote. Although the veto had greater legal validity, the popularity of the bills themselves and those who introduced them won the day, and the first tribes were voting Aye when Camillus arose. "Roman citizens," he said, "you are now being guided not by the authority of the tribunes but by their disregard for it. And the power of the veto, which you won by seceding, is being nullified through lawlessness just as it was gained. For your sakes as much as for the sake of the whole state I shall stand by the veto and shall use my authority as dictator to defend this means for your protection which you now are subverting. Accordingly, if Gaius Licinius and Lucius Sextius are willing to yield to the veto of their colleagues I will not use the powers of a patrician magistracy to interfere with a plebeian assembly. But if they persist in disregarding the veto and trying to impose laws upon the state as if it were conquered in war I shall refuse to allow the tribunician power to destroy itself."

In answer to these words the tribunes contemptuously

continued the roll call, when Camillus in great rage ordered the lictors to eject the plebeians, adding threats that if they persisted he would administer the oath of allegiance to the young men and immediately lead the army out of the city. This intimidated the plebs, but it angered, rather than discouraged, their leaders. But before the question had been finally settled either way Camillus relinquished his office. Some authorities say he did so because of an irregularity in his election; others say that the plebeians passed a measure introduced by the tribunes that if Camillus transacted any business as dictator he should pay a fine of five hundred thousand *asses*. However, the character of the man alone persuades me that it was some flaw in his election that caused his resignation. Moreover, Publius Manlius immediately succeeded him in the dictatorship—and what use would it have been to appoint him to lead a struggle in which Camillus had been defeated? In addition Camillus held the dictatorship again the following year, and surely he would have scrupled to return to an office which had been proven ineffectual in his hands the previous year. Add to this that at the time the fine was proposed either he had the power to nullify the proposal or he could not have prevented even those measures which this proposal was designed to protect. Finally, whatever tests of strength there may have been between tribunes and consuls down to our time, the dignity of the dictatorship always has remained above such controversy.

39. During the period between the resignation of Camillus and the inauguration of Manlius the tribunes dared to call an assembly of the plebs, just as if there had been an interregnum. It now became evident which of the proposals were most pleasing to the plebs and which to the tribunes who introduced them. The people were about to approve the bills concerned with usury and the

distribution of land but reject the one providing for a plebeian consul; this would have been the end of both questions if the tribunes had not then said that they were introducing all the proposals in a package, to be voted on collectively. Subsequently Publius Manlius advanced the cause of the plebeians by appointing Gaius Licinius, a former consular tribune, as his master of horse. I am told that this angered the patricians; the dictator, however, justified his action by citing his close personal friendship with Licinius and asserting that the position carried with it no greater power than that of the consular tribune.

The time for electing tribunes of the plebs had come again. The strategy of Licinius and Sextius was to assert that they no longer wished to remain in office, while at the same time encouraging the plebs to reëlect them to the positions which they professed not to seek. "For nine years," they said, "we have carried on the struggle against the patricians, exposing ourselves to great personal danger but achieving no real benefits for the people. The bills they had introduced and the tribunician power itself have, like us, grown feeble with age. At first we were confronted with the veto of our colleagues against laws proposed in their own best interests, then with the exile of the young men to Velitrae; finally we were threatened by the overwhelming power of the dictatorship. Now we are obstructed neither by the tribunes nor the war nor even by the dictator who himself has provided an omen of the plebeian consulship which is to come by appointing one of our number master of horse. It is you, the plebeians, who are providing obstacles to your own betterment. If you wish we can immediately empty the city and the Forum of usurers, free the land from illegal seizure. But when will you repay the gratitude which is due these kindnesses, if, while embracing the measure which provide these benefits, you deprive the men who

introduced them all hope of high honor? After demanding to be rescued from usury and after receiving land
now unjustly possessed by men of power, it is unbefitting
the integrity of the Roman people to allow the old men
through whom these rights were won to fade into obscurity as ex-tribunes, without honors or hope of honor.
You should therefore settle decisively in your own minds
what you wish and declare your desires when you elect
new tribunes. If you wish to approve the measures which
we have introduced collectively then it may be advantageous to reëlect us as tribunes; we will never abandon
our bills until they are passed. But if each man is only
interested in those measures which will benefit him personally, there is no need for us to expose ourselves to
antipathy by remaining in office."

40. The astonished patricians were struck speechless
with indignation at this forward language of the tribunes.
There was no hope of dissuading the plebs, but it is said
that Appius Claudius Crassus, the grandson of the notorious decemvir, angrily arose to speak against the tribunes. "It would be nothing new or unexpected," said he,
"if I should hear now the charge which seditious tribunes
always make against my family—that from the very
establishment of the Claudian clan we have considered
nothing in the state more important than the primacy of
the patricians and always have acted against the interests
of the plebs. The first of these charges I neither deny nor
confute. It is true that from the day we were adopted into
this nation and the patrician order, we have worked un-
ceasingly to enhance rather than to diminish the dignity
of those houses among whom you wished us to be received. The second allegation I should dare to contest—
unless you think that what is done in the interests of the
whole state is injurious to the plebs, as if they lived in
another city. For I maintain on behalf of my forefathers

and myself that we have never, either as public officials or as private citizens, knowingly acted to the detriment of the plebs; nor can anyone truthfully maintain that we ever have done or said anything contrary to your well-being, although some things may have been against your desires. But if I were not a Claudius and were not born of patrician blood, but were any common citizen who knew no more of my origins than that I was born of two free parents and lived in a free country, could I keep silent at this? Lucius Sextius there and Gaius Licinius, who have permanently arrogated to themselves the tribuneship, have—heaven help us—become so brazen in the nine years of their reign that now they presume to deny you the right to vote as you wish in enacting laws as well as in the elections!

" 'On the condition,' this fellow says, 'that you reelect us tribunes for the tenth time.' Is this different from saying, 'We are so high and mighty that what others strive for we shall not condescend to accept without a large reward?' Well, what reward must we pay for the privilege of having you permanent tribunes of the plebs? 'That you adopt all our bills collectively whether you favor them or not, whether they are good or bad.' I beg you, you Tarquin-like tribunes, think of me as an ordinary citizen calling out from the middle of the assembly, 'Give us your kind permission to choose from these measures those we think advantageous and reject the rest.' 'No,' he says, 'you may not approve the bills concerning usury and land, which are of interest to you, unless you consent to endure the sight of Lucius Sextius and Gaius Licinius as consuls of the city of Rome—a possibility which you abominate and abhor. Take all or nothing!' This is as if someone should place food and poison before a starving man and order him either to do without what he needs in order to live or mix with it what certainly will

kill him. If this were a free state you would have cried
out in unison, 'Go, and take your bills and tribuneships
with you!' What? If the tribunes will not allow the people
to adopt measures which are in their best interests, then
who will? If any patrician or—as the tribunes will tell
you is more reprehensible—if any Claudius should say
'Take all or nothing,' which of you would endure it? Will
you never consider facts rather than personalities? Must
you always listen favorably to what that official says and
disdain to hear what is said by any of us?

"His words, you will admit, are entirely unbefitting a
citizen of a democracy. Well, what kind of bill is this
which they angrily deny you the right to reject? It is a bill
very like their words, Roman citizens. 'I ask,' says this
man, 'that you be forbidden to choose the consuls whom
you wish.' Isn't this the real meaning of a man who would
order that one consul be elected from among the plebs
and refuse to permit you the right of electing two patricians? If today there were wars like the Etruscan war
when Porsinna occupied the Janiculum, or the Gallic war
when the enemy was in possession of all the city except
for the Capitol and the citadel; and if Lucius Sextius over
there were running for the consulship along with Camillus and one other patrician, would you really be able to
endure for Sextius to be assured of being elected while
Camillus was in danger of defeat? And is this what you
call 'sharing' offices—for two plebeians to be able to be
elected consul but not two patricians? Is it imperative that
we elect one consul from among the plebeians while at
the same time it is lawful to defeat any patrician? What
kind of fellowship, what kind of coöperation is this?
When you gain a part of something of which you have
had no part before, is it too little to ask for a part? Must
you have the whole? 'I am afraid,' says he, 'that if it is
possible for two patricians to be elected you will never

elect a plebeian.' What he means is 'Since you will never voluntarily elect unworthy men I shall compel you to do so against your wishes.' What is the logical consequence of this? Simply that if one plebeian runs for office along with two patricians he will feel no obligation to the people at all. He will say he was elected not by your votes but by the law.

41. "Their purpose is to take offices by force, not to solicit votes for them as candidates. They intend to obtain the greatest concessions from you in such a way that they will owe nothing even for the smallest. And they prefer to exploit circumstances to win themselves honors rather than to compete for them on the basis of ability. There are some men who revolt against being scrutinized and evaluated. They seem to think it fair for themselves alone to be assured of honors while others compete strenuously for them. They would exempt themselves from judgment by you. They would make your votes for them obligatory, rather than voluntary—the votes not of free citizens but of slaves. To say nothing of Licinius and Sextius, whose years in constant power you can number as if they were kings in the Capitol—who is there in the city today so lowly that this law would not make the way to the consulship easier for him than it is for us patricians and our children? Indeed you sometimes may be unable to elect us even when you wish, and you may be forced to elect them even when you do not wish.

"But I have said enough about the indignity of this matter. Dignity, after all, is a matter which affects only men. What about religious rites and auspices? Contempt and injury to these is the concern of the immortal gods. Who is there who is not aware that this city was founded under the auspices, that no enterprises at home or in the field, in war or in peace, are undertaken except under the auspices? And whose prerogative is the taking of the

auspices according to the immemorial usage of our forefathers? That of the patricians, of course. For no plebeian official ever is elected under the auspices. And not
only are the patrician magistrates always elected under
the auspices; the auspices are so completely the prerogative of the patricians that we ourselves without the approval of the people often appoint an interrex under the
auspices; we even take the auspices as private citizens,
which plebeians cannot do even as magistrates. The
man, therefore, who proposes to create plebeian consuls
and thus to take away the auspices from the patricians
who alone can have them, wishes to deprive the state itself of them. Let them scoff now at our religious practices: 'What difference does it make if chickens refuse to
eat?' they say. 'Or if they are a little slow to come out of
their coop? Or if the cry of a bird is inauspicious?' Well,
these are small matters. But your ancestors did not build
this great state by neglecting small matters. Now we—as
if we no longer had need of peace with the gods—are
desecrating all religious usages. Let us appoint priests and
augurs and kings of the sacrifices indiscriminately from
the whole population. Let us place the hat of the priest of
Jove upon anyone's head, provided only that he be a human being. Let us discard all questions of piety and en-
trust the sacred shields, the innermost shrines of the gods,
and the care of the gods to whomever we wish. Let us not
bother with the auspices in enacting laws or electing magistrates. Why should the Comitia Centuriata and the
Comitia Tributa have to be authorized by the senate?

"Let Sextius and Licinius rule over the city like Romulus and Tatius, since they are already so generous with
other people's land. It is so attractive to plunder the fortunes of others that it has not entered their heads that one
of these proposals, by driving out the occupants, will
make a vast desert of the countryside. Another will de-

stroy credit, and with it all human society. For all these reasons I ask you to reject these proposals. And may the gods make your decision a happy one!"

42. The speech of Appius served only to postpone the enactment of the tribunes' bills. Licinius and Sextius, after having been reëlected for the tenth time, now succeeded in passing the measure providing for the creation of a commission of ten men, half of them plebeians and half patricians, who should have charge of the Sibylline books. After five patricians and five plebeians had been elected it seemed to the plebeians that they had made a significant step along the path to the consulship. Mollified by this victory, the plebeians ceased to importune the patricians. For the present no further mention was made of plebeian consuls and consular tribunes again were elected. . . .

Rome now was troubled by no foreign wars except for the siege of Velitrae, and the end of this was slow in coming rather than doubtful. Suddenly, however, a report arrived of an approaching Gallic war, which prompted the citizens to declare Marcus Furius dictator for the fifth time. He appointed Titus Quinctius Poenus as his master of horse. According to Claudius, a battle was fought that year [367 B.C.] near the Anio River in which the famous battle occurred between Titus Manlius and a Gaul. After being challenged by the Gaul, Manlius killed him in a single combat which took place between the two armies, then stripped him of the collar he wore.

Contrary to Claudius, however, I am disposed to follow the majority of authors who say that these events took place ten years later and that the battle this year between the dictator Camillus and the Gauls took place near Alba. The Romans won an easy victory despite their great fear, inspired by the memory of their ancient disaster. Many thousands of barbarians were killed in the field and many more after the camp was captured. Others, who made for Apulia, were saved by the distance and because they had become widely separated in their panic and blind wandering. A triumph was decreed to the dictator by the senate and the plebs.

Camillus had scarcely brought the war to an end when a more dangerous, internal crisis claimed him. This time after a vehement struggle he and the senate were defeated and forced to accept the proposals of the tribunes. In the face of aristocratic opposition an election of consuls was held and Lucius Sextius was elected first plebeian consul. But this was not the end of the dissension. When the senate refused to ratify the election, a secession of the plebs almost occurred and other terrible threats were made. Finally, through the intercession of the dictator, the two sides were reconciled on the following terms. The patricians agreed to allow the plebeians their plebeian consul, and they in turn agreed to the election by the patricians of one praetor to administer justice in the city. As a result of this reconciliation between the orders which was finally brought about after such a long dispute, the senate decided that now, if ever, the gods deserved to be honored by a celebration of the Great Games, and that a fourth day should be added to the usual three. When the plebeian aediles refused to take on this burden, the young patricians cried out in unison that they would gladly do it for the sake of honoring the immortal gods. This offer was accepted with gratitude by everyone. The senate then decreed that the dictator should propose to the people the election of two patricians as aediles and that the senate should confirm all elections for that year.

Book 7
3 6 6 - 3 4 0 B C

1. This year [probably 366 B.C.] is noteworthy for the election of a "new man" (the first member of a plebeian family to hold a consulship) as consul, as well as for the institution of two new offices—the praetorship and the curule aedileship. These offices were claimed by the patricians for themselves as compensation for granting one consulship to the plebs. The plebeians gave the consulship to Lucius Sextius who had introduced the law by which it was obtained. The patricians, by their influence at the ballot box, obtained the praetorship for Spurius Furius Camillus, the son of Marcus, and the aedileship for Gnaius Quinctius Capitolinus and Publius Cornelius Scipio, all men of their order. Lucius Aemilius Mamercus was chosen as Sextius' colleague. At the first of the year there were rumors that the Gauls, after being scattered through Apulia, were again assembling and that a revolt was brewing among the Hernici. However, all business was purposely postponed so that the plebeian consul might have no part in the administration of public affairs. The quiet and leisurely atmosphere which resulted made it like a legal holiday, except that the tribunes would let no one forget that for one plebeian consul the patricians had received three magistrates who wore the *toga praetexta* and sat on curule chairs as the consuls did. Indeed, the praetor even administered justice, was considered as a colleague to the consuls, and was elected under the

same auspices. Because of this antagonism the senate thereafter was reluctant to insist that the curule aediles be elected from the patricians; at first an agreement was made to elect plebeians on alternate years, but later aediles were elected from either order without distinction.

The next year, in the consulship of Lucius Genucius and Quintus Servilius, there was neither civil discord nor foreign war; but it seemed that there could never be any respite from fear and danger, for a terrible epidemic broke out. It is recorded that a censor, a curule aedile, and three tribunes of the plebs died, along with a corresponding proportion from the population as a whole. The death of Camillus made this plague especially noteworthy. Although he now was an old man his death caused great sadness, for he was truly singular in every circumstance of fortune. In peace and in war he was Rome's leading citizen before his banishment, and in exile he attained even greater eminence. His unique position was evidenced by the longing with which the captured city had beseeched him to return as well as by the success with which he had restored liberty to his native land. For twenty-five years thereafter—as long as he lived—he retained such respect and honor that he was deemed worthy of being considered the second founder of Rome.

2. The pestilence continued into the next year [364 B.C.], when Gaius Sulpicius Peticus and Gaius Licinius Stolo were consuls. In that year nothing occurred worth recording except that, in order to allay the anger of the gods, a *lectisternium,* or "feast of the gods," was held for the third time since the founding of the city. Yet neither human contrivances nor divine aid seemed to mitigate the fury of the plague, and it is said that people were overcome with superstitious fear. Among other efforts to conciliate the divine wrath, dramas were presented on

the stage—a strange thing for a warlike people whose only previous entertainment had been exhibitions in the circus. However, this drama had a modest beginning, as things usually do, and was of foreign origin at that. There was no singing and no action which told a story by charade. Players imported from Etruria simply danced to the music of the flute in not ungraceful motions, according to the Etruscan manner. Soon the young Romans began to imitate them, adding also rough verses of a jocular character and adapting gestures to their words. This form of entertainment became popular, and with frequent repetition improved in quality. The name *histriones* was given to the local actors, derived from the Etruscan word *ister,* or "player." As the art developed the actors no longer simply tossed out unpolished verses like the Fescennine without regard for continuity; soon they presented medleys all in verse written to the tune of the flute and accompanied by appropriate gestures.

After a few years Livius Andronicus was the first to abandon the loose medley construction and to compose a drama with a plot. This man, like all early playwrights, was an actor as well. It is said that he also originated the practice of using singers to accompany his acting, reserving only the dialogue portions for the actors. His many encores caused his voice to crack, and, with permission of his audience, he posted a boy before the flautist to sing while he acted his part. He found that he was able to act with greater vigor and conviction when free of the restraints necessary for clear diction.

As a result of these improvements, drama was liberated from the level of mere comic and informal mummery and began to become more and more artistic. Then, however, the young Romans began to abandon formal acting to the professionals and return to their original practice of gibing at each other in verse. This was the origin of the *exodia,* or after-plays, which were often attached to the Atellan farces. This particular dramatic genre, which they borrowed from the Oscans, the young men never allowed professional actors to taint. In consequence the rule which still obtains acquired its force: actors in Atellan farces are not disfranchised and may serve in the army; association with the stage does not disqualify them. I have thought it right that the origin of drama should be mentioned along with other history in order to show from what modest beginnings it has burgeoned to such extravagance as can hardly be afforded by wealthy kingdoms.

6. That same year a rift is said to have opened in the middle of the Forum, whether because of a tremor of the earth or other violent force, and to have formed a huge cavern of enormous depth. The abyss could not be filled by throwing earth into it, though everyone carried as much as he could. Eventually the bards foretold that they must dedicate to that phenomenon, if they wished the Roman state to endure forever, that one thing which was the Roman people's particular forte, and investigation was set on foot to determine what that thing might be. The story is that Marcus Curtius, a young man of extraordinary gallantry, chided them for doubting that the Romans possessed any quality higher than arms and valor. In the silence that fell he gazed at the temples of the immortal gods which ringed the Forum and at the Capitol, he spread his hands out now to heaven and again to the deities below in the yawning crevice, and so vowed his own immolation. Then he sat upon a horse decked with the handsomest trappings possible, and so armed cap-a-pie flung himself into the pit. Offerings and fruit were heaped over him by the multitude of men and women. It was after this Curtius, it is said, that the Lacus Curtius got its name, and not from the ancient Mettius Curtius

who served under Titus Tatius. To find the path of truth
in this matter would require careful research, but where
antiquity renders vouchers unreliable we take our stand
on the basis of tradition; it is this more recent legend that
has made the name Lacus Curtius notable.

*The year 343 marked the beginning of war with the
Samnites, a people of central Italy who spoke Oscan, a
language related to Latin. This struggle for supremacy
over the southern half of Italy continued intermittently
until 290 B.C.*

29. From this point my account will be concerned
with wars which overshadowed their predecessors with
respect to their duration, to the might of the enemy, and
to the remoteness of the areas in which they were waged.
In this year [343 B.C.] war was declared against the Samnites, a nation powerful in wealth and in military prowess.
Following the struggle with the Samnites, which was
fought with many vicissitudes, Pyrrhus became the enemy, and after Pyrrhus, the Carthaginians. How many
desperate struggles and near-fatal crises were experienced
in order to extend the empire to its present vast size—
which now it is scarcely able to support!

The trouble with the Samnites, to whom the Romans
had become allied, grew out of the grievances of a third
party, and not from the relations between the two nations.
The Samnites had unjustly attacked the Sidicini simply
because they happened to be weaker. The Sidicini in
their difficulties were forced to turn for help to a nation
of greater strength, and allied themselves to the Campanians. However, the Campanians, who were enervated
by their luxurious way of life, brought only nominal assistance rather than real strength to the defense of their
allies. They were routed in Sidicinian territory by men
who were hardened to warfare by long practice. And by

their intervention they drew the brunt of the Samnite attack on themselves. The Samnites, now disdaining the Sidicini, attacked the very stronghold of the Campanians; for here the victory would be easy and the plunder and glory greater. When they had established a strong position on Tifata, a ridge of hills overlooking Capua, they marched down in battle order onto the plain which lies between Tifata and Capua. There a second battle was fought in which the Campanians were defeated and driven back into the city. With their choicest troops now lost and with no hope of aid in sight, they were forced to seek help from Rome.

30. Their envoys who were presented to the senate spoke in this strain: "Senators, the Campanians have sent us to you to seek aid for the present, but to promise friendship forever. If we had sought this alliance in prosperous times, it might have been arranged more quickly, but would be secured by weaker bonds, for then we should remember that our association was begun on equal terms. As a result perhaps we should be equally friendly, but we also should be less submissive and compliant toward you. As it is, after being won by your pity and defended in a desperate situation by your aid, it will behoove us to respect your kindness or seem ungrateful and unworthy of all human and divine aid. We do not think that the fact that the Samnites are already your allies is any bar to an alliance with us, even though their claims may outweigh ours in priority and importance. For your treaty with the Samnites does not preclude all other alliances.

"To you the mere fact that your friendship was sought has always been a sufficient cause for alliance. Our present circumstances forbid proud words. And yet the Campanians in respect to the size of their city and the richness of their soil yield to no other nation but you;

we should provide, I think, a worthy addition to your prosperity. And whenever your perpetual enemies, the Volscians and the Aequi bestir themselves, we shall be standing at their rear. What you do now for our safety we always shall do for your empire and glory. When those nations which lie between us and you are conquered—a time which your bravery and fortune promises not to be distant—you will hold uninterrupted dominion all the way to our borders. Our fortune forces us to confess a bitter and lamentable truth, gentlemen: we are forced by circumstances to become subject either to our friends or our enemies. If you defend us, we are yours; if not, we belong to the Samnites."

31. When the ambassadors had withdrawn, the senate took the matter into consideration. Many thought that since Capua was the greatest and richest city in Italy, had the richest land, and was situated on the sea, it would serve as a granary for Rome against the vicissitudes of the harvest. But in spite of these advantages loyalty to their word seemed more important. Therefore by direction of the senate the consul answered the ambassadors: "The senate thinks you worthy of assistance, men of Campania, but it is right for us to enter into an alliance with you only on condition of not breaking a previous agreement. The Samnites are allied to us by treaty; thus we must deny you military assistance which would be a breach of faith toward the gods, more than toward the Samnites. But, as is right and just, we shall send ambassadors to our allies to ask that they not attack you." To this the leader of the delegation answered, according to the instructions he had received at home: "Since you do not think it lawful to protect our interests against violence and injury, surely you will protect your own. Therefore we surrender to the authority of the senate and the Roman people the people of Campania, the city Capua, its

land, its temples of the gods, all things human and divine; whatever we suffer, we shall suffer as your subjects."

With these words the Campanians prostrated themselves in the entrance of the curia, stretching forth their hands to the consuls. The senators were moved by the vicissitudes of human fortune at the thought that this nation which had been so wealthy, so famous for luxury and pride, from whom neighbors had recently sought assistance, was now so subdued in spirit that it surrendered itself and all its wealth to an alien power. Moreover they now thought it to be a point of honor not to betray those who had surrendered to them and concluded that it would not be just of the Samnites to attack a city which was now the territory of the Roman people. Thus it was decided to send envoys to the Samnites who should outline to them the Campanians' request, the answer of the senate which had been faithful to the alliance with the Samnites, and the subsequent formal surrender of Capua to Rome. They were to request that the Samnites spare these new subjects of the Romans, in consideration of their alliance with Rome, and not attack a land which was now the territory of the Roman people. But if gentle words had no effect, the ambassadors were to demand in the name of the senate and the Roman people that the Samnites cease their molestation of the city of Capua and the territory of Campania. When the envoys delivered this message to the council of the Samnites, they responded violently. Replying angrily that they would continue to wage war on Capua, their leaders marched out of their senate house, and, while the envoys stood by, summoned the commanders of their cohorts, commanding them in a loud voice to set out immediately for the Campanian territory and to plunder it.

Book 8
3 4 1 - 3 2 2 B C

*Against the Samnites the Romans at first were success-
ful. The following year, however, an insurrection within
the army forced the Romans to agree to a renewal of their
original treaty with the Samnites. The irresolution of the
Romans in this war emboldened the Latin cities, who resented their inferior position, to demand a position of
equality in the Latin League. Roman rejection of this demand in 340 B.C. led to open revolt, in which the Latins
were joined by their allies, the Campanians and the Volscians. The Romans, in turn, were given active support by
the Samnites, who already were engaged in hostilities
with the Latin-Campanian alliance.*

6. The consuls enlisted two armies and set out through
the territories of the Marsi and Paeligni. After joining
the Samnite army, they pitched camp near Capua, where
the Latins and their allies had convened. There it is said
that each consul was visited by a dream in the form of a
man taller and more imposing than any ordinary human. This vision asserted that during the coming battle
the commander of one side and the army of the other
would have to be devoted to the Manes and to Mother
Earth; that army would be victorious whose commander
should devote the legions of the enemy and himself with
them. When the consuls had compared their nocturnal
visions it seemed best to make sacrificial offerings in order
to avert the anger of the gods; then, if the entrails of the

victims should reveal the same warnings which had been portended in the dream, one or the other of the consuls would carry out the behests of fate. The soothsayers conducting the sacrifices confirmed the words of the vision, which the consuls already had felt to be true in their hearts.

First the consuls summoned the legates and tribunes, and informed them of the mandates of the gods, so that the voluntary death of one of the consuls might not terrify the army in the midst of battle. They then agreed between themselves that the consul in command of the front which first began to yield should devote himself on behalf of the Roman people and the Quirites. They also asserted in the council that, if strict obedience and austerity had ever been demanded in time of war, now was the time to return to the military discipline of former days. The consuls were especially anxious because their enemies were the peoples of Latium, whose language, customs, weapons, and above all, military tactics, were very like their own. In the past the common soldiers, centurions, and tribunes on both sides had associated as equals and companions in the same camps and often in the same companies. For fear that the resulting confusion might cause some disastrous error, the consuls issued an order that no one should leave his proper rank to attack the enemy.

7. Squadrons of cavalry were sent out to explore the surrounding countryside. It happened that the commander of one of these was Titus Manlius, the son of the consul. He advanced with his company beyond the enemy camp until he was scarcely a spear's throw away from the nearest guard post. There the cavalry of Tusculum was posted; their commander was Geminus Maecius, a man prominent for his accomplishments as well as his noble birth. As the Roman cavalry approached

Geminus recognized the son of the consul riding con-
spicuously at their head—all of them, especially distinguished men, were acquainted with each other. "Do you
wish to wage war against the Latins and their allies with
one squadron?" he said. "What do the consuls and two
consular armies propose to do in the meantime?" "They
will be here in good time," replied Manlius, "and with
them a mightier ally—Jupiter himself who is witness of
the treaties violated by you. If we gave you your fill of
battle at Lake Regillus, here too we shall make sure that
you find battle with us not greatly to your taste." At these
words Geminus rode out a short distance ahead of his
men. "Well, then," he said, "in anticipation of that day
when you unleash the might of your armies, would you
like to join battle with me so that we may see now how
superior a Latin knight is to a Roman?" The warlike spirit
of the young man was aroused; perhaps it was anger,
or reluctance to shirk a fight, or perhaps the inexorable
power of fate. Neither victory nor defeat in such a contest
would be of any consequence, but forgetting the command of his father and the edict of the consuls, he rushed
headlong into combat.

The rest of the horsemen were moved back as if it
were a spectacle, and in the intervening space the two
opponents spurred their horses against each other. When
their lances struck, that of Manlius grazed the helmet of
his enemy, while Geminus' weapon slipped across the
neck of Manlius' horse. When they turned and charged
again, Manlius sprang forward first and struck Geminus'
horse between the ears. The animal reared up in pain and
shook its head violently, throwing its rider. As Geminus
leaned on his spear and shield and lifted himself up from
his crushing fall, Manlius thrust the lance down his throat
so hard that it emerged between his ribs and pinned him
to the ground. After stripping the body of spoils Manlius

rode back to his men and led his jubilant squadron back to camp. He immediately proceeded to the headquarters of his father, unaware of what awaited him in the future and whether praise or punishment would be his reward.

"Father," he said, "so that all men may say I am truly born of your seed, I bring you these spoils taken from an enemy slain by me." When the consul heard these words immediately he turned his back on his son and ordered an assembly to be sounded on the trumpet. When a crowd had gathered he turned to his son and said, "You, Titus Manlius, have respected neither the consular edict nor your father's authority, and have left your ranks to fight against the enemy. So far as you were able you have undermined the military discipline upon which Roman power has always depended. Because of this you have laid upon me the necessity of forgetting my country or myself. It is better that we be punished for our sins than that the republic suffer to atone for our transgression. We shall be a melancholy example, but a beneficial one, for young men of the future. I am affected by both the inborn love of a father and this token of your courage, which has been led astray by an illusory conception of honor. But the orders of the consuls must either be confirmed by your death or nullified forever by your immunity; I am sure that not even you, if any of my blood is in you, think it wrong for your punishment to reëstablish the military discipline which has been undermined by your wrong-doing. Go, Lictor, bind him to the stake."

All were stunned at this cruel edict. Each man seemed to see the axe raised above his own head. They stood quiet, motionless, as if overcome by astonishment, silenced by fear rather than by respect. Suddenly, when blood gushed out of the severed neck, they broke into unbridled weeping, sparing neither curses nor laments. They covered the youth's body with his spoils, and built a pyre outside the rampart of the camp, where they burned it with full military honors. The "Manlian discipline" not only appalled his contemporaries but became an example of harshness for posterity. 8. Nevertheless this cruel punishment made the soldiers more obedient. Greater care was devoted to sentry duties and watches, and the ordering of guard posts; but, more important, this severe discipline proved to be beneficial during the final battle itself. That battle was very reminiscent of civil warfare: Nothing of the Latins was very different from its Roman equivalent—except their courage.

9. Before marching out to battle the Roman consuls first offered sacrifice. The soothsayer examining the entrails informed Decius that when he sacrificed, the "head" of the liver had been struck in the area related to himself, foreboding his death; in other respects the victim was acceptable to the gods. Manlius' sacrifice was completely auspicious. "It is sufficient," said Decius, "if my colleague's sacrifice has been successful." The soldiers then fell into formation and the army marched forth to battle. Manlius was in command of the right wing, Decius the left. At first both sides struggled with equal strength and courage. Finally, however, the Roman front line was no longer able to stand firm and was forced to fall back. Amid this disorder the consul Decius called in a great voice to Marcus Valerius, "We need the help of the gods, Marcus Valerius. Come then, as pontifex of the Roman people dictate to me the words by which I may devote myself in the army's behalf." The pontifex ordered him to don the toga of his office and, after veiling his head, to reach out from beneath his toga with one hand and touch his chin; then, standing upon a spear he was to recite the following formula: "Janus, Jupiter, father Mars, Quirinus, Bellona, Lares, divine Novensiles, divine Indigetes, gods who have power over us and our

enemies, and divine Manes, I pray to you and I implore, I beseech and I beg, that you may bestow upon the Roman people power and victory and afflict the enemies of the Roman people with fear, terror, and death. Even as I have uttered these words, thus on behalf of the republic of the Roman people, the army, the legions and the auxiliaries of the Roman people, I have devoted along with me the legions and auxiliaries of the enemy to divine Manes and to Earth."

Having completed this prayer he ordered the lictors to proceed at once to Titus Manlius and announce to his colleagues that he had devoted himself on behalf of the army. Then, donning his armor and girdling himself with the Gabinian cincture, he leaped upon his horse and rode headlong into the middle of the enemy. To both armies he appeared a striking figure, more magnificent than any human, as if sent from heaven to appease the anger of the gods and bear ruin away from his own people down upon their enemies. The panic and terror which accompanied him threw the first line of the Latins into disorder, then spread through all their ranks. Wherever he rode on his horse men quailed in terror as if stricken by a pestilential star; but when he fell under a barrage of spears the Latin cohorts openly panicked and fled. At the same time the Roman legions rose up and renewed the battle as if now the signal had been given for the first time.

Book 9

3 2 2 - 3 0 4 B C

During the so-called Second Samnite War (327-304
B.C.) *a Roman force of twenty thousand men was trapped
in a mountain defile and forced to surrender. This hu-
miliating defeat was a great blow to Roman honor, but
the treaty which followed allowed the Romans five years
respite from war during which to rebuild their military
strength. They renounced this treaty in 315* B.C. *and resumed the war, eventually forcing the Samnites to petition for peace.*

1. In the following year, during the consulship of
Titus Veturius Calvinus and Spurius Postumius, came
the Caudine Peace, which marked a momentous disaster to
the people of Rome. The general of the Samnites that
year was Gaius Pontius, whose father, Herennius, was
the shrewdest of men; he was himself an outstanding soldier and general. When the ambassadors whom he had
sent to Rome (after an overwhelming Roman victory) to
offer restitution returned without concluding a treaty, he
said: "Do not think that this embassy has accomplished
nothing; whatever grudge the gods cherished against us
for breaking the treaty [of 341 B.C.] now has been expiated. I know well that the gods who wished to force us
to make reparation for violating the treaty were not
pleased when the Romans so disdainfully rejected our attempted atonement. What more was it possible to do to
appease the gods and conciliate men? We returned the

plunder taken from the enemy, which should have been ours according to the rights of war. The instigators of the war, whom we could not surrender alive, we surrendered dead. All the property of these men we carried to Rome lest anything infected with their guilt remain with us. What more, Rome, do we owe to you? What more to the treaty and to the gods who witnessed it? Whom can I propose to judge your anger and my punishment? There is no nation nor individual whom I should refuse. Do human laws leave no protection for the weak in his struggles with a more powerful enemy? Then I shall turn for aid to the gods who avenge unbearable pride. I pray that they may turn their anger upon the Romans, who are not satisfied with recovering their own possessions and amassing the property of others. Their anger is not satisfied with the death of the guilty, the surrender of their lifeless bodies with all their property, unless we offer them our own blood to drink and our entrails to tear to pieces. War is just, Samnites, to whom it is necessary, and arms are righteous when arms are our only hope. The greatest determining factor in the affairs of men is whether their actions are approved or disapproved by the gods; be sure, then, that in previous wars your greatest enemies have been the gods, not men; but now you shall fight with the gods themselves as your leaders."

2. After uttering these predictions, which were as true as they were auspicious, Pontius led out his army and encamped with the greatest possible secrecy near Caudium. He then sent ten soldiers disguised as shepherds to Calatia where he had heard that the Roman camp was situated. These men were under orders to separate and to graze their flocks not far from the Roman guard posts; when they came upon plundering parties they were all to tell the same tale—that the Samnite legions were in Apulia concentrating all their efforts upon the siege

of Luceria, which they soon would capture. This rumor
already had been purposely bruited about and had
reached the ears of the Romans. But these captives
seemed to increase its credibility, especially since their
stories agreed in particulars. The Romans were quite willing to bring aid to Luceria, which was a good and faithful
ally, for there was danger that all Apulia would defect in
the face of the impending danger. The only question was
the route which they should take.

Two roads led to Luceria. One went through open
country along the coast of the Adriatic, and was safer but
also longer. The other, shorter, route passed through the
Caudine Forks. The nature of the terrain is such that two
deep gorges, narrow and wooded, are linked by a continuous range of mountains on both sides. Enclosed between
these lies a fairly wide grassy plain with plenty of water;
the road runs through the middle of this valley. But before you reach this road you must pass through the first
gorge and from there either go back by the route you
came or, if you wish to proceed forward, continue
through a second, narrower and more obstructed defile.

The Romans marched down through one of the rocky
gorges and out into the valley. From there they proceeded
immediately to the other pass but found it blocked by a
barrier of large rocks and fallen trees. A body of enemy
troops was sighted at the head of the pass, and the artifice
of the enemy now was apparent. The Romans quickly
retreated to the pass by which they had entered, but found
it also shut off by a barrier and armed men. The troops
halted spontaneously without orders from their commanders. Their minds and limbs became paralyzed, and
they stood motionless and silent as if in a trance. Each
of them looked around at the others for guidance as if
he thought them better able to reason than himself. Finally they saw the consuls' tents being set up and some

men taking out the tools for erecting fortifications. They realized that it would be folly to attempt to fortify themselves in this desperate situation, but they were anxious not to seem remiss even in such disaster, and each of his own accord, with no encouragement or orders from anyone, set about fortifying a camp next to the water. All the while the enemy jeered at them arrogantly, and they themselves jested wryly about the uselessness of their labor. The discouraged consuls did not even summon a council, thinking all advice and aid would be fruitless; but the legates and tribunes convened of their own accord and the common soldiers gathered around the consuls' tent demanding help from their commanders which even the immortal gods were scarcely able to grant.

3. Nor could the Samnites immediately decide what should be done in this happy situation, and so agreed that a message should be sent to consult Herennius Pontius, father of the general. Herennius was now advanced in years and had retired from both civil and military life; but even though his body was feeble his mind was as vigorous as ever. When he had been informed that a Roman army had been trapped at the Caudine Forks between the two passes and a messenger from his son had arrived asking his advice, he recommended that they all be released at once unharmed. This proposal was rejected and the same messenger returned to consult him a second time; he then advised that the Romans all be killed. These answers seemed as conflicting and cryptic as responses from an ambiguous oracle, and Herennius' son himself was among the first to decide that his father's mind as well as his body had grown senile. However, popular opinion prevailed upon him to summon his father in person to a consultation.

It is said that the old man did not demur, and was carried to the camp in a wagon. After being called into the council he spoke almost the same words as before, adding only his reasons. Following his first advice, which he considered best, they might use this great benefit to establish a perpetual peace and friendship with a very powerful people. By the other plan, two Roman armies would be destroyed and they would postpone the renewal of the war for many generations while Rome was recovering her strength. There was no third alternative. His son and the other leaders importuned him, asking why they should not take the middle course, releasing the Romans unharmed but exacting conditions upon them as a defeated enemy in accordance with the laws of war. To this Herennius answered, "This is the sort of proposal which neither makes friends nor disposes of enemies. Spare them, if you wish, after branding them with ignominy: the Roman race cannot remain quiet in defeat. Any disgrace which you brand upon them will burn in their bosoms and forbid them to rest until they have exacted a manifold retribution from you." However, neither plan found favor, and Herennius was carried home from the camp.

4. Meanwhile in the Roman camp many efforts to break out had been frustrated and now all supplies had run out. Necessity forced them to send ambassadors who were first to seek a favorable peace, then if peace was not granted, to provoke the Samnites to fight. Pontius answered only that the war was over; and since they did not know how to confess their fate even in defeat and captivity, he would send them under the yoke unarmed and wearing a single garment each. All other conditions would apply equally to conquerors and conquered. If Rome would withdraw from Samnite territory and remove their colonies, the Romans and the Samnites should then live each under their own laws on terms of equality. He was prepared to draw up a treaty with the consuls on these conditions; but if any of these terms were unsatisfactory

he forbade the envoys to come to him again. When these terms were reported to the Romans they received the news with great dejection; it seemed that they would not have been more grief-stricken if it had been announced that they would all meet their deaths on the spot.

A deep silence fell. The consuls were unable to open their mouths either to support such disgraceful terms or to oppose such necessary ones. At length Lucius Lentulus, the bravest and most eminent of the legates, spoke: "Consuls, I have often heard my father say that he was the only member of the senate who opposed ransoming the city from the Gauls. The enemy was very lazy about building fortifications and had not surrounded them with a trench or a rampart, so that they could have broken out —possibly with great peril but still without certain ruin. They were able to rush down upon the enemy with swords raised from the Capitol, just as the besieged often swoop down upon their besiegers. Now if we, whether on favorable ground or not, had even the opportunity of meeting our enemy in battle, I should give you the same spirited advice as my father before me. As for me, I acknowledge that it is a splendid thing to die on behalf of one's country, and I am prepared to sacrifice myself on behalf of the Roman people and their legions or to plunge into the middle of the enemy. But here is my country before my eyes, and here are all the Roman legions; and what can these legions save by their deaths unless they wish to die for their own gratification? 'The roofs of the city,' someone may say, 'and its walls and its population!' On the contrary, all these will be betrayed, not saved by the destruction of this army. . . . 'But surrender is base and shameful,' you may say. This then is love of country —to endure any disgrace just as you would endure death, if necessary, to save it. Therefore let us yield to necessity which not even the gods could avoid and resign ourselves to this indignity, however great. Go, Consuls, and surrender our arms as ransom for the city which our fathers ransomed with gold!"

5. The consuls then went to confer with Pontius. But when he mentioned the treaty they insisted that they were not authorized to make a treaty without the approval of the people or without the fetial priests (who made declarations of war and treaties of peace) and the rest of the established ritual. Therefore the peace of Caudium was not confirmed by a treaty as is commonly believed and as Claudius even writes, but by a verbal covenant. For in the case of a treaty what need would there have been of sureties or hostages? The transaction is completed with the imprecation that if either nation violates the stated terms it may be struck by Jupiter just as the swine is struck by the fetial priests. Moreover, the names of the consuls, legates, quaestors and military tribunes who entered into the covenant are extant; but if a treaty had been compacted the names only of the fetial priests would have been recorded. And because of the necessary delay before a treaty could be approved, six hundred knights were surrendered as hostages who were to suffer death if the Romans did not abide by the terms of the armistice. Subsequently the time was fixed for the surrender of the knights and the release of the unarmed soldiers.

The return of the consuls revived the distress in the camp to the extent that they could scarcely refrain from doing violence to them. It was their impetuosity which had led them into that situation and because of their cowardice escape would be more disgraceful than capture. There had been no guide or scouts; they had been led blindly like beasts into a trap. They first looked around from one to the other, then gazed at their arms which soon must be surrendered, their right hands soon to be empty, and their bodies which soon would be powerless before the enemy. Each could see in his mind the hostile yoke, the jeers of the victors, their looks of scorn, their own march without arms through the midst of the armed enemy, the miserable journey of the humiliated army through the allied cities, and their return to their parents and their fatherland where often in the past they themselves and their forefathers had arrived in triumph. They alone had been defeated without a wound, without a struggle. They had not been allowed to unsheath their swords or join battle with the enemy. In vain had they been endowed with arms, in vain with strength, in vain with courage.

As they fretted with such thoughts as these the destined hour of their disgrace arrived. Reality was to prove more unbearable even than they had pictured it in their imaginations. First they were ordered to leave their fortification unarmed and clad only in a single garment; the hostages then were surrendered and taken away into custody. Next the consuls were commanded to dismiss their lictors and their generals' cloaks were removed. A little while before everyone had been cursing them and asserting that they should be surrendered for torture; now they were so struck with pity that each man forgot his own condition and averted his eyes from the awful sight of the abasement of this great dignity.

6. First the consuls, almost half-naked, were sent under the yoke. The other officers then followed by order or rank, and finally the individual legions. The enemy stood in arms on each side cursing and taunting them. Many even were threatened with swords and some were wounded or killed when their angry expressions offended the victors.

Thus they were sent under the yoke—and what was almost worse, before the eyes of the enemy. When they came out of the defile they seemed to see the light for the first time, like men released from the underworld. But when they looked around at the army's wretched plight the light seemed more bitter than any death. They could have reached Capua before nightfall, but they were uncertain of their allies' fidelity and were held back also by shame. Thus, in spite of their hunger and nakedness they lay down along both sides of the road not far from the city. When news of this reached the Campanians, a proper pity for their allies conquered their native haughtiness. They immediately sent out to the consuls the insignia of their office and to the army weapons, horses, clothing and supplies. All the senate and population of Capua went out of the city to meet them and extended to them both publicly and privately every courtesy due a guest. But the Romans, in response to the friendly words and faces of their allies, not only were unable to speak; they could not even raise their eyes and face their sympathetic friends. Shame as well as grief forced them to avoid all conversation and association with other men.

The next day the young nobles who had been sent to accompany the army to the boundaries of Campania returned and were summoned into the senate. When questioned by their elders they reported that the Romans had seemed much sadder and more dejected than before. The column had marched along in almost complete silence. The old Roman spirit was crushed and their courage had left them with their arms. When greeted they did not respond; they were too dispirited to utter a word, as if their necks still bore the yoke under which they had been sent. The Samnites, they said, had won a lasting as well as a glorious victory; they had captured not only Rome like the Gauls before them but, what was much more warlike, Roman courage and spirit.

7. Upon hearing such words these faithful allies vir-

tually gave up Rome for lost. However, Ofillius Calavius, the son of Ovius, a man distinguished for his birth as well as his accomplishments and then venerable with age, asserted that the very opposite was true. Their stubborn silence, their eyes fixed upon the ground, ears deaf to all solace, their great reluctance to look upon the light—all these things, he said, were signs of great fury seething deep within their breasts. Either he did not know Roman nature or that silence would cause the Samnites bitter tears, and the memory of the peace of Caudium would prove much sadder for the Samnites than the Romans. For wherever they met each side would have its courage to rely upon; but there would not be a Caudine Forks everywhere for the Samnites.

News of the infamous disaster now had reached Rome. They first heard that the army was trapped. Then came news of the ignominious peace—a report which seemed more lamentable than that of the army's danger. At first report of the blockade the citizens had begun to hold a conscription. But when they received word of the shameful surrender they abandoned their efforts and immediately, without any official decree, the city assumed the appearances of a public mourning. Shops around the Forum were closed and business was suspended voluntarily before any edict was announced. Tunics with broad purple stripes and gold rings were laid aside. The citizens were almost more sorrowful than the soldiers. They were angered not only at the commanders who had supported and contracted the covenant of peace but at the innocent soldiers as well. They declared that they should be refused admittance into the city. This resentment was softened, however, by the arrival of the army whose misery even angry men were forced to pity. For they did not return to their native city like men saved beyond all expectation. Bearing the expressions and demeanor of captives they entered the city late at night, and stole away each to his own house; and on the next and each of the days following not one of them ventured to appear in the Forum or the public streets. The consuls went into seclusion and refused to transact any official business except when forced by decree of the senate to appoint a dictator to preside over the elections.

The disaster at the Caudine Forks was redressed by the energy and spirit of Papirius Cursor, whose general-ship was said to be equal to that of Alexander the Great. [The extended digression which follows, in which the achievements of Alexander are disparaged in comparison with those of Roman generals, is thought by some critics to be a schoolboy composition which Livy inserted, somewhat inorganically, into his work. It is the only piece of its kind in his extant work.]

17. From the beginning of this work, I have wished for nothing less than to digress more than necessary from the proper order of events and by adorning my book with variety to amuse my readers and provide respite from my own mental labors. However, the mention of such a great king and great general as Alexander calls to mind certain questions upon which I have often reflected. For this reason I wish now to consider what would have been the consequence for Rome if it had been forced into war against Alexander.

The following considerations are undoubtedly the most decisive in warfare: the numbers and bravery of the troops, the abilities of the generals, and fortune, which is potent in all human activities, but most of all in time of war. When one considers these particulars either sepa-rately or collectively it must be obvious that Alexander, like other kings and peoples, would have found Rome invincible. In the first place, to begin by comparing generals, I do not deny that Alexander was a great military leader; but his reputation owes much to the fact that he was sole commander and that he died while still a young man, at the height of his power, before experiencing any reversal of fortune. Not to mention other famous kings and commanders who furnish noteworthy examples of the vicissitudes of human fortune, consider Cyrus whom the Greeks praise so highly. What besides the length of his life was responsible for his change of fortune? The same is true of Pompey the Great. Now let us survey the list of Roman generals—not every one of every age but only those consuls and dictators with whom Alexander would have had to fight. There was Marcus Valerius Corvus, Gaius Marcius Rutulus, Gaius Sulpicius, Titus Manlius Torquatus, Quintus Publilius Philo, Lucius Papirius Cursor, Quintus Fabius Maximus, the two Decii, Lucius Volumnius and Manlius Curius. A succession of great men followed, in case he had first made war with Carthage and had crossed into Italy as an old man. In each of these was to be found that same courage and ability for which Alexander was famous. Roman military discipline, too, which had been handed down from the founding of the city, had developed into a science with absolute principles, so had the kings waged war, and so the Junii and Valerii who deposed them, and then the Fabii, Quinctii, Cornelii, and Furius Camillus, who still was living when the generals who would have opposed Alexander were young men.

Alexander also was famous for his exploits on the field of battle. Obviously Manlius Torquatus or Valerius Corvus, both of whom were renowned soldiers, would have yielded to him if they had met him in single combat! or the Decii, who had devoted their bodies and rushed into the middle of the enemy! or Papirius Cursor, with his great strength and courage! Obviously that one youth

would have outwitted the whole senate—not to mention
individual members—whom the man who best understood its true nature once called an assembly of kings!
And of course it is likely that he would have been more
skillful at choosing camp sites than any of the men I
have named! or in regulating his supply lines, guarding
against ambushes, choosing the proper time for battle,
forming his battle line or supporting it with reserves! He
would have admitted it was no Darius he had to deal
with; Darius was booty rather than an enemy. He was
conquered without bloodshed simply because Alexander
dared to scorn empty pretension. Italy would have looked
far different to him from India, through which he riotously
led his carousing army. There he would have seen the
passes of Apulia, the mountains of Lucania, and fresh
traces of the disaster where his uncle, King Alexander of
Epirus, had been destroyed.

18. And we are speaking of Alexander before he was
caught in the toils of success, which no man was less capable of bearing. Considering him from the standpoint of his
new fortune, and, if I may use the word, the new character which he had assumed after his victory, he would have
arrived in Italy more like Darius than Alexander; and
he would have led an army which had forgotten Macedonia and had been corrupted by Persian customs. In
speaking of such a great king it grieves me to tell of the
pretentious changes in his dress, his demand that men
prostrate themselves in obeisance—a practice which
would have seemed burdensome to the Macedonians
even in defeat, much less in victory—the brutal punishments, the murder of his friends as they feasted and
caroused, and his empty claims to a divine origin. What if
his love of wine had continued to grow greater day by
day? Or his fierce and passionate temper? I refer to nothing for which there is not overwhelming historical evi-

dence. Should we not consider that these weaknesses detract from his virtues?

The most frivolous of the Greeks, who take the part even of the Parthians against Rome, often assert that the Roman people could not have withstood Alexander's awesome reputation. Of course there was danger of this, when it is doubtful that they had ever even heard of him! In Athens, which had been subdued by Macedon, men dared to speak freely, even when they could see the ruins of nearby Thebes. This is apparent from their speeches which are extant. Are we to suppose, then, that from so many leaders no Roman would have summoned courage to raise the voice of freedom against him?

However preëminent this man may seem to have been, nevertheless this is the greatness of one man, acquired in little more than ten years of success. Some extol Alexander on the grounds that he was never unsuccessful in battle, while the Roman people have lost many battles, although never a war. They do not realize that they are comparing the exploits of one man with those of a nation which now has waged war for four hundred years. When Rome can count more generatons than Alexander's years, should we wonder if its fortune has varied more in this long period than his in thirteen years? Why not compare the one man, or one general, with the other? How many Roman generals I could name who never lost a battle! In the annals and lists of the magistrates it is possible to read through whole pages of consuls and dictators whose ability and fortune never occasioned the Roman people any grief. To make them more remarkable than Alexander or any king, many of them held the dictatorship only for ten or twenty days, and no one remained consul for more than one year. Moreover, their conscriptions were impeded by the tribunes of the plebs. They would go to war at the eleventh hour and were recalled early to preside over elections. The end of the year often caught them in the middle of their undertakings. Sometimes the rashness, sometimes the perversity of their colleagues created obstructions or caused losses. They inherited difficulties caused by the poor management of their predecessors. They were given untrained or poorly disciplined armies. Kings, on the other hand, are free from all restrictions and are masters of time and circumstances. They guide events instead of being guided by them.

Thus the unconquered Alexander would have faced unconquered generals and would have pledged the same stakes on the outcome. On the contrary, his would have been the greater hazard because the Macedonians had Alexander alone, who not only was liable to many dangers but exposed himself unnecessarily. But the Romans had many who were equal to Alexander either in reputation or greatness of achievement; each was ready to live or die in obedience to his fate without imperiling the state.

19. It remains to compare the forces of each with respect to numbers, kinds of soldiers, and numbers of their auxiliaries. The census of that time counted twenty-five thousand people. Thus when all the Latin allies defected, ten legions were levied from the city alone. Often four and five armies would be waging war through Etruria, Umbria (where they also were opposed by the Gauls), Samnium and Lucania. Sometime after, Alexander would have found all Latium, the Sabines, the Marsi, the Paeligni, the Vestini, the Apulians, along with all the Greeks along the coast of the Tuscan sea from Thurii to Naples and Cumae and from there all the way to Antium and Ostia—all these he would have found strong allies of the Romans or subdued by them in war.

He himself would have invaded Italy with an infantry numbering not more than thirty thousand veteran Macedonians and four thousand horsemen, mostly Thessalonians. This was the core of his strength. If he had added Persians, Indians, and other peoples they would have been a greater impediment than a support.

Add to this the fact that the Romans would have had additional troops ready at hand. Alexander would have met Hannibal's fate. He would have watched his army worn away while he waged war on foreign soil. As for arms, the Macedonians would have carried round shields and long lances; the Romans would have carried shields which provided greater protection for the body and a heavy lance which had a much stronger thrust when thrown than the spear. Both armies were trained to fight from a fixed position, preserving their battle order. But the Macedonian phalanx was immobile and composed of soldiers of one kind; the Roman line was divided into several divisions easy to separate or to unite as occasion demanded. And what soldier is equal to the Roman in constructing works or better at enduring hardship? Moreover, if Alexander had been defeated in one battle he would have lost the whole war. But what battle could have vanquished the Romans, whom the Caudine Forks or Cannae did not crush? Even if successful at first, Alexander often would have longed for the Persians and Indians and unwarlike Asians. He would have owned that previously he had made war on women, echoing the fabled remark of King Alexander of Epirus when, lying mortally wounded, he compared the war which Alexander had fought in Asia with that fought by himself.

When I recall that during the first Punic War Rome fought a naval war with Carthage of twenty-four years, I am convinced that Alexander's whole life would scarcely have sufficed for one war. And since Carthage was al-

lied to Rome by ancient treaties, it is possible that fear
would have united these two very powerful cities against
a common enemy and Alexander would have been overwhelmed by a Punic and a Roman war. The Romans have
fought with Macedon in the past—not, I admit, when
Alexander was general but against Antiochus, Philip,
and Perses. Then they not only were never defeated but
were never even exposed to danger. Let my words inspire
no resentment and let civil wars be silent: never have we
been worsted by the enemy infantry; never have we
been defeated in open battle; never on level and certainly
never on favorable ground. A heavy-armed soldier has
reason to fear cavalry, arrows, obstructed defiles, and
country without roads where supplies are difficult to
convey. But Rome has repulsed a thousand armies more
fearful than Alexander's Macedonians; and we shall in
the future if we retain our love of the peace in which we
live and our concern for civil concord.

Epitome of Book 10
3 0 3 - 2 9 2   B C

Colonies were planted at Sora, Alba, and Carseoli. The
Marsi were received in surrender. The augural college
was enlarged, so that there should be nine, whereas there
had been four. A law on appeal was proposed to the people by the consul Murena, for the third time. Two tribes
were added, the Aniensis and the Terentina. War was
declared upon the Samnites, and many successful engagements were fought against them. When war was being

waged against Etruscans, Umbrians, Samnites, and Gauls under the generals Publius Decius and Quintus Fabius and the Roman army was in grave danger, Publius Decius devoted himself on behalf of the army, following his father's example, and by his death gave victory in that battle to the Roman people. Papirius Cursor routed the army of the Samnites; that army had bound itself by an oath before going into battle, so that it might fight with greater fortitude and constancy. The census was taken and the lustrum closed. The count of citizens amounted to 272,320.

Note on Books 11-20
292-218 B C

Between the Samnite Wars, which are concluded in Book 10, and the Second Punic (or Hannibalic) War which begins in Book 21, Rome fought two other great wars. One was against Pyrrhus of Epirus, and resulted in the acquisition of southern Italy, and the other was the First Punic War, and resulted in the acquisition of Sicily. These wars are the principal contents of Books 11-20, which are lost.

The events of the Samnite Wars made it apparent that the Romans intended to extend their sway over all the peninsula. Penetration into southern Italy was resented by the rich Greek city of Tarentum, for it boded interference in her own sphere of influence. When Thurii, another Greek city in southern Italy, requested the assistance of Rome against attacks by Lucanians, Tarentum took umbrage and applied to King Pyrrhus of Epirus for support. Pyrrhus was an experienced and skillful general, and his army of 25,000 men supported by twenty elephants was trained in the Macedonian manner. The success of the "barbarian" Romans against such an army was significant of the future of Mediterranean history.

With Rome unquestionably a power in the Mediterranean, it was inevitable that she should eventually come into conflict with Carthage, the other great power in the west. In 264 B.C. Hiero of Syracuse laid siege to the Sicilian city of Messana, then in possession of a group of Campanian mercenaries who called themselves Mamertines, or "sons of Mars." To rid themselves of Hiero the Mamertines asked for a garrison from Carthage, but subsequently found their Carthaginian guests equally difficult to dislodge and turned for assistance to Rome.

Although fully aware that intervention would lead to war with Carthage, Rome sent an expedition to Sicily, which defeated both the Carthaginians and Hiero. To drive the Carthaginians from Sicily and protect Italian coasts against Carthaginian sea power, the Romans were forced to acquire a navy. In their first essay at naval warfare they defeated the Carthaginians off Mylae, in 260 B.C. Encouraged by this success, the Romans sent a force under Atilius Regulus, in 256 B.C., to invade Africa itself. At first Regulus was successful, but in 255 B.C. his army was all but annihilated and he himself was captured. In 249 B.C. he was sent to Rome with an offer of peace, but loyally advised the Romans to reject the Carthaginian terms and returned to Carthage to inevitable death by torture.

Rome met with further reverses, after the defeat of Regulus, especially against the formidable Hamilcar Barca, who became Carthaginian commander in Sicily in 247 B.C. Rome nevertheless persisted with great tenacity, and in 242 B.C. a Roman fleet under command of Lutatius Catulus defeated a Carthaginian force in the battle of the Aegates Islands. Carthage relinquished Sicily and paid an indemnity.

During a revolt of Carthaginian mercenaries in 238 B.C. Rome took advantage of Carthage's vulnerability, and seized the islands of Sardinia and Corsica. These and Sicily in 227 became Rome's first transmarine provinces.

Book 21
2 1 8 B C

1. It is fitting and proper for me to preface this part of my history with a remark which many historians have made at the beginning of their entire works: I am about to describe the most memorable of all wars—the war waged by Hannibal and the Carthaginians against the Roman people.

No two more powerful countries ever made war against each other. At this time the military power of both was greater than ever before; never had their defensive posture been stronger. Moreover, in the First Punic War each had become well acquainted with the other's military techniques. Thus the fortune of the war so varied and the conflict was so uncertain that at first the victors came nearer destruction than the conquered. The bitterness with which both sides fought was almost greater than their power. The Romans were angry that the conquered presumed to attack their conquerors; the Carthaginians believed Roman domination avaricious and tyrannical.

There is a tradition that at the age of nine, after Carthage's African war, Hannibal saw his father sacrificing in preparation for crossing his army to Spain. When he began coaxing Hamilcar to take him along, his father led him to the altar, laid his hand on the victim, and made him swear that as soon as he was able he would make war on Rome. The loss of Sicily and Sardinia tortured Hamilcar, who was a man of great pride. He thought that Sicily had been given up prematurely in a fit of despair and that Rome had unscrupulously taken advantage of Carthage's African uprising to steal Sardinia and impose a tribute upon his people.

2. Although he constantly fretted with such thoughts as these, he was occupied five years with the African war (which occurred immediately after peace was made with Rome) and nine years more with extending Carthaginian sovereignty in Spain. But during all this time he conducted himself in a manner which made it plain that he was planning a much greater war than he was fighting. If he had lived longer he rather than Hannibal would have led the Carthaginian invasion of Italy.

Hamilcar's death was very opportune for Rome, because Hannibal's youthfulness postponed the war. Between Hamilcar and Hannibal, Hasdrubal held command of the army for five years. They say that this man first became a favorite of Hamilcar because of his youthful beauty; later because of other qualities (undoubtedly those of the mind) he was chosen as his son-in-law. As Hamilcar's son-in-law he was placed in command of the army. This was done against the will of the nobles through the influence of the Barcine faction, which carried great weight among the soldiers and the common people. This Hasdrubal accomplished things by diplomacy rather than force. He did not extend Carthaginian influence in Spain by military conquest, but through friendly relations with chieftains and by conciliating new tribes through friendship with their important men. Yet peace afforded him no great security. For an angry native whose master he had executed publicly assassinated him. When seized by bystanders this man looked as happy as though he had escaped; and when tortured he even seemed to smile, as though his happiness were overcoming his pain. Because of Hasdrubal's wonderful success in conciliating tribes and joining them to his empire, Rome renewed its treaty with him, establishing the Ebro River as the boundary between the two empires and leaving Saguntum free as a buffer state.

The young Hannibal, who had come to Spain as little more than a boy in order to gain knowledge of military service, was chosen as the new commander-in-chief.

4. Upon his first arrival in Spain Hannibal became the center of attention in the whole army. The veterans imagined they had recovered a rejuvenated Hamilcar: they saw the same energetic expression, the same piercing eyes, the same features and visage. But very quickly his resemblance to his father was a negligible factor in winning approval. Never were high aptitudes for obeying and commanding—very different qualities—combined to such a degree in a single character. It was not easy to decide whether the general or the army loved him best. It was Hannibal that Hasdrubal chose to put in charge of any business that required courage and energy, and it was under Hannibal that the soldiers displayed greatest confidence and daring. He was fearless in undertaking dangerous enterprises, he was prudent in discharging them. Toil could not weary his body or subdue his spirit. Heat and cold he endured alike. He ate and drank to satisfy nature, not pleasure. Hours for sleeping and

waking were not determined by the clock; whatever time was left after work was done he devoted to sleep. Nor was sleep wooed by soft couches and stillness; often he could be seen lying on the ground among the sentries and pickets, covered with a soldier's cape. His dress was no different from his contemporaries', but his arms and horses were preëminent. Among horse and foot alike he was far the best; he was the first to engage in a battle, the last to leave the engagement. But great as the man's merits were, his enormous faults were as great—inhuman cruelty, faith worse than Punic, no scruple to truth or sanctity, no fear of gods, no respect for oaths or religion. He served three years under Hasdrubal, omitting nothing which should be seen or done by one destined to be a great general.

5. From the day Hannibal was declared general he conducted himself as if he considered Italy had been allotted to him as a province and he himself ordered to make war on Rome. He was afraid that if he delayed his life might unexpectedly be cut off like those of Hasdrubal and his father Hamilcar.

Thus he decided to make war upon Saguntum at once. But since he realized that an attack on Saguntum undoubtedly would provoke immediate war with Rome, he decided first to occupy the territory of the Olcades, a tribe located south of the Ebro in Carthaginian territory which the Carthaginians had not yet subjugated. In this way he hoped it would seem that he had not intended to attack Saguntum but had been drawn into war with them by a series of events in the process of extending his empire. After the wealthy city of Cartala, the capital of the Olcades, had been taken by storm and sacked, the smaller cities were so intimidated that they voluntarily capitulated. The army then victoriously returned with their booty to New Carthage, where they spent the win-

ter. There Hannibal generously divided the booty and
faithfully paid up all back wages so that he firmly secured
the good will of all the soldiers.

At the beginning of spring he advanced into the territory of the Vaccaei, and took their cities, Hermandica
and Arbocala. However, the large population of Arbocala fought tenaciously and was able to defend the city
for some time. Fugitives from Hermandica together with
exiles from the Olcades, who had been conquered the
summer before, had aroused the Carpetani. This alliance
attacked Hannibal not far from the Tagus River as he
was returning from his invasion of the Vaccaei. Since
his army was weighted down with booty, at first they created considerable confusion. However, Hannibal avoided
a pitched battle and fortified a camp on the river bank.
After nightfall, as soon as the enemy camp became silent,
he quietly crossed the river by a ford. When he constructed
his rampart on the other side he took care to allow
the enemy space to cross, with the intention of attacking
them as they forded the river. He ordered the cavalry to
attack the enemy infantry as soon as they were in the
stream. His forty elephants he stationed along the bank.
With their allies, the Olcades and Vaccaei, the Carpetani
numbered one hundred thousand—an irresistible force if
Hannibal had attempted battle on the open plain. The
natives believed that the enemy had retreated out of fear,
and the only obstacle delaying their victory was the river.
Being naturally savage and confident in their numbers,
they immediately raised the battle cry, and all along the
bank everyone spontaneously rushed into the river at the
nearest point. From the opposite bank a large force of
cavalry charged against them. When they met in mid-
stream the contest was very uneven. The foot soldiers
were so unsteady in the water that they could have been
knocked down even by unarmed horsemen riding hap-

hazardly at them; but the horses were steady even in the middle of the current, and their riders were free to fight either at long range or at close quarters. A large number of natives were drowned; some were caught up in the swirling current and borne to the opposite bank, where they were trampled by the elephants. Those in the rear were able safely to retreat to their own bank. But before they had regrouped and had recovered from the shock Hannibal's infantry crossed the river and routed them from the bank. Hannibal then began devastating their fields, and within a few days the Carpetani capitulated. With their surrender, all the territory south of the Ebro except Saguntum belonged to Carthage.

6. Hannibal was not yet at war with the Saguntines, but had begun stirring up quarrels between them and their neighbors, especially the Turdetani. When the man who had created the quarrel sided with the Turdetani it became apparent that he was not interested in justice but in a pretext for war. Therefore the Saguntines sent ambassadors to Rome to ask for aid for the war which was obviously imminent. The consuls that year were Publius Cornelius Scipio and Titus Sempronius Longus. When the Saguntines had spoken before the senate, it was decided to send ambassadors to Spain to look into the affair. If there seemed to be sufficient reason they were empowered to caution Hannibal to leave the Saguntines alone, since they were allies of the Roman people. They were then to sail to Africa and report the complaints of the Roman allies to the Carthaginians. However, even before the envoys had left Rome and sooner than anyone expected word arrived that Saguntum was under siege. The matter was then once more referred to the senate. Some thought the consuls should be sent both to Spain and to Africa, and that Rome should prepare for both naval and land operations. Others thought they should

concentrate their attack on Hannibal in Spain. Finally, there were some who thought the situation too grave to take unnecessary risks and that they should await the return of the envoys from Spain. This course of action seemed most prudent and so was adopted. Publius Valerius Flaccus and Quintus Baebius Tamphilus were sent at once to Hannibal in Saguntum. If he refused to abandon his offensive they were to continue on to Carthage and demand the surrender of Hannibal himself in punishment for the breaking of the treaty.

7. While the Romans occupied themselves with these deliberations, Hannibal was pressing the siege against Saguntum. That city, which was located about a mile from the sea, was the richest south of the Ebro. It is supposed to have been settled by colonists from the island of Zacynthus along with some Rutulians from Ardea. These settlers may have owed their wealth to commerce, or to agriculture, or to the increase in their population, or perhaps to the moral integrity which prompted them to stand by their allies until they themselves were destroyed; at any rate, as I said, they quickly grew prosperous.

When Hannibal invaded their territory, he first ravaged the countryside, then marched on the city, which he attacked from three sides. One bastion of the city wall faced onto a part of the plain which was more level than the rest. Here, under the protection of mantelets, Hannibal attempted to move up battering rams to the wall. But although the ground was level for some distance from the wall, this attempt to bring up mantelets was unsuccessful. A high tower overlooked this sector, and since the terrain made the wall vulnerable here, it was built up higher than elsewhere. Moreover, this position, where the danger seemed greatest, was defended by the best of the Saguntine fighting men. At first they repulsed the enemy with missiles from the wall and made it impossible for the mantelets to approach. Later, besides attacking from the battlements, they ventured to make forays outside the walls against the enemy siege works. In these irregular battles there were as many Carthaginian as Saguntine losses. Even Hannibal himself was struck in the thigh by a javelin when he rashly approached too close to the wall. This caused such great panic and confusion that the siege works were almost deserted.

8. For a few days, while Hannibal's wound was healing, the siege was not actively pressed. This time was devoted to the building of siege works, and soon the fighting was renewed more fiercely than ever. Mantelets and battering rams were moved up against the wall at many points, even in places where the rough terrain made this almost impossible. The size of the Carthaginian army, which numbered about one hundred fifty thousand, was overwhelming, and when the townsmen began to divide up their forces to defend many points their numbers proved to be inadequate. Thus, the walls began to be battered by the rams, and in many places were weakening. Then at one point a long breach was made in the wall as three towers with the sections of the wall between them came down with a crash. The Carthaginians believed the town as good as captured when this gap was made. But the Saguntines rushed to the attack just as if the wall had been protecting both armies. This was nothing like the irregular forays which it is customary for both sides to make during sieges wherever the opportunity arises. Between the ruins of the wall and the houses a short distance away formal battle lines were drawn up just as if they stood on an open plain.

Hope inspired the Carthaginians, who believed that with a little effort they would capture the city. The Saguntines were driven by despair as they placed their own bodies between the enemy and their city denuded

of its walls; no one dared take a step backward for fear
of admitting an enemy into the spot which he had quit-
ted. The more fiercely they fought and the more closely
they packed together, the more men were wounded, for
wherever a missile fell it hit some shield or body. The
Saguntines had a javelin called the *phalarica,* with a shaft
of fir which was round except at the end where the head
was fixed. This head, which was four-sided like that of
the *pilum,* they wrapped with tow and covered with
pitch; and since it was more than three feet long it could
pierce through both the shield and the body. But even
when the head stuck in the shield and did not penetrate
the body it still was an effective weapon. For when the
tow was set afire and the javelin thrown, the flame was
fanned high by the motion and forced the soldier to
throw down the shield which protected him.

9. For a long while the fighting remained indecisive.
The Saguntines, since they had been fighting against all
hope, took courage; if the Carthaginians were not yet
victorious, they were as good as defeated. Suddenly the
townsmen raised a shout and pushed the enemy back
among the ruins of the wall, then drove them back to
their camp in complete rout.

Meanwhile the envoys from Rome arrived. But messengers from Hannibal met them at their ships and advised them that it would be unsafe for them to come into
the camp among the half-savage native troops. Moreover,
Hannibal, they said, had no time to listen to embassies
during such a crisis. Since Hannibal knew that if no re-
ception was granted them they would continue on to Carthage, he sent messengers ahead of them to caution the
leaders of the Barcine party to rally their supporters and
prevent the opposing party from making any concessions
to Rome.

10. The only achievement of the mission to Carthage,

therefore, was that there it received a hearing. Hanno alone of all their senators spoke for the preservation of the treaty. Because of his great authority his listeners received Hanno's words in silence, but without enthusiasm. He beseeched the senate on behalf of the gods who witness treaties not to take on the additional burden of a war with Rome. He had warned them, he said, not to send a son of Hamilcar to the army. Neither the man's shade nor his offspring was at peace, nor could the treaty with Rome ever rest undisturbed as long as anyone of Barcine lineage remained alive. "You were heaping fuel on a fire when you sent that stripling to command your armies. He is burning with desire for a throne and he sees one way to achieve that end—to surround himself with armed legions and to instigate one war after another. You have fed this fire which is burning you. Your armies surround Saguntum contrary to the terms of the treaty. Soon the Roman legions will surround Carthage and those same gods will lead them who helped them avenge a broken treaty once before. Are you unaware what an enemy you are opposing? Or do you not know yourselves or the fortunes of both nations? That peerless general of yours refused to receive friendly ambassadors who came on behalf of allies. He flouted international law. These ambassadors were repulsed from a place where even enemy envoys receive admission. Now they have come to you seeking redress in accordance with your treaty. They are demanding the perpetrator of the crime as a token of the good faith of our people. But I am afraid that the more mildly they act in the beginning the more relentless they will be when they anger. Think of Eryx and the Aegatian Islands, and the trials you suffered by land and sea for twenty-four years. This boy was not your general, but his father—the 'second Mars' as they call him. Then we were the aggressors at Tarentum—that is to say, in Italy—just as now we are the aggressors at Saguntum. Thus we were conquered by the gods as well as men, and our difference of opinion—which nation had broken the treaty—was settled by the outcome of the war; like an unbiased judge it gave victory to those who had justice on their side. Hannibal is moving up his mantelets and towers against Carthage as well as Saguntum. He is shaking the walls of Carthage with the battering ram. The ruins of Saguntum (may I be a false prophet!) will fall on our heads, and besides the war with Saguntum we must fight with Rome.

" 'Well then, shall we surrender Hannibal?' someone may ask. I know that in this matter my influence is negligible because of my feud with his father. But I rejoiced when Hamilcar died, because if he had lived we would be at war with Rome; and in the same way I detest this young man, this Fury who is setting his torch to this war. I think not only that he should be deported to the farthest corner of the earth, but banished to a place where word of him will never reach our ears and he will never again disturb the peace of our country. Therefore, let us send envoys to Rome to give satisfaction to the senate while dispatching others to command that our army be withdrawn from Saguntum and that Hannibal be surrendered to Rome. Let us then send a third embassy to make compensation to Saguntum."

11. When Hanno had finished speaking no one thought it necessary to answer him, so entirely was the senate partisan to Hannibal. They asserted that he had spoken with greater antagonism than the Roman ambassador, Valerius Flaccus. Subsequently they replied to the envoys that the Saguntines had started the war, not Hannibal, and that Rome would act unjustly if it gave preference to Saguntum over Carthage, its oldest ally.

Hannibal's soldiers were exhausted with fighting and

building siege works. So while the Romans were wasting time sending ambassadors, he set up guard posts to protect the works and gave them a few days rest. Meanwhile, he bolstered their courage by arousing their anger against the enemy and by promising great rewards. When he proclaimed before the assembled army that all the spoils of the city would be theirs, they were so aroused that if the signal for battle had been given at once it seemed that nothing could resist them. But to the Saguntines, their respite from battle meant no rest; they were laboring night and day to repair the breach in the wall which exposed their city.

Soon Hannibal renewed the assault, with much greater intensity than before. Since the clamor of the battle echoed everywhere it was impossible for the Saguntines to tell where help was needed first or most urgently. Hannibal was taking a personal part in the battle, encouraging the men who were rolling up a huge tower, taller than all the city's defenses. As soon as the catapults and *ballistae* which were mounted on its platform had driven the defenders from one of the walls, Hannibal sent five hundred Africans with picks to undermine the wall. This was not difficult, since the stones were not held by cement but were filled in with mud according to the ancient method. Because of this an even larger section of the wall fell than had been undermined, and armed men poured through the breach into the city. Once in the city they seized an elevated position where they assembled their catapults and *ballistae*. This position they surrounded with a wall so that they had a fortress within the city which towered over it like a citadel.

The Saguntines also built a wall inside the city wall around the section of the city not yet occupied. Both sides were desperately fighting and building fortifications. But as the Saguntines shortened their line of defense they made their city smaller day by day. At the same time necessities of all kinds were growing more and more scarce as the blockade continued and hope of any outside aid was dying. Rome, their only hope, was far away and they were completely surrounded by the enemy. For a short time, however, their waning courage was revived by the departure of Hannibal. Two tribes, the Oretani and the Carpetani, had been aroused by the rigor of the Carthaginian levy and had imprisoned the recruiting officers. This threatened to develop into open rebellion, but the natives were taken unawares by Hannibal's unexpected arrival and laid down their arms.

12. Meanwhile the assault on Saguntum was being prosecuted as vigorously as ever by Maharbal, the son of Himilco, whom Hannibal had left in command. Neither his own army nor the enemy felt the absence of the general. Maharbal fought several successful battles and with three battering rams destroyed a large section of the enemy's walls. Upon Hannibal's return he was able to show him a wide area covered with the debris of the wall. Accordingly Hannibal immediately led the army against the citadel of Saguntum itself. There a savage battle took place, with great losses on either side, and part of the citadel was taken.

Although there now was small hope of a peace treaty, attempts at mediation were made by two men, Alco of Saguntum and Alorcus, a Spaniard. Alco crossed over into Hannibal's lines by night without the knowledge of the Saguntines. He thought that he might accomplish something by entreaties, but his tears had no effect and the conditions offered were harsh, as might be expected from an angered conqueror. Therefore instead of ambassador he became a deserter and remained with the enemy; for he was sure that anyone proposing a peace under those conditions would be executed by the Saguntines. The conditions proposed by Hannibal were as follows: that the Saguntines should make restitution to the Turditani; that they should surrender all their silver and gold; and that they should depart from the city wearing only a single garment each and resettle wherever Hannibal should order.

Alco declared that the Saguntines would never accept such terms, but Alorcus asserted that the spirit surrenders where all else is conquered, and promised to act as mediator. At that time he was a member of Hannibal's army, but he also enjoyed the status of "guest" of the Saguntine state. Therefore he openly surrendered his sword to the enemy sentry, crossed the lines, and was taken to the Saguntine commander at his own request. Immediately a huge crowd gathered around him; but all were removed except for the senate, and Alorcus delivered the following speech:

13. "If your fellow citizen Alco, who went to Hannibal to seek peace, had reported Hannibal's terms to you, my mission would be unnecessary and I should come to you neither as an ambassador nor as a deserter. But he has remained with the enemy either because of his deficiency or your own. It is his if he has counterfeited his fear, but yours if it is so dangerous simply to report facts to you. Therefore, out of consideration for our long friendship, I have taken it upon myself to come to you so that you might be informed that Hannibal offers you terms of peace and safety. What I have to say I shall say for your sake alone, and for no other reason. While you had strength to resist and were still hoping for aid from Rome I never mentioned peace to you. But now there is no hope from Rome, and your walls and your arms can no longer defend you; I am offering you a peace which is necessary, if not favorable to you. . . . Although these

terms are severe, the enemy is victorious and your fortune forces your acceptance. I have hopes that when you have agreed he will relax some of his demands. But certainly you should submit to them even as they are rather than allow yourselves to be butchered and your wives and children dragged away before your eyes."

14. A crowd had gradually collected to hear Alorcus' words and the populace had crowded in among the senators. Suddenly, without giving any answer, the city's leaders withdrew. After gathering together in the forum all the gold belonging to themselves and to the state they threw it all into a fire which they had hastily made. Many also flung themselves into these same flames. This desperate act created panic and confusion throughout the city. Suddenly, however, a second uproar was heard in the citadel. A tower which had long been pounded by the rams finally fell and through the breach rushed a company of Carthaginians. When they discovered that the usual guards within the city were not at their posts they informed their general. Hannibal was quick to seize his opportunity, attacking immediately in full force; in a moment he was master of the city and had given the order to kill all the adult inhabitants. This was a cruel order, but proved to be almost unavoidable. For how could people be spared who locked themselves inside their houses with their wives and children and burned the houses down on top of themselves, or who seized their swords and fought to the death?

15. A huge amount of booty was captured with the town. It is true that a great many valuables had purposely been destroyed by their owners; the furious soldiers also had slaughtered the natives indiscriminately without regard for age. The comparatively few captives who were taken were given to them as booty. Neverthe-

less historians agree that a large profit was made from the goods which were sold and a great deal of valuable furniture and clothing was sent home to Carthage.

According to some sources Saguntum was taken after a siege of eight months; thereafter Hannibal returned to winter quarters in New Carthage; and after he departed again from that city it took him five months to reach Italy. But if this is true Publius Cornelius Scipio and Tiberius Sempronius Longus cannot have been consuls. For these men were consuls when the ambassadors arrived from Saguntum, yet they also met Hannibal in battle during their term of office—one of them at the River Ticinus and both together at the Trebia a short time after. Either all of these events were of considerably shorter duration or the capture of Saguntum rather than the commencement of the siege took place at the beginning of their consulship. The battle at the Trebia could not have occurred as late as the consulship of Gnaeus Servilius Geminus and Gaius Flaminius Nepos. For Nepos began his consulship at Ariminium, and the consular elections were presided over by Sempronius, who came to Rome *after* the battle at Trebia to supervise the election, then returned to his army in winter quarters.

16. At almost the same time the envoys returned from Carthage to report the hostility they met there, and news arrived of the destruction of Saguntum. The senators were besieged by a variety of emotions: grief and pity for the undeserved destruction of their allies, shame at their own failure to bring aid, anger toward Carthage, and fear for the fate of Rome. So upset and confused were they that instead of planning for the future they trembled as if the enemy were at the gates. It seemed to them that they never had met a more aggressive and warlike foe and never had Rome been so apathetic. The Sardinians, Corsicans, Istrians and Illyrians each had cre-

ated a disturbance but had not really put Roman military power to the test; the conflict with the Gauls had
been a police action rather than a real war. On the other
hand the Carthaginian army which now was crossing the
Ebro was a veteran force of twenty-three years' arduous
service in Spain without a defeat. It was trained by a
very able general fresh from the capture of a wealthy
city; accompanying it were many Spanish tribes, and it
would be joined by tribes of Gauls who were always willing to go to war. This war, they thought, would be
fought against the whole world, in Italy and before the
very walls of Rome.

17. The consuls were ordered to draw lots for their
respective theaters of action. The senate already had
determined what these would be. Spain went to Scipio,
and Africa along with Sicily to Longus. Six legions were
authorized for that year, along with as large a force of
allies as seemed necessary and as large a fleet as could
be mobilized. Twenty-four thousand foot soldiers were
enlisted and eighteen hundred horsemen, in addition to
forty thousand allied infantry and forty-four hundred
cavalry. Two hundred and twenty heavy warships and
twenty cutters were launched. The motion then was
introduced in the assembly to authorize war against Carthage; sacrifices and prayers were offered throughout the
city that the war declared by the Roman people might
end prosperously.

18. After these preparations had been made, a second embassy was sent to Carthage in order that all the
preliminaries to the war might be concluded in due
form. This embassy, which consisted of men advanced in
years . . . was to inquire whether Hannibal had attacked Saguntum on the authority of the government. If,
as seemed probable, the Carthaginians would affirm that
this was so, they were formally to declare war upon

that state. When they had arrived in Carthage and been admitted before the senate, Quintus Fabius asked nothing more than the one question which he had been instructed to ask.

To this, one of the Carthaginians replied: "Your first embassy was overhasty, Romans: you demanded Hannibal's surrender as if you thought he was attacking Saguntum on his own authority. This time your words so far are more moderate, but your real intentions are more ominous. At that time you accused Hannibal and demanded his surrender; now you are trying to exact from us a confession of guilt and are demanding immediate compensation, just as if we had confessed. I think you should ask not whether the government authorized the siege of Saguntum but whether it did so justly or unjustly. It is up to us to question and punish our own citizen if he has exceeded his authority. Your only consideration should be whether this was permissible under the terms of the treaty. Well, since you wish to make a distinction between what generals do on their own responsibility and what they do upon the authority of the people, your consul, Gaius Lutatius Catulus, once signed a treaty with us which protected the allies of both states; that treaty contained no provision about Saguntum because they were not yet your allies. 'But,' you may object, 'Saguntum was included in our treaty with Hasdrubal.' My only answer to that is one which I have learned from you. You claimed that you were not bound by the treaty which your consul Catulus made with us; it was not authorized by the senate or the popular assembly, you said. Because of this a new treaty was made with the sanction of your government. But if a treaty is not binding upon you unless it is authorized by your government, we are not obligated to honor the second treaty, which Hasdrubal made without our knowledge. So come now, forget about Saguntum and the Ebro and say what you have been itching to say."

At these words the Roman gathered his toga up to form a pouch and said: "Here we have for you either war or peace: take whichever you wish." To this the senate shouted angrily that he might give them whichever *he* wished. Dropping the pouch of his toga as if to pour out its contents, he said that he gave them war. To this they answered that they accepted, and would wage it with the same courage as they had accepted it.

19. This straightforward declaration of war seemed more befitting the dignity of the Roman people than wrangling about the validity of the two treaties.

Before returning to Rome the ambassadors traveled through Spain and Gaul, unsuccessfully seeking allies for their war with Hannibal.

21. After the capture of Saguntum Hannibal returned to winter quarters in New Carthage. There he was informed of what had taken place at Rome and Carthage —finding that he himself was not only the commander for the coming war but the cause of it as well. Thinking that he should delay no longer, he divided up or sold the remainder of the booty and called his soldiers of Spanish origin to an assembly, where he spoke to them as follows:

"I am sure that you are aware that now, since all the tribes of Spain have been subdued, our campaign is over; we must disband the army or carry the war into new territories. The benefits of peace and prosperity can be Spain's—but only if we seek booty and glory from other nations. Therefore, since war is threatening far from home and it is uncertain when you will see everything that is dear to you again, I grant furlough to anyone who wishes it. My only stipulation is that you return at the first of spring. Then we will begin a war, which, with the help of the gods, will yield us great profit and great renown." This permission to visit their homes, which Hannibal had offered of his own accord, was accepted gratefully by almost everyone. They already were longing to see their families, and they foresaw a long absence in the future. They were exhausted by their long labors, but the winter's rest renewed their strength and their courage to suffer new hardships. At the beginning of spring they returned as commanded.

22. Subsequently Hannibal set out toward the Ebro along the coast past Onussa. There is a tale that when he arrived there he was visited by a dream in his sleep. He dreamed he saw a youth who resembled a god, who declared that he had been sent to guide him into Italy. This vision ordered Hannibal to follow, keeping his eyes fixed upon him. At first Hannibal was fearful, and followed without looking around in any direction. Soon, however, he was overwhelmed by curiosity to know what it was he was forbidden to see and could no longer control his eyes. He saw an immense serpent following behind, which left a wide swath of fallen trees and bushes in his path. Behind the serpent rolled a thundering storm cloud. When he asked what this incredible portent signified, he was told that it was the devastation of Italy; he was now to proceed onward and to ask nothing more, but to allow his fate to remain unknown.

23. Elated by this vision, Hannibal sent his troops across the Ebro in three divisions, first sending ahead men to buy the good will of the Gauls through whose territory they would be passing and to explore the passes of the Alps. He crossed the Ebro with ninety thousand foot soldiers and twelve thousand horsemen. From there he proceeded to subjugate the Ilergetes, the Barguisi, the Ausetani, and Lacetania, which lay at the southern base

of the Pyrenees. This whole territory he placed under the command of Hanno in order to insure control of the passes between Spain and Gaul. To Hanno was allotted a garrison of ten thousand foot soldiers and one thousand horsemen. After the army had begun to cross the Pyrenees, the rumor grew more insistent that their destination was Rome. Because of this rumor three thousand of the Carpetanian infantry deserted. It was discovered that the prospect of the war did not alarm them so much as the length of the journey and the hopelessness of trying to cross the Alps. Hannibal was reluctant to bring them back or detain them by force for fear of exciting the ferocious tempers of the rest of his troops. For this reason he sent home over seven thousand additional men who, he had observed, were discontented with military service, pretending that he had voluntarily discharged the Carpetani also.

24. With the remainder of his army he then resumed his journey at once for fear that they would begin to fret with the tedium of delay. After crossing the Pyrenees he pitched camp near the town of Iliberri. The Gauls had been assured that the invasion was directed only against Italy, but they had heard that the Spaniards beyond the Pyrenees had been subdued and a large garrison stationed in their territory. Fearing that they would be enslaved, several tribes took arms and assembled at Ruscino. When this was reported to Hannibal the threat of war did not disturb him, but he was alarmed at the prospect of delay. Ambassadors were sent to their chieftains to announce that Hannibal wished to confer with them in person. He requested that they come into Iliberri or allow him to advance to Ruscino in order to make their conference more convenient. He would receive them in his camp or would be glad to meet in theirs. He had come as a guest of the Gauls, he said, not as an en-

emy, and would never draw his sword, if they would allow it, before he reached Italy. The Gallic chieftains were quite willing to meet with Hannibal and moved their camp to Iliberri without delay. There they were persuaded through bribery to allow the Carthaginians to pass the town of Ruscino and to march through their territory without meeting resistance.

25. Meanwhile, no news of Hannibal had reached Rome except for the report by envoys from Massilia that he had crossed the Ebro. Suddenly, however, the Boii revolted. This insurrection was inspired not so much by the traditional enmity of these tribes toward the Roman people as by Rome's recent colonization of Placentia and Cremona in Gallic territory near the Po. They made a sudden attack on this district and created great panic and disorder. The rural population along with the Roman commissioners who were allotting homesteads feared that the walls of Placentia were inadequate, and fled to Mutina, which the Gauls invested. But since they were inexperienced in siege operations and too lazy to build siege works, they merely blockaded it without attacking the walls. At length they pretended an interest in making peace, and their leaders asked the Romans to send representatives to a conference. These delegates, however, they made prisoners, in violation of international law and the pledge of immunity which had been given. The Gauls refused to release them unless the hostages were returned which they had given after their last war with Rome.

When the report arrived that the delegates had been seized and that Mutina and its garrison were in danger, the praetor, Lucius Manlius, angrily and hurriedly set out to bring relief to the city. Most of the area was uninhabited and forests lined both sides of the road. Failing to reconnoiter, Manlius rushed headlong into an ambush, and many of his troops were killed before they could struggle through to open land. Here he built a fortified camp, which the Gauls were loath to attack. The diffidence of the Gauls heartened the soldiers, even though it was determined that about five hundred of their comrades had been killed. When they resumed their march there was no sign of the enemy as long as they remained in open country. But when they reëntered the forest, the Gauls again attacked their rear, causing great panic and confusion. Seven hundred soldiers were killed, and six standards captured. Only when they had made their way out of the thick and pathless forest was there an end to the fearful depradations of the Gauls. Once in open country where they could ward off attacks, they hurried to Tannetum, a village on the Po. There with the help of the Brixian Gauls they erected a temporary fortification, and with provisions brought in by the river, they were secure for the moment. But the numbers of the enemy were growing daily.

26. When reports of this sudden uprising reached Rome and the senators learned that they were faced with a Gallic as well as a Punic war, they ordered the praetor Gaius Atilius to go to Manlius' assistance. He was given one legion and the five thousand soldiers of the allies who had been enrolled by the consul in the latest draft. With these he reached Tannetum without resistance, since the enemy retreated in fear.

Meanwhile, Publius Cornelius Scipio levied a new legion in place of the one sent with the praetor and set out from the city in sixty warships, sailing along the coast of Etruria and Liguria and by the mountains of the Salyes until he reached Massilia. Here, at the nearest mouth of the Rhone (the river divides into several channels before flowing into the sea), he pitched camp, scarcely believing that Hannibal had already crossed the Pyrenees. Much to his surprise he discovered that Hannibal already was considering how to cross the Rhone. Scipio was uncertain where to meet him and his own troops had not yet recuperated from their tossing-about on the sea; for the time being, therefore, he contented himself with sending out three hundred picked horsemen and a number of Gallic mercenaries with Massilian guides for the purpose of exploring the countryside and observing the enemy from a safe distance.

After conciliating the other Gallic tribes by intimidation and bribery Hannibal reached the territory of the Volcae, a powerful nation. Although the Volcae lived on both sides of the Rhone, they were afraid that they would be unable to defend the western bank. Therefore, they transported most of their belongings to the farther bank, where the river would afford some protection, and prepared to defend themselves. However, Hannibal bribed others who lived along the bank of the river, and even some of the Volcae who had refused to leave their homes, to gather together boats from around the neighborhood and to build more. The natives also were prompted by a desire for the army to be transported across so that their country might be relieved of the burden of so vast a number of soldiers as soon as possible. The Gauls accordingly collected a large number of boats and rough homemade skiffs and began to make new ones by hollowing out tree trunks. Soon the abundance of timber and the easiness of the work induced the soldiers to follow their example. Although the boats which they had hacked out were shapeless dugouts, their only concern was that these be capable of floating and carrying burdens well enough to ferry themselves and their equipment across.

27. When all preparations for crossing had been made Hannibal was still deterred by the menace of the enemy, who occupied all the bank opposite. Realizing that he

would have to drive them away he directed Hanno, son
of Bomilcar, to set out during the night with a company of
troops—mostly Spaniards—and to make a one day's
journey upstream. He directed Hanno to cross the river
as soon as he was able to do so with a maximum of secrecy
and to outflank the enemy so that at the proper moment
he might attack them from the rear. The Gauls assigned
to Hanno as guides for this expedition informed him that
there was an island about twenty-five miles upstream;
there the river widened where it divided, and hence was
shallower and could be easily crossed. There the soldiers
quickly cut timber and constructed rafts in which to transport themselves, their horses, and other equipment. The
Spaniards without further ado stuffed their clothes into
inflated skins, and lying upon their wicker shields which
they had placed upon the skins, they swam across the
river. The rest of the army crossed on the rafts which they
had constructed and pitched camp by the side of the river.
Their general was eager to carry out his task at the proper
time, and although they were wearied by their night
march and laborious toil, he allowed them only a single
day for rest. The following day they set out again and from
an elevated point indicated to Hannibal by a smoke signal
that they had crossed and were not far away. When Hannibal saw this signal he immediately seized his opportunity and gave the order to cross.

By posting large boats athwart higher upstream in order
to break the force of the current, he afforded a smooth
crossing to the skiffs below. The horses swam across, led
by halters from the stern of the boats; some, ready
bridled and saddled, were conveyed in the boats so that
they would immediately be available to the cavalry when
they disembarked on the farther bank.

28. With discordant whoops the Gauls broke into their
war chant and charged toward the river bank, shaking

their shields above their heads and brandishing their spears. Opposite them the Carthaginian soldiers and boatmen were struggling mightily against the current while others on the shore cheered on their companions in the boats. In spite of the Gauls' bravado they were alarmed when they saw the large number of ships and heard the mighty roar of the river and the clamorous shouting. They were already intimidated by the scene before them when suddenly a more frightening clamor arose at their rear, as Hanno fell upon their camp. Soon Hanno's troops were upon them; they found themselves beset by danger from two fronts, with a large force of soldiers disembarking from the boats and another, unexpected, attack pressing at their rear.

After trying to attack in both directions, and finding themselves repulsed, they began to break through wherever they could see an opening and to scatter in panic for their villages. Hannibal then crossed the rest of his forces at leisure, paying no more regard to the Gauls.

Various methods probably were used to transport the elephants—certainly several accounts are given. Some say that the herd was gathered together on the bank and the fiercest of them was goaded by his driver who fled into the water. As the elephant pursued the swimming man he drew the whole herd with him. The current of the stream alone carried each panic-stricken beast to the opposite bank when he could no longer touch bottom and lost his foothold. But it is more generally believed that they were transported on rafts. Since this would have seemed the safer method before the attempt, it seems most likely that it was the method used. They extended from the bank into the river a raft two hundred feet long and fifty feet wide. To keep this raft from being carried downstream they secured it with several strong cables higher up on the bank. It was then covered over with earth like a bridge so that the elephants would not hesitate to step on it, thinking it was land. To this was attached a second raft, of the same width and one hundred feet long, which was equipped for crossing the river. Then the elephants, led by the females, were driven onto the stationary raft; when they all had reached the smaller raft, immediately the cables by which it was lightly attached were loosened and it was drawn by tugs to the opposite shore. The beasts showed no signs of fear so long as they were on what seemed to be a continuous bridge; they first began to panic when the raft was loosened from its moorings and swept into the current. Then, pushing each other as those nearest the edge shied away from the water, they created a great disturbance, until their very terror at the water all around them again made them quiet. Some stampeded and fell overboard, throwing off their drivers. But because of their weight they were not carried downstream and, finding a foothold, they walked to shore.

29. While the elephants were being carried across, Hannibal sent five hundred Numidian horsemen to the Roman camp, to spy on their numbers, their location, and their movements. This company happened upon three hundred Roman horsemen sent, as I have said, from the mouth of the Rhone. The battle which took place was much fiercer than one would expect from the number of combatants. Besides the many wounded, losses were almost equal on either side; only the eventual panic and flight of the Numidians gave the completely exhausted Romans claim to victory. About one hundred sixty Roman troops, some of them Gauls, were killed, along with two hundred of the enemy. This was both the beginning of the war and an omen of its outcome; it foretold a successful conclusion, but also a bloody victory after a difficult and uncertain struggle.

After this battle, when the horsemen reported to their

respective generals, Scipio could decide on no course of
action except to formulate his plans in accordance with
those of the enemy. Hannibal, likewise, hesitated whether
he should continue his journey straight into Italy or stop
and fight with this, the first Roman army which he had happened upon. While he was in this uncertainty, envoys
from the Boii, including a petty chieftain named Magalus,
arrived in camp, offering to serve as guides. These natives
asserted that they would follow Hannibal into any danger,
but advised him to avoid giving battle before he reached
Italy, so that he might arrive with his army at full strength.
The troops had not forgotten the previous war and still
feared the enemy; but they were more afraid of the long
journey across the Alps—a formidable ordeal, they had
heard, at least for the inexperienced.

30. And so when Hannibal had decided to proceed on
his journey to Italy without delay, he called a meeting of
the troops and undertook to inspire them by both encouragement and reproof. "I am amazed," he said, "at
the sudden terror which has seized you. Through so many
victorious years you have always fought fearlessly and
did not leave Spain before stretching the Carthaginian do-
main from one sea to the other. Now, in indignation because Rome has demanded that all who besieged Saguntum be surrendered, as if it were a crime, you have crossed
the Ebro to destroy the name of Rome and free the whole
world. No one thought the journey far when it stretched
from the setting of the sun to its rising. But now you see
the greater part of the journey completed; you have sur-
mounted the passes of the Pyrenees, through the most
ferocious tribes. In spite of the opposition of thousands
of Gauls you have crossed the great river Rhone and conquered the very force of its current. Now you see the Alps
before you, and beyond them lies Italy. Now do you stop
exhausted at the very gates of the enemy? What do you

think the Alps are but high mountains? Suppose they are higher than the Pyrenees: surely no land touches the sky and is insurmountable to mankind. The Alps are even inhabited and cultivated; living things are born and thrive there. If they can be crossed by individuals they are passable to armies. Do you think these ambassadors you see here were lifted up on wings and soared across the Alps? And the ancestors of the Boii were not natives of Italy but immigrants who safely crossed those very Alps in hordes along with their wives and children: To the soldier carrying nothing but his weapons what can be impassable or insuperable? What toils, what dangers you went through for eight months to capture Saguntum! Can there be anything so difficult or arduous as to stop men whose object is Rome, the capital of the world? Once even Gauls captured that city which you despair of being able to reach. Confess yourself less courageous than this race which you have so often conquered of late, or let your goal be the field between the Tiber and walls of Rome."

31. After these words of exhortation Hannibal ordered the men to eat and rest, and to prepare for their journey. The next day he set out along the bank of the Rhone toward inland Gaul. This was not the shortest route to the Alps, but he wished to avoid battle with the Romans before he reached Italy, and believed he would be less likely to encounter them the further he was from the sea. On the fourth day he arrived at the "Island." Here is the confluence of the Isere and Rhone rivers, which flow from widely separate parts of the Alps. The name "Island" has been given to the area between the two rivers. Nearby live the Allobroges, who were even then one of the wealthiest and most famous of the Gallic tribes.

At this time the tribe was split by dissension, with two brothers contending for the throne. The elder of these, a certain Braneus, had previously been in power; he had been illegally but successfully deposed by his younger brother and a junta of young men. This dissension proved to be opportune for Hannibal, who was chosen to act as arbitrator. He restored the elder brother to the throne, concurring with the opinion of the senate and tribal leaders, and in return for this favor they furnished him with supplies of all kinds, especially clothing. This would be essential in the notoriously cold Alps. After settling the dispute of the Allobroges, Hannibal resumed his march toward the Alps, not by a straight route but veering leftward toward the land of the Tricastini. From there he marched along the boundaries of the territory of the Vocontii into that of the Tricorii, encountering no obstacle until he reached the Druentia river. This river also rises in the Alps, and is by far the most difficult of all the rivers of Gaul to cross. Although it is very large, it is not navigable, for it keeps within no permanent banks but flows in several channels, which are always shifting. Because of this it is constantly developing new shallows and new deep spots, which makes it hazardous even to men on foot, and it carries along stones and gravel so that nowhere does it offer any firm or solid footing. The river was then in flood, moreover, because of recent rains. The crossing was accompanied by the greatest disorder, and the men increased their confusion by their own agitated clamor.

32. About the third day after Hannibal had departed from the bank of the Rhone, the consul Publius Scipio reached Hannibal's camp with his army, marching in fighting order and ready to do battle without delay. When he found the camp's defenses deserted and realized that the enemy had such a head start that he could not easily overtake them, he returned to the sea and his ships. He was sure that he could meet the enemy with less danger and difficulty after he had crossed the Alps. Nevertheless,

he did not wish to leave Spain, the province allotted to him, without a Roman garrison. He therefore sent most of his troops under the command of his brother Gnaeus to oppose Hasdrubal. The strategy in Spain which he decided upon was not just to protect the old allies and gain new ones, but to attempt to drive Carthage out of Spain completely. He himself returned with a small number of troops to Genoa with the intention of defending Italy with the army stationed in the area of the Po.

Meanwhile Hannibal set out from Druentia over level country toward the Alps, which he reached without harassment from the Gallic natives. Rumor tends to exaggerate, and the army had been told what they would find. Nevertheless, when they saw the height of the mountains before them, the snow almost blending into the sky, primitive huts perched on cliffs, cattle and draft animals pinched with cold, men squalid and unshaven, objects both animate and inanimate rigid with cold, and everything else too horrible for description—then their terror returned. As the army began to ascend onto the first slopes, mountaineers were seen occupying the hills above. If they had hidden themselves in the valley, they might have ambushed the column, causing great panic and destruction. Halting the column, Hannibal sent ahead a scouting party of Gauls. When he was informed that no passage could be found, he pitched camp in the widest level place he could find in this steep and rugged area. Since these Gauls were very similar to the mountaineers with respect to language and customs, they were sent to infiltrate their lines and attend their councils of war. Hannibal was informed by them that the mountaineers maintained their blockade only by day, and at night dispersed to their homes. The next day at dawn he proceeded toward the hills as if intending to force a passage openly by daylight. That day he spent confirming this impression, and then he fortified a camp at the place where he had stopped. As soon as he was sure that the mountaineers had abandoned their posts he made more fires than were needed for the number remaining in the camp. Then, leaving the cavalry and most of the infantry behind with the baggage, he took a troop of light-armed soldiers consisting of his bravest men and hurried rapidly through the pass. There he took possession of the very hills the enemy itself had occupied.

33. At dawn the rest of the troops began to break camp and to advance. In response to a signal the mountaineers now were gathering from their strongholds to man their accustomed stations. Suddenly they caught sight of enemy soldiers occupying their own citadel, while the rest of the enemy army now was crossing the pass. Seeing both these sights at once, they were momentarily stupefied. Then, when they saw the disorder and confusion in the defile below, especially the fright of the horses, they thought that anything they could add to the panic would spell disaster. Knowing the terrain well, they dashed down everywhere over the rocks, where there were trails and where there were not. The Carthaginians now had to cope simultaneously with the enemy and the rugged ground. As each man strove to get clear of the danger they struggled more with each other than with the enemy. The horses especially endangered the column. They were terrified by the dissonant clamor, which reverberated from forests and gorges; and when one was struck or wounded they created havoc among the men and the baggage. The pass was precipitous on each side, and in the turmoil many animals and men—some of them armed soldiers—were pushed over the edge. Baggage animals with their burdens went tumbling down like stones from a toppling wall.

Although this was horrible to see, Hannibal held back his men for some time for fear of adding to the disorder and confusion. Finally he saw that the column was being

cut in two and that it would be useless for the army to
negotiate the path safely if all its supplies were lost.
Hurrying down from his higher position he swept away
the enemy by the force of his charge, but increased the
panic among his own soldiers. After the path was cleared
of the mountaineers, the tumult abated immediately. Soon
the whole column had gone through the pass without
harassment and in virtual silence. Hannibal then seized
the stronghold which was the capital of this district along
with several nearby villages, and captured enough food
and cattle to feed his army for three days. Since neither
the mountaineers, once they had been routed, nor the
nature of the land presented any great obstacle, he traveled a considerable distance in those three days.

34. Now he reached another canton, which was thickly
populated for a mountain district. There he came near to
destruction, not in open battle, but through deception and
ambuscade, his own favorite devices. Elders from the
mountain stronghold came as envoys. They declared that
they had learned from the misfortunes of others that it
was better to seek the Carthaginians' friendship than experience their might. They were prepared, they said, to
carry out his commands, and wished to provide him with
provisions, guides, and hostages as guarantee of their
good faith. While Hannibal was not quick to trust them
blindly, he did not wish to reject their offer summarily
for fear they would then become openly hostile. He gave
them a gracious reply, and accepted their hostages as well
as the supplies they had carried down to the road of their
own accord. But to follow their guides he drew up his
forces in preparation for battle—not as though marching
through a friendly territory. The elephants and horsemen
made up the first column; he himself followed with the
main body of infantry, keeping a cautious watch in every
direction.

When they reached a narrow pass lying along a ridge overhanging one side, suddenly the natives rose up everywhere, in front and in the rear. They attacked at close quarters and from a distance, rolling huge boulders down into the line of march. The heaviest attack was in the rear; there the infantry turned about and made it clear that if the rear guard had not been strengthened they would have sustained great losses in that pass. Even so they were in grave danger and almost incurred disaster. Hannibal hesitated to send his division further ahead into the narrow pass since the infantry, which was protecting the cavalry, had no guard to protect its own rear. Thus the mountaineers, making a charge against his flank, established themselves in the breach between segments of the column of march, and Hannibal spent a full night cut off from his cavalry and baggage.

35. On the next day the natives attacked with less ferocity. The army was able to reunite, and made its way through the pass. Considerable losses still were suffered, but more pack animals perished than men. After this the mountaineers attacked in smaller numbers, more like highway robbers than soldiers. They would make rapid forays, first in the front, then in the rear of the column— wherever the terrain afforded an advantage, or men venturing too far ahead or straggling behind offered an opportunity. Although the slowness of the elephants in the narrow pass was exasperating, they protected the column wherever they went; for the natives were afraid of coming too near to these unfamiliar beasts.

They now proceeded through many trackless regions, often losing their way because of the treachery of their guides or, when they became skeptical of them, because of their own blind conjectures. On the ninth day they arrived at the highest point of the Alps; there they pitched camp, and for two days the soldiers rested from their toil and fighting. Several of the pack animals which had slipped and fallen among the rocks found their way into camp by following the track of the column. During this encampment there occurred a fall of snow—for it was now late October—and this too dismayed the exhausted and demoralized soldiers. At daybreak of the third day, when the army began to move through the deep drifts of snow, resignation and despair were written on every face. Advancing to the head of the column, Hannibal halted the troops on a projecting height and pointed to Italy and the valley of the Po below. "You are surmounting the walls not only of Italy," he said, "but of the city of Rome itself. The rest will be level or downhill. In one—or at most, two —battles you will be in possession of the capital and citadel of Italy." The column now resumed its march, no longer bothered by the enemy except for occasional trifling ambuscades. But the descent was even more trying than the ascent, for on the Italian side the Alps fall sheer. The whole way was precipitous, narrow, and slippery, so that they could not keep from slipping nor stick to their tracks if they stumbled: men and beasts rolled one on top of another.

36. A cliff they reached was so narrow and perpendicular that a soldier without pack could scarcely lower himself by feeling his way and holding on to bushes and roots. A recent landslip had deepened the precipice to nearly a thousand feet. At this impasse the cavalry halted, and when Hannibal wondered what was delaying the column he was told that the rock was impassable. He went to inspect the situation in person and found the column would have to detour through a pathless and untrodden tract. But this was found impracticable. The first few who attempted to pass could find footing in the new snow which covered that hard packed below, but when the tramp of men and beasts ground this to slush they trod on

the naked ice below. Men floundered and struggled. The slippery ice afforded no grip, and was the more treacherous as it was downhill; if a man rose on his hands or braced himself on his knees he would collapse together with his supports, and there were no stumps or roots against which he could buttress himself. Thus they kept wallowed in the slush on the smooth ice. Sometimes the pack animals, stamping their hoofs against falling, broke through, and were stuck in the hard, deep-frozen ice as if trapped and fettered.

37. Finally, after the men and animals had exhausted themselves to no good end, the top of a ridge was cleared of snow with great difficulty and camp pitched there. The soldiers were then put to work opening a road through the cliff, their only possible route. After felling some large trees round about and cutting off their branches they made a great stack of logs. When the wind rose high enough for a fire they kindled the logs, then after the rock had grown red hot poured vinegar on it, causing it to crumble. Using implements of iron they now cut a path through the fiery-hot rock, and even eased the steep grade of the hill with zig-zag gradients so that not only the pack animals, but even the elephants could pass through. Four days were spent working on the rock, and during that time the pack animals almost starved; for these peaks were almost bare of vegetation, and what grass there was was covered with snow. Lower down they found valleys, sunny slopes and streams flowing by woods—places more and more suitable for human habitation. There the animals were put out to pasture and respite given to the men after building the road. Then in three days they descended to the plain where they found a more agreeable country and a pleasanter population. 38. This was the character of Hannibal's march into Italy, which took, according to

some authorities, five months, fifteen days of which were spent crossing the Alps.

In the valley of the Po river Hannibal found himself confronted by a Roman army commanded by Publius Scipio who had returned from the mouth of the Rhone. Subsequently a battle took place near the Ticinus, a tributary of the Po. The speeches supposedly given by the two commanders before the Battle of Ticinus River are reported in the following chapters.

40. In order to embolden his men before leading them into battle Scipio addressed them as follows: "Men, if I were leading into battle the army which I commanded in Spain, I should have considered it superfluous to address you. For what would be the use of exhorting those horsemen who so brilliantly conquered the enemy cavalry near the Rhone, or those legions with whom I pursued this same enemy as he admitted defeat by his very flight? But now that army which was levied for duty in Spain is serving there under the command of my brother, in the province assigned it by the senate and the Roman people. But, to give you a consul to lead you against Hannibal and the Carthaginians, I volunteered for this command.

"As your new commander it is proper for me to say a few words to you, so that we may become better acquainted and so that you may not be ignorant of what kind of war and what kind of enemy you are facing. This is an enemy whom you have conquered on land and on sea, from whom for twenty years you have exacted tribute, from whom you took Sicily and Sardinia as prizes of victory. Thus you will go to battle with the assurance gained by habitual conquest, they with the dejection caused by customary defeat. They are not now going to battle because they dare, but because they must; for more of them, almost, have perished in the Alps than still survive. Or do you believe that an army which avoided battle while it was at full strength has more hope of victory with two-thirds of its forces lost while crossing the Alps? But, you may say, these few are men of strength and courage whose offensive power and endurance it is scarcely possible to withstand. No! These are mere shadows of men, half-dead with hunger, cold, filth and squalor, bruised and crippled on the rocks and cliffs. Their limbs are frost-bitten, their muscles stiffened by the snow, their bodies shriveled by frost, their weapons shattered and broken, their horses weak and lame. This is the cavalry, this the infantry which opposes you. You will have facing you not an enemy but an enemy's last remains. I fear nothing more than that after you have fought Hannibal people may say that it was the Alps which defeated him. But perhaps it is proper for the gods without human assistance to undertake and almost finish a war against a general and a people who have violated their treaties, and for us, who next to the gods have been most wronged, only to bring to an end the work which they have accomplished.

41. "I am not afraid anyone will think that I am only speaking in grandiloquent terms for the sake of inspiring you, while I myself feel quite differently. I could have gone with my army into Spain, my own province, where I had started. There I should have had my brother as adviser and ally, Hasdrubal as enemy instead of Hannibal, and surely a less demanding war. Instead, when I heard news of this enemy as I sailed along the coast of Gaul I disembarked at once, sent my cavalry ahead, and pitched camp near the Rhone. When I was lucky enough to meet the enemy cavalry I routed them. The enemy infantry, which levanted like a rout of fugitives, I could not overtake, so I returned to my ships and sped over land and sea as quickly as I could to meet this timorous foe. Does it look

as if I had blundered upon this enemy while trying to avoid a fight, or as if I had been dogging his steps in order to provoke one? I wish to see whether the earth has produced a new breed of Carthaginians during these twenty years, or whether this is the race which fought at the Aegates Islands and whom you allowed to leave Eryx under ransom, at the price of eighteen denarii a head. And I would like to know whether Hannibal is emulating the journey of Hercules, as he says, or was left by his father bound to pay tribute and taxes as a slave of the Roman people. If his crime at Saguntum had not driven him senseless he would show regard, if not for his conquered country, at least for his home, his father Hamilcar, and the treaties Hamilcar himself wrote, at our consul's bidding, when he withdrew his garrison from Eryx. Upon Carthage's defeat he accepted our conditions, with wailing and gnashing of teeth, and upon his departure from Sicily he agreed to pay tribute to the Roman people.

"And so I bid you fight with your customary spirit, soldiers, but also with indignation and resentment, as if you suddenly saw your slaves up in arms against you. When they were under siege at Eryx we might have killed the Carthaginians by starvation, the most horrible of all human deaths. We might have sailed our victorious fleet to Africa and without resistance destroyed Carthage within a few days. But we showed mercy to their prayers; we released them from investment; we made peace when they were conquered; and we took them under our protection when they were hard-pressed by the African war. In return for these kindnesses they have come following an insane youth to wage war on our country.

"I wish that this battle was for your glory and not your safety! We are not fighting for the possession of Sicily and Sardinia as once we fought. It is for Italy that now you must fight. There is no other army to our rear to stop the enemy if we are beaten, nor any more Alps to delay his approach while we levy new forces. Here we must stand firm, soldiers, just as if we were fighting before the walls of Rome. Let each one of you bear in mind that he is protecting not his own body with his arms, but his wife and small children. And let him not consider his own domestic cares alone, but let him recall again and again that today the senate and the Roman people are depending upon our right hands. The fortune of that city and of the Roman empire will be as secure as we are strong and courageous."

42. These were the words of the consul before the Roman soldiers. Hannibal, on the other hand, thought that his soldiers should be aroused by deeds rather than words. After gathering his army around in a circle for an exhibition, he placed in the middle the captive mountaineers bound in shackles. Then, throwing some Gallic weapons at their feet he ordered an interpreter to ask if any of them would wish to fight, on condition that the victor would be set free and given a horse. To a man every one volunteered, and when lots were cast to choose the combatants, each hoped that fortune would pick him. When a man's lot came up he would snatch up arms with great jubilation amid the congratulations of his comrades, dancing in glee according to the custom of his country. And when they fought, not only the captives but even the spectators at large felt that the lot of the men who died bravely was not less admirable than that of the victors.

43. When the men had watched several duels and had grown expectant he dismissed the Gauls. Then, it is said, he called an assembly and spoke as follows: "If you assess your own position with that same attitude with which you watched others decide their fate, we are victorious. For that was not merely a spectacle for entertainment but an illustration of your own condition. Perhaps fortune has

laid upon you stronger chains and necessity more desperate than theirs. On the right and the left we are bound by
two seas without even a ship available for flight. Before
you is the Po, a river wider and more violent than the
Rhone; behind you the Alps, which you scarcely managed
to cross when you were many and strong. Here you must
conquer or die in your first combat with the enemy. But
the same fortune which places the necessity of fighting
upon you, places before you rewards for victory greater
than any which men dare hope for—even from the hands
of the immortal gods. If it were possible to recover only
Sicily and Sardinia which were stolen from our parents,
still the prizes would be ample enough. But all that Rome
has won and amassed through so many triumphs now will
be yours, along with those who amassed it. Come, then,
take arms and with the help of the gods earn this rich
reward. Long enough have you followed the flocks over
the mountain wastes of Lusitania and Celtiberia, realizing
no profit for such great toils and dangers. Now, after trek-
king over so many mountains and rivers, through so many
lands, it is time to draw abundant wages, to win a great
reward for your toil. Here fortune grants you the end
of your labors; here with your service ended, she affords
you worthy compensation.

"But do not think that victory will be so difficult because the war is with an enemy of great reputation. Often
a despised enemy offers a bloody resistance, and many
famous kingdoms have been conquered with small effort.
Aside from the glory of the Roman name, how can your
enemy be compared with you? Not to mention your courageous and successful service for twenty years, you have
victoriously made your way here from the Ocean and the
farthest corners of the world through many savage tribes
of Spain and Gaul. You will face an army of recruits
which this very summer was cut to pieces, conquered and

besieged. Moreover, this army still is unknown to its general and unacquainted with him. I was born virtually in the tent of my father, who was a renowned general, and was reared there. I have conquered Spain and Gaul, the Alpine tribes, and—a much greater deed—the Alps themselves. Should I compare myself with a general of six months who has deserted his army? If you would take away the standards today and show him the Carthaginians and the Romans he would not know which was his army. It seems to me of no small importance that before the eyes of every one of you I have performed many a soldierly exploit; and there is not one to whose deeds of prowess and glory I could not bear witness and describe, even to the date and place of each. I was your foster son before I was your commander, and I shall go into battle with men whom I have praised and rewarded a thousand times, against enemies who are strange to each other.

44. "Wherever I cast my eyes I see nothing but courage and strength. I see a veteran infantry, cavalry of the noblest nations, you, our faithful allies, and you, Carthaginians—all going to battle for your country inspired by the most just indignation. We have the offensive in this war as we descend upon Italy in hostile array; and we shall fight more bravely because hope and courage are greater in those who attack than in those who defend. Moreover, our spirits rage with anger at our persecution and humiliation. They demanded first me, your general, and then all of you, in punishment for our siege of Saguntum; if we had been surrendered they would have inflicted upon us the most exquisite tortures. They are a proud and cruel race, and consider all the world their own. They claim the right to decide with whom we may make war, with whom we must have peace. They crib and confine us within the boundaries of rivers and mountain ranges, beyond which we must not go; yet they do not ob-

serve their own limits: 'Do not cross the Ebro. Leave Saguntum alone.' Is Saguntum on the Ebro? 'Well, don't move a step anywhere.'

"It is not enough to have taken my ancient provinces Sicily and Sardinia. You are taking Spain as well, and if I yield in Spain you will cross over into Africa. Do I say *will* cross? You already have crossed. You have sent one of the consuls elected for this year to Spain, the other to Africa. There is nothing left to us anywhere except what we defend by force of arms. They can afford to be cowards who have some refuge, who may flee over safe and peaceful highways back to their own land. It is necessary for you, men of Carthage, to be brave men, with the certain conviction that there is no alternative but victory or death. You must now either conquer, or if fortune wavers, seek death in battle rather than in flight. If this conviction is implanted in all your minds, again I say: You are victorious. No keener incentive to victory is given by the immortal gods than contempt of death."

45. Inspired by these speeches, the soldiers on both sides prepared for battle. The Romans erected a bridge over the Ticinus, along with a redoubt to protect it. While they were thus occupied Hannibal sent Maharbal with a division of five hundred horsemen to ravage the fields of the allies of Rome, ordering him to spare the land of the Gauls as much as possible and to encourage their leaders to defect. When the bridge was finished the Roman army was led over into the territory of the Insubrians and took up a position five miles from the village of Victumulae, where Hannibal had his camp. When Hannibal saw that the battle was imminent he quickly recalled Maharbal and his cavalry. Then, thinking no encouragement before battle too much, he called an assembly and proclaimed specific rewards for which the soldiers would fight. Each man would receive land wherever he wished,

in Italy, Africa, or Spain, which would be tax-free for the recipient and his children. Those who preferred money to land would receive silver. Those allies who wished might become Carthaginian citizens. For those who desired to return home he would make it his business to see that they would never envy any of their countrymen or wish to change places with them. To the slaves who had accompanied their masters he offered liberty, and to the masters two slaves to take the place of each of these. Then as a guarantee of his good faith he took in his left hand a lamb and in his right a flint knife. Praying to Jupiter and the other gods, if he should fail to keep his promises, to slay him as he would slay the lamb, he struck its head with the stone. At this they all cried out for battle with a single voice. Each felt that the gods were guaranteeing his desires and that only the start of battle was delaying their fulfillment.

46. In the Roman camp there was by no means such great eagerness. Among other things the soldiers had been terrified by recent ill omens. A wolf had entered the camp and had escaped unharmed after slashing everyone it came upon. A swarm of bees had settled in a tree overhanging the consul's tent. After expiating these omens by sacrifice, Scipio set out for the camp of the enemy with his cavalry and light-armed spearmen to observe at short range the numbers and description of its forces. Soon he happened upon Hannibal himself, who had gone out with his cavalry to reconnoiter the countryside. At first neither party saw the other, but soon the dense dust rising from the feet of so many men and horses gave the signal that the enemy was approaching. Each column stopped and prepared for battle. Scipio stationed the spearmen and the Gallic horsemen in front, holding the Romans and the heavy cavalry of the allies in reserve. Hannibal put his Numidians on each wing, with the rest of the cavalry

between them. Scarcely had the battle cry been raised when the Roman spearmen turned and fled into the midst of the reserves in the second line. For a while the fighting was even on either side. But the foot soldiers who had retreated among the horses agitated them, causing many riders to fall off; others jumped from their horses, seeing their fellows hard-pressed, and soon the battle was being chiefly fought on foot. Suddenly the Numidians, who had flanked the Romans, appeared in the rear, causing great panic. Their agitation was increased by the wounding of the consul, who was saved from danger only by the intervention of his son, at that time scarcely more than a boy. This was the youth who was destined to achieve the glory of ending that war and who was subsequently styled "Africanus" for his brilliant victory over Hannibal and the Carthaginians. The spearmen, who had returned to the rear and were the first to be attacked by the Numidians, were routed. The cavalry, however, gathered in close order around the consul, to protect him with their arms and their persons, then retreated to their camp without alarm or confusion. Coelius assigns the glory of saving the consul's life to a Ligurian slave; but I should prefer to believe the version which names his son. This is the version which is transmitted by most authorities and is confirmed by tradition.

47. This was the first battle with Hannibal. It proved conclusively that the Carthaginian cavalry was superior and therefore that the open plain, such as that between the Alps and the Po, was strategically unsuitable for battle to the Romans. On the following night, therefore, the troops were ordered to pack their gear in silence, and camp was hurriedly moved from the Ticinus to the Po, where the troops crossed over the pontoon-bridge without confusion and without harassment by the enemy. They already had reached Placentia before Hannibal

had realized that they were gone from the Ticinus. Nevertheless he did capture about six hundred of the rear guard who were slow about loosening the end of the bridge. Hannibal was unable to use the bridge to cross since the ends were unfastened and the whole thing was carried downstream.

48. The following night the Gallic auxiliaries in the Roman camp mutinied, but caused more panic and disorder than bloodshed. About two thousand horsemen and foot soldiers killed the guards at the gates and deserted to Hannibal. He received them with friendly words, and after assuring them of great rewards he sent them home to incite their countrymen to revolt. Scipio perceived that this incident portended the revolt of all the Gauls, and that all those infected by this lawlessness would rush to arms like maniacs. So even though he was tormented by his wound, the next night at about the fourth watch he silently broke camp and moved into a hilly area near the Trebia river, where cavalry could not easily maneuver. But this time he did not escape Hannibal's vigilance as he had at the Ticinus. Hannibal first sent his Numidians, then the rest of his cavalry, in pursuit. These would have thrown at least the rear of the army into disorder if their greed for plunder had not diverted them to the empty Roman camp. While they wasted time searching through the camp and found nothing to compensate for the delay, the enemy escaped from their grasp. When they found the Romans they had already crossed the Trebia and were laying out their camp, and they were able to overtake only a few stragglers who had not yet crossed the river.

Because of his wound Scipio could no longer endure the discomfort caused by the jostling of the march. Since he had heard that his colleague had been recalled from Sicily, he thought that he should wait for him. Choosing the safest position he could find near the river, he established a permanent camp.

Hannibal also pitched camp, not far away. He was cheered by the victory of his cavalry but anxious because of the lack of grain. Since he was traveling through enemy country where there was no regular source of provisions his supply was growing shorter day by day. At length he sent a force to Clastidium, a village where the Romans had laid up a large store of grain. As they were preparing to attack, they received word that the commander of the garrison, one Dasius of Brundisium, was willing to surrender Clastidium for the small sum of forty pieces of gold. This furnished the Carthaginians with a grain supply while they remained near the Trebia. The soldiers in the captured garrison were not harmed, since Hannibal wished to establish a reputation for clemency from the very beginning.

49. Military activity on the mainland had virtually come to a halt. However, around Sicily and the islands off the Italian coast the consul Sempronius was busily engaged in land and sea operations. 51. After arranging affairs in Sicily Sempronius took ten ships and sailed along the coast of Sicily for Ariminum. Disembarking there, he marched his army to the river Trebia to join his colleague.

52. The fact that both consuls and all of the forces Rome had at hand were pitted against Hannibal meant that if these troops could not maintain Roman autonomy no hope was left. Nevertheless there was dissension in the army. One consul, who was ill and had been bested in a cavalry battle, wished to postpone further action. The other, who was still confident and therefore more venturesome, would brook no delay.

The area between the Trebia and the Po at that time was inhabited by Gauls. In this contest between two powerful nations these would commit themselves to neither side, quite clearly wishing to be on good terms with the victor. This was acceptable to the Romans, provided the Gauls committed no overt act, but it angered Hannibal, who asserted that he had come to free the Gauls at their request. Because of this displeasure (and because he needed booty to maintain his troops) he dispatched two thousand foot soldiers and one thousand horsemen—mostly Numidians, along with a few Gauls— to plunder their territory all the way to the Po. Until that time the Gauls had remained doubtful; but now necessity forced them to turn from those who had misused them to those who would protect them. Thus they sent envoys to the consuls, asking for assistance and asserting that the cause of their suffering was their loyalty to Rome. Scipio did not think that their motives or the present situation warranted Roman intervention. He was suspicious of the Gauls because of their many disloyal acts in the past, and, if time had obscured these, by the recent treachery of the Boii. On the other hand, Sempronius asserted that the surest way to keep faithful allies was to protect the first who asked for assistance. When his colleague demurred, Sempronius sent his cavalry and almost one thousand spearmen across the Trebia to defend the territory of Gaul. These troops fell on the enemy unexpectedly when they were dispersed and weighted down with booty. After causing great panic and killing many they pursued them all the way to the guard posts before their camp. Their allies in the camp poured out and drove the Romans back, but the Roman reserves stayed the retreat. The battle then wavered back and forth, ending undecisively. However, since the losses of the enemy were heavier, it was called a Roman victory.

53. But to the consul Sempronius it seemed a great and decisive victory. He was elated that he had been

victorious in a cavalry battle while his colleague had been defeated. He said that the courage of the troops was restored and no one but Scipio himself wanted to postpone battle; Scipio was sick more in mind than in body and the memory of his wound made him fear the perils of battle. . . . He spoke such things as this while sitting by his sick colleague and repeated them to the soldiers before his tent almost as if he were making a speech. The time of the elections was drawing near, when new consuls would assume charge of the war; and the sickness of his colleague provided an opportunity of winning all the glory for himself. So, regardless of Scipio's objections, he ordered the soldiers to prepare for battle.

Hannibal saw what policy would be most advantageous to the enemy, and had little hope that the consuls would do anything rash or imprudent. But he had heard that one of them was hotheaded and impulsive by nature and had discovered by experience that this was true. He also believed that Sempronius' success against his raiding party would make him even more impetuous, so that he was hopeful that an opportunity for battle was soon to come. He took great pains not to miss any opportunity while the enemy soldiers were still unseasoned and the morale of the Gauls was still good; for he knew that the further his men were led from home the more reluctant most of them would be to follow. With these thoughts in mind, he intended even to provoke a battle if the enemy should demur. Soon, however, his Gallic scouts—they were safer for reconnaissance since Gauls were serving in both armies—reported that the Romans were preparing for battle. Upon receiving this report Hannibal began to look around for a place for ambush.

54. Between Hannibal and the Romans flowed a small stream with very high banks which were covered with the marsh grass, briars, and bracken which usually

overrun uncultivated land. After riding around this place and finding it adequate even for concealing cavalry, he said to his brother Mago, "Here is where you will take your position. Select one hundred men each from the infantry and cavalry and report to me at the first watch. Now let us eat and rest." With that he dismissed his staff.

Soon Mago returned with the men he had chosen and Hannibal addressed them, "I see here the strength of my army," he said, "but numbers are necessary as well as courage. Each of you select nine men from the cavalry and infantry like yourselves. Mago will show you the position which you will occupy. You will have an enemy who is completely unfamiliar with tactics of this sort." At dawn, after Mago had departed with the infantry and cavalry, Hannibal sent out his Numidian cavalry with orders to cross the Trebia river and ride up to the gates of the enemy camp. There they were to provoke a battle by hurling javelins at the enemy guard posts and then, gradually retreating, to draw them across the river. The other officers were ordered to direct their men to have breakfast and to await the signal for battle armed and with their horses saddled.

Sempronius already was determined to fight and was eager for battle. When the Numidians began their disturbance, he first led out all his cavalry, in whom he had great confidence; then six thousand of the infantry; and finally all his forces. Winter had now arrived. It was snowing that day in the area between the Alps and the Apennines and the nearby rivers and marshes made it extremely cold. Moreover, the men and horses had been hastily sent out without first eating or making any preparations against the cold. They had no heat in them, and as they approached the river the wind blew colder and colder. A rain the night before had caused the river to rise to chest-height. As the troops entered the water

behind the retreating Numidians, and especially when
they came out again, their bodies became so stiff with
cold that they could scarcely hold their weapons. At the
same time they grew faint with weariness and, as the day
progressed, with hunger.

55. Meanwhile Hannibal's troops had built fires in
front of their tents and had dined at leisure; oil had been
distributed to them with which to make their joints sup-
ple. When it was reported that the enemy had crossed
the river they were prepared in mind as well as body;
eagerly snatching up their arms, they marched out to
battle. . . .

Hannibal's light-armed Balearics began the battle, but
when they were confronted with legions who were more
heavily armed they were quickly withdrawn and sent
to the wings. This immediately endangered the weary
Roman cavalry. These numbered only four thousand,
and even before had hardly been able to withstand the
ten thousand horsemen of the enemy, most of whom
were still fresh. Now they found themselves almost
buried under a cloud of javelins thrown by the Balearics.
Moreover the unaccustomed odor as well as the sight of
the monstrous elephants stationed on the wings caused
the horses to panic and break. As for the infantry, although they were equal to the Carthaginians in courage,
they were not so in strength. For the enemy was fresh
and had prepared their bodies for battle, while the Romans were hungry, exhausted, and stiff with cold. They
might still have successfully resisted by dint of courage
alone if they had been opposed only by infantry; but
soon the Balearics had routed the cavalry and were directing their missiles upon the infantry's flanks, while the
elephants charged into the middle of their line. Meanwhile Mago and the Numidians, as soon as the Romans
had passed their hiding place, attacked their rear and

created great panic. But despite these dangers from every side, the infantry held steady for some time—best of all, surprisingly, against the elephants. Light-armed soldiers posted for that purpose turned them aside by throwing javelins, then struck them under the tail where the hide is soft.

56. The elephants were about to stampede their own lines when Hannibal ordered them to be driven away from the middle of the battle line toward the Romans' Gallic auxiliaries on the left wing. There they caused an immediate rout; and the terror of the Romans was increased when they saw their auxiliaries put to flight. The Romans were now fighting in a circle. About ten thousand men, finding they could not get away in any other direction, cut their way through the middle of the Africans and their Gallic auxiliaries, killing a large number. Since they were cut off from their camp by the river, and they could not see for the driving rain where they could bring assistance to their fellows, they set out straight for Placentia. Several other groups broke through in different directions. Those who made for the river were either drowned in the flood or cut down by the enemy as they hesitated to enter. Those who scattered through the fields followed the tracks of the retreating ten thousand to Placentia. Fear of the enemy inspired others to brave the river, and they succeeded in crossing and returning to their camp. Many men and pack animals and almost all the elephants died from the rain mixed with snow and the unbearable cold. The Carthaginians ended their pursuit at the Trebia, and returned to camp so numbed with cold that they felt no elation at their victory. The following night the garrison from the camp and the fugitives who had survived, most of whom were unarmed, crossed the Trebia on rafts. Either the enemy heard nothing in the beating rain, or fatigue

and wounds made them unable to move and they pretended not to hear. Scipio led the army in silence to Placentia without molestation from the Carthaginians. From there he crossed the Po and proceeded to Cremona, so that one provincial town might not be taxed with furnishing winter quarters for two armies.

57. The report of this defeat caused such terror at Rome that the people believed the enemy would appear before the city at any moment. They could see no hope nor any aid by which to repulse an attack on the walls and gates. After one consul was defeated at the Ticinus, the other had been recalled from Sicily. But with the defeat of two consuls and two consular armies, what other legions were there for them to summon? With the city in this state of terror the consul Sempronius arrived. Although the enemy cavalry was dispersed over the whole countryside in search of booty, he had managed to get through by reason of his daring rather than by shrewdness or any hope of eluding the enemy or of resisting if he failed to escape. After holding consular elections—the most urgent business at the moment—he returned to his winter quarters. The consuls elected were Gnaeus Servilius and Gaius Flaminius, for his second term.

The Roman army was afforded no respite even in winter quarters. The Numidian cavalry was ranging far and wide, and where the ground was too difficult for them, the Celtiberians and Lusitanians substituted. All supply lines were cut off in every direction except for the Po, where provisions were brought in by boat. Near Placentia was their market place, heavily fortified and occupied by a strong garrison. In the hope of taking this stronghold Hannibal made an expedition there with his cavalry and light-armed troops. Since his hope of success lay in concealing his intentions, he attacked at night. But he did not manage to surprise the sentries. Such a great uproar arose that it was heard as far away as Placentia. As a result the consul arrived by daybreak, with his troops marching in battle order. Before this a cavalry battle had begun, in which Hannibal was wounded and forced to retire from the battle. This so demoralized the enemy that the attack was easily repulsed.

After resting a few days Hannibal then set out to attack Victumulae, even before his wound had sufficiently healed. This had been a Roman market place during the Gallic war. Afterwards, since it was a fortified town, it had been peopled by a mixed population of settlers from nearby tribes; and at this time fear of rapine had driven many there from outlying rural areas. This hybrid population was inspired by the news of the courageous defense of the garrison near Placentia; snatching up their arms they marched out to meet Hannibal. They met him on the road in anything but battle order. Since there was nothing more than a disorderly mob on one side, while on the other there was mutual confidence between the soldiers and their general, about thirty-five thousand men were routed by relatively few. The next day the city surrendered and opened its gates to a garrison. After the inhabitants were ordered to lay down their weapons and had complied, the signal was given to the victors to sack the city, just as if it had been taken by assault. Every atrocity occurred which historians consider worth recording on such an occasion. The miserable population suffered every example of inhuman arrogance and savage lust. This was Hannibal's winter campaign.

58. While the cold was unbearable Hannibal allowed his soldiers a brief rest; but at the first uncertain signs of spring he set out from his winter quarters for Etruria, intending to annex that state either willingly or under compulsion just as he had treated the Gauls and Ligurians. As he crossed the Apennines he was caught in a storm so

violent that even the evils of the Alps would not rival it. At first wind and rain blowing in the faces of the soldiers forced them to halt; for either they had to drop their weapons, or if they pressed on against the blast it twisted them around and hurled them headlong. Then, when the wind became so strong that it stopped their breath, they were forced to sit down with their backs to it for some time. Suddenly a loud thundering shook the heavens, and lightning lit up the sky. They were so deafened and dazzled that they were prostrated with fear. Finally the rain stopped, but the wind continued to blow stronger than ever. It was decided that their only course was to pitch camp just where they had halted.

But this only began their labors anew, for it was impossible to unroll or set up a tent; and if anyone succeeded, the wind ripped it apart and blew it away. Soon it began to hail and snow, when the moisture carried by the wind began to freeze as it passed over the cold mountain ridges. At this the men dropped everything and threw themselves on the ground, where they were enveloped rather than sheltered by their tents. Such bitter cold followed that whenever anyone wished to get up from that miserable cluster of men and animals, for a long time his muscles would be so stiff that he would not be able to bend his joints. Finally, however, they began to force themselves to move, and their spirits began to return; here and there fires were built and everyone who could not help himself sought help from others. Many men as well as pack animals died, and seven of the elephants who had survived the battle of the Trebia perished.

59. Hannibal then descended from the Apennines and set out in the direction of Placentia. After proceeding about ten miles he stopped and pitched camp. The next day he advanced against the enemy with twelve thousand

infantry and five thousand cavalry. The consul Sempronius (who now had returned from Rome) was not reluctant for battle and that night the two armies camped only three miles apart. The following day a furious but indecisive battle was fought. At the first onslaught the Roman attack was so successful that they not only turned back the enemy but put them to flight and pursued them into their camp. Soon they were besieging the camp itself. Hannibal, however, stationed only a few men to defend the rampart and the gates. The rest he assembled in close order in the middle of the camp, commanding them to be ready to charge out when the signal was given.

It was now about the ninth hour of the day [about three o'clock] and the Roman soldiers had exhausted themselves to no purpose. The consul, giving up hope of taking the camp, gave the signal to withdraw. When Hannibal heard the signal and saw that the fighting was slackening and the soldiers retreating, he immediately sent out his cavalry from the side gates, while he himself led the main body of his infantry out the center. Seldom has there been so fierce a fight or so bloody a slaughter as that would have been if daylight had permitted it to continue. However, darkness stopped the battle while it was still raging furiously. As a result the numbers killed belied the ferocity of the battle. And just as the battle was indecisive, the loss of lives on either side was almost equal. No more than six hundred infantry and three hundred cavalry fell on either side. But the Roman loss was great in proportion to the numbers; several knights, five military tribunes, and three prefects of the allies were killed. After this battle Hannibal withdrew into Liguria and Sempronius to Luca. When Hannibal arrived in Liguria, the populace surrendered to him two Roman quaestors, Gaius Fulvius and Lucius Lucretius, along with two military tribunes and five knights—most of them

sons of senators—whom they had waylaid and captured.
Through this action they hoped to convince him of their
peaceful intentions and friendly attitude towards him.

62. During that winter [218 B.C.] many prodigies
occurred in and around Rome; or at least—as usually
happens once men become concerned with the supernatural—many were reported and readily believed. One
was that in the vegetable market a free-born infant six
months old had cried out, "Victory!" Another that in
the cattle market a bull had climbed of its own accord
up to the third story of a house, then thrown itself to the
ground when frightened by the inhabitants. It was also
said that a fleet of ships was seen shining in the sky. The
temple of Hope, which is in the vegetable market, was
struck by lightning. At Lanuvium the spear on the statue
of Juno had moved. A crow had flown into the temple of
Juno and lighted on her couch. In the neighborhood of
Amiternum, phantoms of men dressed all in white had
been seen in many places from a distance; but never did
they approach near to anyone. In the district of Picenum
there had occurred a shower of stones. At Caere the
oracular tablets had shrunk. And in Gaul a wolf had
stolen a sentry's sword from its scabbard.

Concerning the other portents the decemvirs were ordered to consult the Sibylline books; for the shower of
stones, a festival of nine days was proclaimed. Following
this festival almost the whole city devoted itself to the
expiation of the other portents. First the city was purified; then full-grown victims were sacrificed to the gods
which had been designated by the Sibylline books. An
offering of forty pounds of gold was carried to Lanuvium
and presented to Juno, and the matrons dedicated a
bronze statue to Juno on the Aventine. A *lectisternium,*
or feast of the gods, was ordered for Caere, where the
oracular tablets had shrunk; and a ceremony of suppli-

cation was to be made to Fortune on Mount Algidus. At Rome a *lectisternium* was ordered for Juventas and a supplication at the temple of Hercules specifically, and then for people generally at all the shrines of the gods. Five full-grown victims were sacrificed to Genius; and Gaius Atilius Serronus, the praetor, was commanded to make certain vows to be fulfilled if the state should abide in its present condition for ten years. These expiatory rites and vows largely dispelled the religious qualms of the population.

63. To one of the two consuls elect, Gaius Flaminius, had been allotted the legions in winter quarters at Placentia. He sent a letter to the present consul instructing him to have this army in the camp at Ariminum on March 15th. His intention was to assume the duties of consul there; for he was sensible of his long-standing quarrel with the senate. This had begun while he was tribune of the plebs and had continued during his former consulship when the senate had first attempted to invalidate his election, then to deny him a triumph. He also was disliked by the patricians because of a new law which a tribune of the plebs, Quintus Claudius, had passed against the senate's opposition. Flaminius alone of all the senators had supported him. This law provided that no senator or son of a senator might possess a. sea-going vessel with a capacity of more than three hundred amphorae; this was estimated as sufficient for transporting produce from the fields, and it was considered improper for senators to engage in trade. This law, which was passed only after the greatest controversy, offended the nobility very much, but it made its proponent popular among the common people and was responsible for his second consulship. Because of this situation he was sure the senate would try to keep him in the city by misrepresenting the auspices or postponing the Latin Festival (at

which he was required to offer sacrifices) or other such hindrances. He therefore pretended he had to take a journey and left for his province before his term of office began.

When this became known it moved the senate to new anger: "Gaius Flaminius," they said, "has declared war not only upon the senate but upon the immortal gods as well. Previously he was elected consul against the auspices, and when gods and men recalled him from the very battle line he refused to obey. Now, conscious of his sacrilege, he has fled from the Capitol and the established vows so that on the day of his inauguration he might not enter the temple of Jupiter Optimus Maximus; so that he might not see and consult the senate which hates him and which he alone hates; so that he might not proclaim the Latin Festival or make the traditional sacrifice to Jupiter Latiaris on the Alban Mount; so that he might not take the auspices, and after making the customary vows on the Capitol, journey in state to his province dressed in his general's cloak and attended by lictors. He preferred to go like some camp follower, secretly and furtively without the symbols of his office and unaccompanied by lictors, as if he were going into exile. Obviously it was for the sake of dignity that he is entering office at Ariminum rather than at Rome and is donning the *toga praetexta* of a consul in a public inn rather than in the presence of his own household gods!"

The senate decreed unanimously that Flaminius should be recalled and compelled to perform all his duties to gods and men before he returned to his province. It was decided to send envoys to inform him of this decree. But when the envoys, Quintus Terentius and Marcus Antistius, reached him he paid this delegation no more regard than he had the letter sent by the senate in his previous consulship. A few days later he entered office. During the ceremony, as he was sacrificing a calf, it slipped out of the hands of those who were holding it and sprinkled many of the bystanders with blood. There was even greater agitation and confusion among those some distance away who did not know the cause of the disturbance. This was considered by most as an omen of disaster. After assuming command of the two legions under the command of Sempronius, the consul of the previous year, and the two commanded by Gaius Atilius, the praetor Flaminius set out through the passes of the Apennines.

Book 22
2 1 7 - 2 1 6 B C

In the spring Hannibal left his winter quarters to move southward into Etruria. He elected to take the shorter of two possible routes, through the swamp of the Arno. But a recent overflow of the river had made progress very difficult.

3. After many men and pack animals had been lost under these wretched conditions the army finally emerged from the swamp. As soon as a spot of dry land was found they pitched camp, and through scouts who had been sent ahead it was ascertained that the Roman army was stationed around the walls of Arretium. He then carefully set about finding out the plans and the temper of the consul, the geography and roads of the region, the resources for obtaining provisions and other things important to know. This region, the plains of Etruria which

lay between Faesulae and Arretium, was among the most
fertile in Italy and produced an abundance of grain and
cattle as well as all other supplies. The consul was arrogant as a result of the successes of his previous consulship and did not have sufficient reverence for the laws
or the dignity of the senate or even for the gods. This
arrogance which was inherent in his nature had been
fostered by his victories in both the political and military
spheres. It was apparent that in all cases he would act
recklessly and precipitously without first consulting either gods or men. In order to make him more susceptible
to these weaknesses Hannibal set out to irritate and
arouse him. Turning away from the enemy on his left
he bypassed Faesulae and set out to ravage the plains
of central Etruria, leaving the utmost devastation which
he could effect for the consul to see.

Flaminius would have taken action if the enemy had
not; but now he saw the possessions of the allies being
pillaged and destroyed almost before his very eyes. He
considered it a disgrace to himself for Hannibal to be
allowed to wander around central Italy and without any
resistance to march up to attack the very walls of Rome.
Everyone else in the council of war favored conservative
rather than spectacular action, urging him to wait for
his colleague so that they might unite their forces and
act coöperatively; meanwhile he could use his cavalry
and light-armed troops to curb the unrestrained plundering by the enemy. Enraged at this advice, he stalked out
of the council and ordered the signal given for marching
and for battle. "By all means let us sit before the walls
of Arretium," he said, "for here is our city and our household gods. Let Hannibal slip through our fingers and
devastate Italy until he arrives at Rome with his pillag-
ing and burning! Let us not move from here until the
senate summons Flaminius from Arretium as they once

called Camillus from Veii!" Inveighing against them in this way, he ordered the troops to hurry and pull up the standards. He himself leaped on his horse, but as he did so the animal stumbled, pitching the consul head over heels. Everyone was alarmed at this, taking it for a bad omen betokening evil for the campaign. Their alarm grew when a messenger reported that the standard could not be pulled up no matter how hard the standard bearer tried. At this Flaminius turned upon the messenger and said, "Are you also bringing letters from the senate forbidding me to act? Go and order them to dig up the standard if their hands are so numbed with fear that they cannot pull it up!" With these words he led the column forward. The officers, besides disagreeing with his strategy, were terrified at the double omen, but the soldiers in general were delighted with their commander's boldness; for they considered only his confidence, not his grounds for it.

4. In order to provoke the anger of his enemy further and make him more eager to revenge the injuries to his allies, Hannibal completely devastated the whole area between Cortona and Lake Trasumennus. He now arrived at a spot naturally suited for ambush, just where the mountains of Cortona come nearest to the lake. The passage between the two is very narrow, as if the space were left by design for a road. Further on it opens into a somewhat wider plain followed by hills. In this valley Hannibal established a camp in full view, where he himself encamped along with his African and Spanish troops. The Balearics and the other light-armed troops he sent around behind the mountains; the cavalry he stationed at the very mouth of the pass where they were well concealed by hillocks. Thus, when the Romans should enter, the cavalry would block the pass and they would be trapped by the lake and mountains.

Flaminius reached the lake at about sunset but did not bother with reconnoitering. The next morning he passed through the narrow defile almost before daylight, and when the column began to debouch on the open plain, all they saw was the enemy directly before them. The ambuscade in the rear and above them escaped their notice. When Hannibal saw that he had the enemy where he wanted him, trapped between the hills and lake, and surrounded by his troops he gave the signal for them to attack simultaneously. The attack caught the Romans even more unawares because of a mist which had arisen from the lake and lay thicker on the plain than on the hills. But the different enemy companies, running down from the hills each by the shortest route, were visible to each other and could coördinate their attack. From the clamor which arose from all sides the Romans sensed that they were surrounded, but still could not see their attackers. They were charged on their front and flank before they could draw up their line or put on their armor or even draw their swords.

5. The consul himself remained reasonably calm and unruffled, considering the terrifying circumstances. His ranks had become confused and disordered as the men turned here and there to face the various shouts. He marshaled them as well as the critical situation permitted, and wherever it was possible to go and be heard he encouraged his men to stand and fight. "You will not be able to escape by vows and prayers to the gods," he said, "but only through strength and courage! The sword will clear a path through the enemy line! The less you are afraid the safer you will be!"

But in the confusion and the turmoil neither his encouragement nor his orders could be heard. The soldiers had scarcely the presence of mind to hold their swords, much less keep their lines and positions. Some were cut down because their armor encumbered rather than protected them. The thick fog made ears more useful than eyes; but the soldiers constantly turned to look wherever they heard groans of the wounded, blows on body and armor, and the confused din of crashes and screams. Some tried to flee, but were caught in the throng of fighters; others trying to return to the fight were driven back by the mass of fugitives. Sorties were attempted in every direction and it became clear that they were trapped by the mountains and lake and the enemy line. Everyone then realized that there was no hope left except in his right hand, and as each man became his own general and steeled his courage for battle, the fighting began anew. The columns were not in proper battle order, nor was each soldier in his proper company; but wherever they were gathered together by circumstances, each man's inclination dictated to him whether to fight in the van or the rear. During the battle an earthquake occurred which demolished large parts of many Italian cities, turned great rivers from their course, caused the sea to backwash into the rivers, and leveled mountains in great landslides. But so great was their fervor and absorption in the battle that none of the combatants were aware of it.

6. For three hours the battle raged on. The fighting was vicious everywhere but was most intense around the consul. Followed by the bravest of his troops he tirelessly brought assistance wherever he saw his forces in trouble. But he was easily distinguishable because of his armor and was constantly and furiously attacked by the enemy. The Romans continued to stave off this attack, until at last a certain Insubrian horseman, Ducarius by name, who knew the consul by sight, recognized him. "Look," he said to his companions, "there is the man

who slaughtered our legions and devastated our city and our fields. With my own hands I will offer him up as a victim to the spirits of our shamefully murdered countrymen." Spurring his horse, he plunged into the thick of the enemy. First he cut down the armor-bearer, who threw himself in his way, then ran his lance through the consul. He attempted, but was not able, to despoil the body, which the Roman reserves protected with their shields.

The death of the consul routed most of the army. Now neither lake nor mountains stood in their way. They fled as if they were blind over defiles and precipices; arms and men tumbled one over the other as they fell. A large number who were cut off from the hills ran into the lake until the water reached up to their heads and shoulders. Blind fear drove others to try to swim to safety, but this was hopeless because of the size of the lake. They either became exhausted and were drowned or miserably returned to the shallows to be cut down by the enemy cavalry riding into the water. About six thousand men in the first line gallantly forced a passage through the enemy and escaped through the defile. They took up a position on a small hill, where they listened to the clamor of battle and crash of arms, but in the fog they were unable to see how the contest was going. At length, as the fighting subsided, the heat of the sun dispelled the fog, and the sunlight beaming on the hills and plain revealed the disastrous slaughter of the Roman army. Then for fear that they might be seen in the distance and pursued by cavalry, they turned and retreated as quickly as possible. Maharbal overtook them during the night with all his cavalry; the next day he offered to let them go with a single garment each if they gave up their weapons. In addition to their other woes they were threatened by starvation, so they surrendered themselves. But this promise Hannibal kept with Punic faith and clapped them all in chains.

7. This was the famous battle of Lake Trasumennus, the most notable of the few disasters suffered by Rome. Fifteen thousand Romans were killed on the battlefield. Ten thousand others scattered through Etruria and made their way back to Rome. Twenty-five hundred of the enemy fell in battle, and many later died of their wounds. Other sources make the losses many times greater on either side. However, I wish to avoid the useless exaggeration to which many historians are so prone, and in preference to others I have taken Fabius Pictor, who lived during the time of the war, as my authority. Hannibal set free all of the allies who were captured, but threw the Romans into chains. He then ordered the bodies of his own men to be sorted out from the piles of the enemy dead and buried. A careful search was also made for the body of Flaminius in order to bury it, but it could not be found.

When the first news of the disaster reached Rome a confused and terrified crowd of people collected in the Forum. Women wandered through the streets asking everyone they met what sudden catastrophe had been reported and if anything had happened to the army. The crowd collected like a great assembly before the Comitium and the curia, calling for the magistrates. Finally, just before sunset, the praetor Marcus Pomponius appeared and announced, "We have been defeated in a great battle." Although nothing more concrete was to be gotten from him, the crowd was rife with rumors; each person went home with the news that the consul had been killed with a large number of his troops, but that a few had survived and were scattered throughout Etruria or captured by the enemy.

The fears and forebodings of the relatives of the men who had served under Flaminius were in proportion to the casualties suffered by the army. Each one wondered if those dear to him were alive, and no one knew whether to hope or fear. On the next day and for several days following a great crowd, largely of women, collected at the gates waiting for one of their relations to arrive, or for some news about them. They poured around everyone who came along, questioning him; they could not be torn away, especially from those they knew, until they had inquired into every particular. As each questioner turned away, the news he had received—whether good or bad—was written on his face. He then would turn home surrounded by a throng of friends congratulating or comforting him. The joy and grief of the women was especially moving. It is said that when one of them suddenly came upon her son at the gate safe and unhurt she died in his embrace. Another, who sat at home grieving at the false news of her son's death, died with joy as she saw him walk in the door. For several days the praetors kept the senate from sun-up to sun-set debating what general and what forces could stop the victorious Carthaginians.

Quintus Fabius Maximus, later surnamed "Cunctator" for his delaying tactics against Hannibal, was declared dictator. He enrolled two additional legions and took command of the army of the other consul, Gnaeus Servilius.

12. After receiving the army of the consul from the legate, Fulvius Flaccus, the dictator marched through the Sabine territory to Tibur, where he had set a day for the new recruits to assemble. From there he marched to Praeneste, and cutting across country, came out on the Via Latina. He then advanced in the direction of the en-

emy, always carefully reconnoitering ahead, resolved never to commit his forces to battle anywhere unless forced to do so. On the first day that he pitched camp within sight of the enemy, not far from Arpi, Hannibal at once drew up his battle line and offered battle. But soon he saw that all the enemy camp was quiet and there was no flurry of preparation. He then retired again to his own camp, saying with derision that the martial spirits of the Romans were crushed, that they were conquered and had openly renounced all claim to valor and glory. In fact, however, he was deeply concerned in his heart, since now he realized he would have a general far different from Flaminius and Sempronius to deal with. The Romans had finally learned a lesson from adversity and had chosen a general equal to Hannibal himself.

The dictator's caution he feared at once; but his resolution he had not yet experienced, and so began to badger him in order to try his temper. He constantly moved his camp and devastated the fields of the allies before his very eyes. Now he marched quickly out of sight, now halted suddenly at some turn of the road and hid to see if he could catch him as he descended to the plain. But Fabius continued to lead his troops along high ground at a moderate distance from the enemy; in this way he never lost sight of him while also avoiding battle. He kept his troops in camp except for such duties as necessity required. Parties sent for forage and wood were never small and these were under orders not to venture far. By keeping a company of cavalry and light-armed infantry drawn up in readiness against sudden forays he protected his own foraging parties and made it dangerous for the enemy to scatter far in search of plunder. His troops had been demoralized by their former disasters. For this reason he would never stake everything on a single general engagement; but by undertaking light skirmishes from a safe position with a place of refuge close at hand, he gradually persuaded his troops to place more confidence in their own courage and in the outcome of the war.

This conservative policy vexed Fabius' own master of horse as much as it did Hannibal. He was a rash and violent man, and immoderate in his language. Only his reluctance to disobey a superior prevented his plunging the state into ruin. At first before small groups, then openly so that all could hear, he vilified Fabius, calling his delaying tactics laziness, his caution timidity. By deriding his superior and imputing to him faults which resembled his virtues—a contemptible practice which has often been successful—he aggrandized himself.

13. From the Hirpini, Hannibal proceeded into Samnium, devastated the territory of Beneventum, and took the city of Telesia, intentionally provoking the Roman general and seeking to draw him into open battle in anger at this destruction. Among the prisoners from the Italian allies whom Hannibal had released at Trasumennus were three Campanian knights who had been bribed by Hannibal to undertake to conciliate their fellow citizens to his cause. These three reported to Hannibal that if he advanced into Campania he would have an opportunity to take Capua. Hannibal was uncertain whether to trust them or not, since it was a difficult and important matter to attempt upon the authority of such men. Finally, however, he was persuaded to move from Samnium into Campania. After warning them again and again to make their promises good with deeds he dismissed them, ordering them to return with more of their people, including some nobles.

Meanwhile he ordered his guide to conduct him into the territory of Casinum, for he had been advised by men who knew the area that if he occupied the pass there

he could prevent the Romans from bringing assistance
to their allies. However, Latin was difficult for the Punic
tongue to pronounce, and the guide misunderstood Casinum for Casilinum; he therefore turned from the proper
route and led Hannibal through the territories of Allifae,
Calatia, and Cales down into the plain of Stella. When
Hannibal saw this valley enclosed by mountains and
rivers, he called the guide and asked what territory he was
in. When the guide answered that he would be in
Casilinum by nightfall, then at last the error was discovered and he learned that Casinum was far off in a different direction. He had the guide scourged and crucified as
an example, and after fortifying a camp sent Maharbal
with the cavalry to ravage the territory of Falerii. This
devastation extended all the way to the Baths of Sinuessa.
The Numidians created havoc and spread alarm and
terror even more widely. Yet in spite of this terror and
with all they possessed aflame with war, the allies remained resolute in their loyalty, undoubtedly because
they were ruled with justice and moderation. Never did
they hesitate to obey their superiors—which is the one
real pledge of fidelity.

14. The Carthaginians had encamped at the Volturnus River, and the most delightful countryside in all
Italy was scarred with flames. As Fabius passed by along
the ridge of Mount Massicus villas were seen smoldering
far and wide, and sedition in his army almost flared up
anew. It had subsided for a few days, because of the belief, when a sudden march was ordered, that they were
hurrying to prevent the devastation of Campania. As
they reached the last ridge of the mountain they could
see before their eyes the enemy burning the houses
of the Falernian countryside and of the colonists of
Sinuessa. When still no mention was made of battle,
Minucius exclaimed, "Have we come to watch the burning

and slaughter of our allies as an entertainment? These are our fellow citizens whom our fathers sent as colonists to safeguard this frontier from the Samnite enemy. If nothing else shames us, are we not mortified that their homes are now being ravaged, not by their Samnite neighbors, but by strangers from Carthage whom our indolence and delay have allowed to come here from the ends of the earth? Are we so inferior to our fathers that we are to watch their land overrun with Moorish and Numidian enemies? They thought it a disgrace for Carthaginian fleets to sail along its coast. . . . It is stupidity to think that the war can be ended by sitting still and praying. It is your duty to take arms and go down onto the plain to meet the enemy in battle man to man. Rome has grown great by action and daring—not by this indolence which the timid call discretion." A crowd of tribunes and Roman knights gathered to listen to Minucius' harrangue; these violent words even reached the ears of the common soldiers. It was positively asserted that if the question could be submitted to the soldiers, they would elect Minucius general in preference to Fabius.

15. Fabius did not waver in his resolution, but watched both his own men and the enemy with equal care. He knew that his delaying tactics were disliked in Rome as well as in his own army, but he steadfastly continued to adhere to that same course of action through the rest of the summer. Eventually Hannibal gave up hope of battle, which he had so keenly wished for, and began to look around for a location for winter quarters; the area which he was in was planted entirely in vineyards and orchards, producing pleasant fruits but not a permanent, staple food supply.

This information was reported to Fabius by scouts. When he was sure that Hannibal would withdraw by the same narrow passes by which he had entered the

Falernian district, he established a fairly large garrison on Mount Callicula and another at Casilinum. This town, which is divided by the Volturnus river, marks the boundary between Falerii and Campania. He himself led the main army back to the same mountain ridges by which he had come, sending Lucius Hostilius Mancinus ahead with four hundred horsemen as a scouting party. Hostilius was one of the young men who had often listened to the violent tirades of the master of horse. At first he confined himself to the duties of reconnoitering, observing the enemy from a safe distance. But soon he saw the Numidians scattered through the villages in search of plunder and killed a few when opportunity offered. After this he became carried away and forgot the commands of the dictator, who had ordered him to proceed only so far as he could in safety, then to retreat before he was seen by the enemy. As party after party of Numidians attacked and retreated they succeeded in tiring his men and their horses and gradually drawing him almost to their camp. Then Carthalo, their cavalry commander, charged at full speed, routing the Romans before he came within spear's throw, and pursued them for about five miles without stopping. When Mancinus saw that the enemy would not give up the chase and there was no hope of escape, he rallied his men and turned to fight, even though his troops were greatly outnumbered. Thus he himself and the bravest of his troops were surrounded and slaughtered. The rest fled in disorder first to Cales, then made their way back to the dictator over almost impassable mountain paths.

It happened that that day Minucius had rejoined Fabius after being sent to establish a garrison at a pass above Tarracina which dwindles into a narrow defile as it approaches the sea. This was to cut off Hannibal from the Appian Way by which he could reach Roman territory from Sinuessa. After joining forces, Fabius and his master of horse moved down onto the road along which Hannibal would advance, at a point about two miles away from the enemy camp.

16. The next day the Carthaginian army set out and filled the whole road between the two camps with its column of march. The Romans had established themselves in a much more strategic position just below the rampart of their camp. Nevertheless Hannibal approached with his cavalry and light infantry and tried to provoke the enemy with repeated sallies, quickly advancing then retreating. However, the Romans stood their ground and the fighting was only spasmodic—more to the advantage of Fabius than Hannibal. Two hundred Romans were killed and eight hundred of the enemy.

With the road to Casilinum blockaded Hannibal now seemed to be trapped. While the Romans had wealthy allies like Capua and Samnium to their rear to furnish them with supplies, Hannibal would have to winter among thick forests between the cliffs of Formiae and the sands and swamps of Liternum. It did not escape Hannibal that he was now being hounded by his own tactics. Finding it impossible to escape through Casilinum, he realized that he would have to make for the mountains and cross the ridge of Callicula in order to avoid being attacked while boxed up in the valleys. He therefore devised a maneuver which would deceive and terrify the enemy, and would allow him, while they were thus occupied, quietly to withdraw to the mountains during the night. This artifice was as follows. He had collected, among the plunder from the countryside, about two thousand head of cattle, some of which were broken to the yoke and some not. To the horns of these cattle he tied faggots of branches and dry brushwood collected from all the country around. Hasdrubal was given the duty of setting fire to their horns when darkness fell and driving them up the mountains—if possible above the passes occupied by the enemy.

17. At nightfall the Carthaginians silently decamped, driving the cattle a little ahead of their column. When they reached the narrow passes at the foot of the mountains the signal was given immediately to set fire to the horns and to drive the herd up the mountains ahead. The cattle stampeded madly as the flames blazed from their horns and the heat penetrated to the base of their horns, burning them to the quick. Their useless shaking of their heads only fanned the flames, but this gave the appearance of men running in every direction; and as they began running frantically to and fro it looked as if the forests and mountains were in flames. When the Romans blockading the pass saw flames on the hilltops above them they thought that they had been surrounded and abandoned their post. They made for the tops of the ridges, taking what seemed to be the safest route, in the direction in which they saw the fewest flames, and they stood terrified at this supernatural vision; but when they saw that it was an artifice devised by men they concluded that it was an ambush and fled in even greater panic. They then encountered some light-armed troops of the enemy; but both sides were afraid to fight in the darkness and they refrained from battle until dawn. Meanwhile Hannibal led his whole army through the pass, and after surprising some of the enemy in the defile itself, pitched camp in the territory of Allifae.

18. Fabius heard this uproar. But he was sure that it was an ambush and was hesitant to fight at night anyway, so he held his men within their camp. At dawn there

was a battle just below the ridge of the mountain with the light-armed troops of the enemy who had been cut off during the night. The Romans with their superior numbers would have gained an easy victory if Hannibal had not sent a company of Spaniards to their aid. These men were more accustomed to mountain warfare than the Romans and better suited for skirmishing among rocks and cliffs; their physical agility and light armor made them able easily to baffle a heavily armed enemy used to the stationary tactics of the open country. After a one-sided battle they separated and withdrew to their respective camps. The Spaniards were almost all unhurt but the Romans had suffered some casualties.

Fabius also proceeded through the defile and pitched camp in a naturally fortified height above Allifae. Hannibal then turned back through Samnium, laying the countryside waste all the way to Peligni, as if he intended to march upon Rome. Fabius proceeded along the ridges between Hannibal and the city, neither avoiding battle nor attacking. Turning, Hannibal marched back through Apulia to the city of Gereonium. The inhabitants of this city fearfully evacuated it since part of its wall had fallen in ruins. The dictator fortified a camp near Larinum. Subsequently he was called back to Rome on religious business. Before leaving he not only commanded Minucius, but advised him as a friend and virtually pleaded with him to trust prudence rather than chance, and to follow his own precedent rather than that of Sempronius or Flaminius. He urged him not to think that nothing had been accomplished from a full summer of frustrating Hannibal. Physicians, he said, sometimes found rest more beneficial than activity. In this case it was of no small value to have ceased being defeated by an enemy who had so often been victorious and to have gained a breathing spell from the constant disasters. After these fruitless admonitions to the master of horse he set out for Rome.

While Fabius was in Rome, according to some authorities, Minucius fought a pitched battle with the Carthaginians in which losses were almost even on either side. However, the report reached Rome of a splendid victory, and this led to further discontent with the dictator's military policy.

25. These affairs caused much discussion both in the senate and in the assembly. In this atmosphere of rejoicing only the dictator refused to believe the rumor and the message from Minucius. And he remarked that even if it should be true, he feared success more than failure. At this Marcus Metilius, a tribune of the plebs, exclaimed that this attitude was not to be endured. "The dictator," he said, "not only has opposed attempting any successful action while with the army, but he is against it even now after its accomplishment; he is purposely protracting the war in order to remain longer in office and hold supreme command in the city and in the army. One consul has been killed in action, the other banished far from Italy on the specious pretext of pursuing the Carthaginian fleet. Two praetors are assigned to Sicily and Sardinia, and neither province needs a praetor at this time. Marcus Minucius, his master of horse, has virtually been held in confinement in order that he might not undertake active operations. Not only Samnium, which was yielded to the Carthaginians as if it were some territory across the Ebro, but even the fields of Capua, Cales, and Falerii have been devastated while the dictator sat at Casilinum safeguarding his own farm with the legions of the Roman people. The master of horse and the soldiers, who wished to fight, were almost held prisoner in the camp.

Their arms were taken as if they were enemy captives. At last, when the dictator left for Rome, they marched out of the camp like men freed from a siege and immediately routed the enemy. If the Roman plebs still retain their traditional spirit, therefore, they should fearlessly enact that the dictator be deposed. As it is, I will propose a moderate bill to divide the authority between the master of horse and the dictator. Even so Quintus Fabius should not be allowed to return to the army before he has appointed another consul to succeed Gaius Flaminius."

The dictator himself avoided speaking before the assembly, since his policies were not at all popular. He created prejudice even in the senate when he praised the abilities of the enemy and said that the disasters of the last two years were due to the irresponsibility and ignorance of the Roman commanders. The master of horse, he said, should be called to account for fighting against his orders. And if he were allowed to retain the supreme authority he would soon make it apparent to everyone that under a good leader luck was of no great weight; the decisive factors were prudence and reason. He considered it more honorable to have preserved the army in a time of crisis without disgrace than to have killed many thousand men. Speeches of this kind fell on deaf ears. Fabius therefore appointed Marcus Atilius Regulus consul, and then, the night before the proposal to limit his authority was to be voted on, he left the city in order to avoid any personal role in the dispute.

The assembly of the plebs was held at dawn. Although dissatisfaction with the dictator was widespread and the master of horse had become a popular idol, no one had courage enough to introduce this measure. Thus, although the bill was extremely popular it found no active support among their influential leaders. Finally one proponent of the bill was found—G. Terentius Varro, who had been praetor the year before. He was a man of not merely humble, but even base, parentage. It is said that his father was a butcher who peddled his own wares, and employed his son in servile pursuits of that trade.

26. As soon as this young man inherited the money earned by his father at this occupation, he began to hope for a more honorable career, and he elected to become an advocate. He first attracted public notice by haranguing against the interests and the reputations of worthy citizens on behalf of the lowest kinds of men and causes. He subsequently sought public office; after being elected quaestor, both plebeian and curule aedile, and finally praetor, he was now ambitious to become consul. Thus he craftily undertook to win popularity by exploiting the unpopularity of the dictator, and he received sole credit for the passage of the decree. This bill was considered by the dictator's friends and his foes, in the army and at Rome—by everyone except the dictator himself —as a censure of his policies. He bore the wrong done to him by the people with the same patience with which he had endured the slurs of his enemies abusing him before the multitude. For he realized that an increase in ability did not necessarily accompany an increase in power. While still on his journey he received the dispatch from the senate regarding the division of his command, but he returned to the army with his courage undaunted by either the enemy or his fellow citizens.

After receiving his share of the command Minucius soon risked a battle with Hannibal and was saved from complete destruction only by Fabius' intervention. In 216 B.C. the military command reverted to the hands of the two consuls for the year, Lucius Aemilius Paulus and the demagogue Gaius Terentius Varro.

44. Hannibal had pitched his camp near the village of Cannae, with the wind called Vulturnus at his back; the region is parched and dry, and the wind carries clouds of dust. The position was not only comfortable but would bring a distinct military advantage when they formed for battle, for they would have only their backs exposed to the blasts and fight against an enemy blinded by enveloping dust. The consuls were careful enough in scouting the route as they followed the Carthaginians, but when they arrived at Cannae and had the enemy in sight they built separate camps, at a considerable distance from one another, and divided their troops as they had done previously. The river Aufidus flowed past either camp and afforded approach to the watering parties of each, but they had to watch for opportunities and sometimes fight. The lesser camp was on the other side of the Aufidus, and there water could be fetched more freely because the enemy had no guard on the farther bank.

The terrain was suitable for cavalry action, in which arm Hannibal was invincible, and he conceived hopes that the consuls would afford him an opportunity for battle; he marshaled his forces, therefore, and provoked his opponents by flying charges of Numidians. Again the Roman camp was embroiled by insubordination and by disagreement between the consuls. Paulus chided Varro with the foolhardiness of Sempronius and Flaminius, and Varro instanced Fabius as the specious model for timid and slow-moving generals. He called gods and men to witness that it was in no way his fault that Hannibal had assumed squatter's rights in Italy: he was tied down by his colleague, and the soldiers who were indignant and eager to fight had sword and buckler taken from their hands. Paulus protested that if mischance befell the legions when they were exposed to ill-advised and imprudent battle he would be free of blame though he would share the consequences. Men whose tongues were so nimble and rash, he warned, must have hands equally vigorous when it came to fighting.

45. While the Romans were frittering time in altercation rather than deliberation Hannibal had kept his troops in formation till late in the day; now he withdrew them to his palisade and sent the Numidians across the river to attack a watering party from the lesser camp. This disorganized group the Numidians routed by their shouting and turbulence before they had well reached the opposite bank, and their rush carried them to an outpost in front of the rampart and even to the very gates of the camp. The Romans were outraged that their very camp should be menaced by a disorderly troop of mere auxiliaries; all that kept them from crossing the river forthwith and forming for battle was the circumstance that the supreme commander that day was Paulus. But on the day following, when it was Varro's turn, Varro posted the battle signal without consulting his colleague, formed his troops, and led them across the river. Paulus could refuse approval but not support, and so he followed.

After crossing the river they were joined by the troops from the smaller camp. Then drawing up their line, they placed the Roman cavalry on the right wing nearer the river and next to them the infantry. The cavalry of the allies held the extreme left, with their infantry between them and the Roman legions. The javelin men along with the rest of the light-armed troops made up the front line. The two consuls commanded the wings, Varro the left and Aemilius the right, while Geminus Servilius had charge of the center.

46. At daybreak Hannibal crossed the river after sending ahead the Balearics and the other light-armed troops. He located each division in the battle line in the order in which it had crossed. On the left wing, opposite

the Roman horsemen, he placed the Gallic and Spanish cavalry, and the Numidians on the right. The infantry
formed the center, with the Spaniards and Gauls in the
middle between the Africans on each side. The Africans
were armed with the equipment captured at Trebia and
at Trasumennus and had almost the appearance of a Roman division. The shields of the Gauls and Spaniards
were almost alike, but their swords were very different
both in size and in shape; the blades of the Gauls were
very long and had no points, while the Spaniards, who
were accustomed to fight by thrusting rather than cutting,
had short and efficient pointed weapons. The costumes
of these peoples as well as their great stature gave them
an extremely formidable appearance: the Gauls were
naked above the waist, while the Spaniards were dressed
in purple-bordered tunics of remarkable whiteness. The
total number of infantry in the Carthaginian line was forty
thousand, with ten thousand cavalry. The left wing was
commanded by Hasdrubal, the right by Maharbal, while
Hannibal himself with his brother Mago had the center.
Whether the lines were so disposed intentionally or not,
as it happened the Romans faced the south and Hannibal
the north so that the sun shone in the eyes of neither army.
But the wind, which the natives called the Volturnus, was
against the Romans and, blowing dust in their eyes, made
it difficult for them to see.

47. The auxiliaries charged with a shout and the
fighting began with the light-armed troops. Next, the Roman right wing clashed with the Carthaginian left. They
were obliged to meet head on and could not resort to the
usual cavalry tactics, since the river on one side and the
infantry on the other left no room to maneuver. Each
side drove straight ahead and the horses were brought to a
standstill in a tight press. The riders could only grapple
with their enemies and drag them to the ground. Soon

most of the horsemen were fighting on foot; the battle was violent but brief and soon the Roman cavalry turned and fled in defeat. Just as the horsemen were routed the infantry began to fight. At first the Gauls and Spaniards fought fiercely and bravely, as long as they maintained their line unbroken. But finally after long and repeated efforts the compact and even Roman front pushed back the thin projecting wedge of the enemy line. As the enemy was hurled back and retreated in panic the infantry pressed forward without stopping through the line of unresisting fugitives, until they came even with the African reserves on the wings which were slightly behind the middle of the line. As the center was pushed back, the enemy line first straightened, then yielding further bulged inward and formed an arc with the Africans standing on each end. As the Romans rushed recklessly forward into this pocket the African wings extended around, enclosing them in the rear. At this the Romans were forced to turn from the Gauls and Spaniards, whom they had been pursuing and cutting to pieces, and begin the contest anew with the Africans. The battle now was extremely unequal, for not only were the Romans surrounded, but after fruitlessly winning one battle they were exhausted, while their enemy was fresh and vigorous.

48. Now the fighting had commenced sporadically on the Roman left, where the cavalry of the allies was opposed by the Numidians. The Carthaginians began the battle with a trick. Five hundred Numidians hid swords under their corselets in addition to their regular arms and pretended to desert, riding forward from their lines with their shields behind their backs. When they reached the Roman lines they leaped from their horses and flung their shields and spears at the feet of the enemy, who received them into the Roman lines and ordered them to take their place in the rear. Until the fighting became widespread

they kept still; but as soon as everyone was occupied with
fighting, they snatched up shields which lay everywhere
among the piles of bodies, and attacked the rear of the Roman line. By cutting at the backs of the Romans and ham-
stringing them they caused great injury and even greater
panic and confusion. The Romans now were routed in one
area and in another were struggling hoplessly in a desperate situation. The fighting on the right wing now was slow;
so Hasdrubal, who was commander in that area, sent some
of the Numidians from the middle of this wing in pursuit
of Roman fugitives. The Spanish and Gallic cavalry he
sent to aid the Africans, who had exhausted themselves
with killing rather than fighting.

49. On the Roman side Paulus had been wounded by a
sling at the beginning of the battle. Nevertheless time
and again he confronted Hannibal; leading a compact
division of cavalry he restored the battle in several
places. As he became too weak even to control his mount
the horsemen were finally forced to abandon their horses
in order to protect him. When Hannibal was informed that
the consul had ordered his cavalry to dismount, he is said
to have exclaimed, "I would prefer him to deliver them
to me in chains!" However, the dismounted cavalry fought
like men who knew they would be conquered and chose to
die in their tracks rather than flee. The victors were enraged at them for dragging on the battle and cut to pieces
those whom they could not rout. Finally, however, the
few wounded and exhausted survivors were routed and
dispersed; those who were able caught their horses and
fled.

As Gnaeus Lentulus, a military tribune, rode by on his
horse he discovered the consul, covered with blood, sitting
on a rock. "Lucius Aemilius," he cried, "you are the one
man whom the gods should consider innocent of blame for
today's misfortune. Here, take this horse while you still

have the strength and I am here to help you up and protect you. Do not make this day more disastrous because of a consul's death. Even without that there is enough grief and tears." To this the consul replied, "You are a brave man, Lentulus. Heaven be with you. But don't waste time pitying me or you won't be able to escape from the enemy. Go, tell the senators publicly to fortify Rome before the conqueror arrives. Tell Quintus Fabius privately that Lucius Aemilius lived and died mindful of his precepts. Let me die here among my slaughtered soldiers. Better this than to be prosecuted after my consulship, or to accuse my colleague to protect my own innocence." As the consul said this a crowd of fugitives suddenly appeared, pursued closely by the enemy. Not realizing who the consul was they cut him down, while Lentulus escaped on his horse in the confusion. The Romans now were totally routed.

Seven thousand men fled to the smaller camp, ten thousand to the larger. Almost two thousand fled into the village of Cannae, but since the village was unfortified were immediately captured by Carthalo and his cavalry. The other consul, either by chance or purpose, managed not to fall in with any group of these fugitives but escaped to Venusia with about fifty horsemen. It is said that forty-five thousand infantry and twenty-seven hundred cavalry were killed, of whom about half were allies. Among these the quaestors of both consuls, Lucius Atilius and Lucius Furius Bibaculus, twenty-nine military tribunes, and several former consuls, praetors, and aediles fell. These included Gnaeus Servilius Geminus and Marcus Minucius, the master of horse of the previous year, who also had been consul several years before. In addition there were killed eighty senators and men who had held offices which qualified them for the senate. It is said that the captured numbered three thousand infantry and fifteen hundred cavalry.

50. This was the Battle of Cannae, a disaster as famous as that at Allia. Its consequences were less serious because the enemy was slow in pursuing his advantage; but the loss of lives was more appalling. For while the flight to Allia proved fatal to the city, it saved the army. At Cannae barely fifty men followed one consul in flight; almost all the rest joined the other in death.

51. All Hannibal's officers surrounded him, hailing him victor. As a reward for completing this great war they persuaded him to allow his exhausted men to rest the remainder of the day and overnight. On the other hand, Maharbal, the commander of the cavalry, did not think they should delay a moment. "No," he said, "you must realize what has been accomplished in this battle. In five days you will feast victoriously in the Capital. Follow me. I will go ahead with the cavalry and they will learn of your arrival before they know you are coming." However, to Hannibal his victory seemed too great and fortunate to comprehend immediately. He answered that he appreciated Maharbal's eagerness, but he needed time to think about what should be done. To these words Maharbal replied, "The gods do not grant all their gifts to one man, Hannibal. You know how to conquer but not how to use your victory." The delay of that day is thought to have been the salvation of the city and of the empire.

The next day at daybreak they set to work collecting the spoils and examining the results of their slaughter—a horrible sight even for enemies. Many thousands of Romans, cavalry and infantry, lay heaped indiscriminately, as chance had united them in battle or in flight. Some were aroused as the early morning cold stung their wounds and rose up from the carnage covered with blood, only to be cut down by the enemy. Some they found who were still alive but had their thighs or tendons cut through; these bared their necks and throats and begged them to drain whatever blood was left. Some were found with their heads buried in the ground who had apparently suffocated themselves by digging holes, and covering earth over their heads. They were especially awed at the sight of a Numidian with torn ears and nostrils who was pulled still alive from beneath a dead Roman. The Roman had been unable to hold a weapon in his hands and died frantically rending his enemy with his teeth.

Epitome of Book 23
2 1 6 - 2 1 5 B C

The Campanians defected to Hannibal. Mago was sent to Carthage to carry word of the victory at Cannae, and at the entrance of their senate house poured out the golden rings taken from the bodies of the slain; it is said that they amounted to more than a peck. After the message was delivered, Hanno, a member of the Carthaginian nobility, tried to persuade their senate to seek peace of the Roman people. He could not carry his point, for the Barcine faction protested loudly. The praetor Claudius Marcellus fought a successful engagement against Hannibal at Nola, making a sortie out of the city. Casilinum, which was under Carthaginian siege, was so afflicted with famine that the besieged ate thongs, skins stripped from shields, and mice. They sustained life with nuts sent down the river Volturnus by the Romans. The senate was filled out with 197 men drawn from the order of knights. The praetor Lucius Postumius and his army was cut down by the Gauls. Gnaeus and Publius Scipio defeated Hasdrubal in Spain and made it their own. The remnant of the army at Cannae was relegated to Sicily and forbidden to leave there before the war was finished. The consul Sempronius Gracchus smashed the Campanians. The praetor Claudius Marcellus won a decisive victory over Hannibal's army at Nola; he was the first to give the Romans, who were exhausted by so many disasters, brighter hope of the war. An alliance was made between Hannibal and Philip, king of Macedonia. This book also contains successful operations against the Carthaginians carried out by Publius and Gnaeus Scipio in Spain and by the praetor Titus Manlius in Sardinia. These men captured the general Hasdrubal and also Mago and Hanno. Hannibal's army lived so luxuriously in winter quarters that it was enervated in spirit and energy.

Epitome of Book 24

2 1 5 - 2 1 3 B C

Hieronymus king of the Syracusans, whose father Hiero had been a friend of the Roman people, defected to the Carthaginians, and was killed by his own men because of his cruelty and arrogance. The proconsul Tiberius Sempronius Gracchus fought successfully against the Carthaginians and their general Hanno at Beneventum; he was greatly helped by the slaves, to whom he gave freedom. In Sicily, which had almost wholly defected

to the Carthaginians, the consul Claudius Marcellus laid
siege to Syracuse. War was declared against Philip king
of the Macedonians; he was defeated and put to flight in
a night battle at Apollonia, and escaped with his army
virtually disarmed. Assigned to wage this war was the
praetor Marcus Valerius. This book also contains the
operations of Publius and Gnaeus Scipio against the Carthaginians in Spain. The Scipios won Syphax king of Numidia over to friendship. Syphax had been fighting for
the Carthaginians and had been defeated by Masinissa
king of the Massylians; he crossed over to Scipio in Spain
with a large force, from a point opposite Gades, where
Africa and Spain are separated by a narrow strait. The
Celtiberians also were received into friendship; Roman
camps had mercenary soldiers for the first time when these
were enrolled as auxiliaries.

Epitome of Book 25
213-212 BC

Publius Cornelius Scipio, later styled Africanus, was
made aedile before the legal age. With the help of Taren-
tine youths who pretended they were going hunting by
night, Hannibal captured the city of Tarentum, except
for the citadel, in which the Roman garrison had taken
refuge. The Apollinarian Games were instituted, in accordance with the oracles of Marcius, in which the disaster at Cannae had been foretold. A successful battle
against Hanno, general of the Carthaginians, was fought
by the consuls Quintus Fulvius and Appius Claudius. The
proconsul Tiberius Sempronius Gracchus was drawn into

into an ambush by his Lucanian host and killed by Mago.
Centenius Paenula, who had served as centurion, petitioned the senate to give him an army, promising a victory over Hannibal if he obtained his suit. He received
eight thousand soldiers, was made general, fought a
pitched battle with Hannibal, and was cut down along
with his army. Capua was besieged by the consuls Quintus
Fulvius and Appius Claudius. The praetor Gnaeus Fulvius fought against Hannibal unsuccessfully; twenty thousand men fell, and Fulvius himself escaped with two hundred cavalry. Claudius Marcellus took Syracuse by storm
in the third year, and comported himself as a great man.
In the tumult of the captured city, Archimedes was intent
on figures which he had drawn in the sand, and was killed.
The many successes of Publius and Gnaeus Scipio in
Spain had a sad ending; in the eighth year of their campaigns there they were cut down with virtually their whole
armies. Possession of that province would have been lost
had not the remains of the armies been drawn together
by the energy and courage of Lucius Marcius, a Roman
knight; by his encouragement two camps of the enemy
were taken by storm. About twenty-seven thousand were
killed, about eight hundred, with enormous booty, were
captured. Marcius was named general.

Book 26
2 1 1 - 2 1 0 B C

1. As soon as the consuls, Gnaeus Fulvius Cen-
tunalus and P. Sulpicius Galba entered office on March
15 [211], they called a meeting of the senate in the Capi-

tol to consult with them on public business, the conduct
of the war, and the allotment of the provinces and armies.
The commands of Quintus Fulvius and Appius Claudius,
the consuls of the previous year, were extended. They
were authorized by decree to remain in command of their
armies and directed not to withdraw from their siege at
Capua until they reduced it. This siege was a matter of
the greatest concern to the Romans. They were motivated
not so much by anger, although no state deserved it more,
as by policy, for the defection of this important and
powerful state had influenced other nations to follow suit,
and they hoped by its recovery to revive respect for the
sovereignty of Rome. The praetors of the previous year,
Marcus Junius in Etruria and Publius Sempronius in
Gaul, were retained in command, each with the two
legions which he now had. It was decreed that Marcus
Marcellus should continue as proconsul for the remainder
of the war in Sicily with his present army. If he needed
reinforcements he was to get them from the forces in Sicily under the command of the propraetor, Publius Cornelius; but he was to take none of the survivors of Cannae, who were forbidden by the senate to be discharged
or to return home before the end of the war. The
two legions which Publius Cornelius had commanded
were assigned to Gaius Sulpicius, the praetor for Sicily,
as well as reinforcements from the army of Gnaeus Fulvius, which had been routed and humiliated in Apulia
the year before. These soldiers had received the same term
of military service as the survivors at Cannae; as an
added disgrace it was decreed that soldiers of neither of
these armies might winter in towns or build winter quarters within ten miles of any town. To Lucius Cornelius
were assigned the two legions in Sardinia commanded
by Quintus Mucius, and the consuls were ordered to en-
list reinforcements if they were needed. Titus Otacilius

and Marcus Valerius were ordered to patrol the coasts
of Sicily and Greece with the legions and fleets under
their command; to Greece had been assigned fifty ships
and one legion, to Sicily one hundred ships and two
legions. The combined military and naval forces on active
duty that year numbered twenty-three legions.

4. Meanwhile Rome's military efforts were concentrated on Capua. However, the Romans were content
to blockade the city tightly instead of pushing active assault; the slaves and commoners were able to endure
their hunger no longer nor could they send messengers
through the concentrated Roman guard to Hannibal. At
last a Numidian was found who promised to take a message through the Roman line and proved as good as his
word. His escape through the Roman lines during the
night inspired the Campanians to attempt to break
through in all directions while they still had strength
left. But in many skirmishes, although their cavalry was
usually successful, their infantry was worsted.

Any pleasure the Romans might have felt at their
successes was nullified by their chagrin at being beaten
in any respect by a besieged and virtually conquered
enemy. Finally they hit upon a tactic by which to compensate for their lack of cavalry strength. The swiftest and
nimblest young men were chosen from all the legions.
These were given shields smaller than those of the cavalry, and each man received seven spears four feet long
with iron points, like those on the javelins of light-armed
troops. By practicing with the cavalry they trained themselves to ride behind the horsemen and to jump down
quickly on a given signal. When daily practice had taught
them to do this adroitly, they rode out to oppose the Campanian horsemen in the area between the camp and the
city wall. When they were within a spear's throw the signal was given and the skirmishers jumped down. Running

forward, they quickly flung their javelins, one after the other. Many horses and men were wounded under this fusillade, and the sudden and unexpected nature of the maneuver caused the greatest panic. Amid their consternation the cavalry then charged upon and pursued them back to the city gates, inflicting heavy losses. From that time the Roman cavalry as well as the infantry was superior to the enemy and these light-armed troops were made a permanent division of the army. It is said that a centurion, Quintus Navius, suggested this maneuver of combining cavalry and infantry, for which he was honored by the general.

5. With affairs in Capua in this state, Hannibal was torn between the desire to seize the citadel of Tarentum and the desire to keep possession of Capua. At length his concern for Capua prevailed. For he realized that the attention of all his allies and enemies were fixed upon this city, and its fate would be considered an example of what befell those who revolted from Rome. Therefore, he left his baggage and his heavy-armed troops, which would slow him down, in Bruttium and set out rapidly for Campania with a picked group of cavalry and infantry. In spite of his haste he also took along thirty-three elephants. He encamped in a hidden valley behind Mount Tifata, which overlooks Capua, and immediately took the fortress at Galatia. He then directed his attack against the blockade at Capua, sending ahead messengers to the inhabitants to inform them at what time the assault would begin so that they would be ready to coördinate their attack. The Romans were panic-stricken at this onslaught; simultaneously the Campanians, along with the Carthaginian garrison under Bostar and Hanno, poured out of every gate, and on the other side Hannibal assaulted their flanks.

But in this desperate situation the Romans divided their forces in order to avoid leaving any area undefended in the disorder and confusion. Appius Claudius opposed the Campanians and Fulvius Hannibal; the propraetor Gaius Nero guarded the road leading to Suessula with the cavalry of the six Roman legions, while Gaius Fulvius Flaccus with the cavalry of the allies took a position facing the Volturnus river. As the battle began the Romans were distracted by a terrific barrage of noise. To add to the usual din of horses and men and arms, the Campanians who were not fighting stood along their walls beating bronze vessels, as people do in the silence of the night during an eclipse of the moon. Appius easily repulsed the Campanians from his rampart, but on the other side Hannibal was pressing Fulvius harder. There the sixth legion was pushed back and a Spanish company with three elephants broke through the Roman line and advanced all the way to the rampart. Here they hesitated whether to force their way into the camp and risk being cut off from their own forces.

When Fulvius saw the rout of the legion and the danger to the camp he cried out to Quintus Navius and other centurions of the first rank to charge the Spaniards. "The situation is critical," he cried, "we must either give way to them or kill them before they scale the rampart. For they will break into the camp more easily than they penetrated the concentrated battle line. It will not be hard; there are few of them and they are cut off from support. If the battle line which was broken now turns on the enemy it will trap them between two attacks." Hearing these words, Navius seized the standard of the second maniple of spearmen from its standard bearer and charged toward the enemy, threatening to throw himself in their midst if the soldiers did not quickly follow and support him. He was a large man and a commanding figure in his armor; as he raised the standard aloft every eye turned toward him. When he reached the Spanish standards from everywhere javelins showered upon him, and almost the whole line turned upon him alone. But neither the numbers of the enemy nor the deluge of their javelins could stay the force of his charge.

6. The legate M. Atilius now charged against the company of Spaniards with the first maniple of the second line. The legates in charge of the camp, Lucius Porcius Licinus and Titus Popilius, fought gallantly on the rampart and even killed the elephants as they tried to cross over it. These fell into the trench before the rampart, furnishing a bridge for the enemy to cross over, and a bloody battle took place over the bodies of the dead elephants. On the other side of the camp the Campanian and the Carthaginian garrison had been repulsed; the battle continued up to the very gate of Capua which now leads to Volturnum. Here the Roman attack was checked not by the arms of their opponents but by stones ejected from engines mounted above the gate. Their zeal was also dampened by the wounding of their commander, Appius Claudius, who was struck by a javelin in the chest just under his left shoulder as he led a charge. Many of the enemy were killed before the gate and others were driven panic-stricken into the city.

When Hannibal saw the company of Spaniards massacred and realized that the camp was being defended with great determination he abandoned the assault and began to retreat, using the cavalry to cover his rear against the attack. The soldiers were eager to pursue the enemy, but Flaccus, too, ordered the retreat to be sounded; he was confident that enough had been done to make the Spaniards and Hannibal himself realize that Hannibal could not do much to protect them. Some sources say that eight thousand men in Hannibal's army were killed along with three thousand Campanians, and

that fifteen Carthaginian and eighteen Campanian standards were taken.

I have found other authorities who report that the battle was much less important and that there was more confusion than fighting. According to these accounts the Nu-
mudians and Spaniards along with the elephants burst
unexpectedly into the Roman camp. When the elephants
rushed through the middle of the camp, knocking down
tents and causing great pandemonium, the pack animals,
too, broke their tethers and stampeded. To increase the
turmoil Hannibal sent men who knew Latin into the Roman camp dressed as Italians. These warned the soldiers
that the camp was lost and the consul had ordered them
to flee for their lives into the hills nearby. This ruse was
quickly discovered and suppressed, and many of the
enemy were killed; the elephants were driven from the
camp with fire.

Regardless of how it began or ended, this was the last
battle before the capitulation of Capua. That year the
medix tuticus, the highest official of the Campanians, was
Seppius Loesius, a man of humble origin and little wealth.
It is said that once when his mother was expiating a
portent on behalf of her son, whose father was dead, the
soothsayer prophesied that he would hold the chief magistracy in Capua. Since she could see no hope for this
she answered, "Truly, you are speaking of an evil day for
Capua when the highest magistracy falls to my son." Her
jest at this prophecy proved to be itself prophetic. For
when the city was oppressed by famine and the sword,
and there was no hope left of repelling the enemy, all
those who were qualified by birth refused public office.
Loesius, however, accepted, complaining that Capua was
betrayed by its leaders; he was the last of all the
Campanians to hold the supreme magistracy in the city.

7. Hannibal saw that the enemy could not be enticed into further battle and that it was impossible to force a passage through their camp to Capua. Since he also was apprehensive that the new consuls in Rome might cut his own supply line he decided to abandon his vain undertaking and move his camp away from the city. As he pondered where he should go next the idea occurred to him to attack Rome, the source of his opposition. This was a thing he had always wished to do, but he had let his opportunity slip, after the battle of Cannae, as others complained and he himself admitted. He now thought that in the panic and confusion of his sudden arrival he could occupy some part of the city, and he was sure that if Rome were endangered one or both of the generals and their armies would abandon Capua. If the Roman forces were divided each would be weakened and this would give either him or the Campanians a chance of success. His one concern was that the moment he left the Campanians would capitulate. Therefore he bribed a Numidian to enter the Roman camp pretending to be a deserter, and then from the opposite side to slip quietly away to Capua with a message. The message was full of encouragement: his departure would save them by diverting the Roman army and generals away from the blockade of Capua to defend Rome. They should not lose hope, for by holding out a few days they would rid themselves of the siege. He then ordered the boats to be collected from the river and taken upstream to a bridgehead which he had previously built on the river. Word soon arrived that there was enough shipping to transport his whole army in one night. After provisions for ten days were prepared, he led his troops down to the river by night and all crossed over before dawn.

8. Even before Hannibal's departure Fulvius Flaccus learned of his project from deserters and informed the

senate at Rome. Men were affected by this news in various
ways according to each one's temper. Since the situation
was so critical the senate was called immediately. Publius
Cornelius Asina wished to disregard Capua and everything else and to recall all the troops in Italy to protect
the city. Fabius Maximus thought that it would be
shameful to abandon Capua and to run around in a panic
at Hannibal's every nod or frown. "Even after his victory
at Cannae he did not dare to march on the city. Now after
being repulsed at Capua can he have any hope of taking
Rome? He is not coming now to besiege Rome but to
free Capua from blockade. Jupiter and the other gods,
witnesses of the treaties violated by Hannibal, will protect us with only the help of the army now stationed in the
city." Publius Valerius proposed a compromise between
these two opposing opinions, which was accepted. With
due regard both for besieging Capua and defending
Rome, he advised that a message be sent to the generals
at Capua telling them the size of the garrison in the city;
they themselves would know the size of Hannibal's force
and how large an army was needed for the seige of Capua.
Thus, if one of the generals could be sent with part of the
army while effectively maintaining the blockade, Claudius
and Fulvius could decide who would go and who would
stay. When this decree of the senate arrived at Capua, Fulvius, whose colleague was incapacitated by his wound,
set out for Rome, crossing the Volturnus with fifteen thousand foot soldiers and one thousand cavalry. When he had
discovered that Hannibal intended to proceed to Rome by
the Via Latina, he sent ahead messengers to the towns on
and near the Appian Way—Setia, Cora, and Lanuvium—
with instructions for the inhabitants to have provision for
the army prepared in their cities and to bring them down
to the road from the fields. Each city also was ordered to
collect a garrison so that it might see to its own defense.

9. On the day Hannibal crossed the Volturnus he pitched camp not far from the river. The next day he advanced beyond Cales into the Sidicinian territory. After delaying there one day to devastate the fields he marched through the districts of Suessa, Allifae and Casinum along the Via Latina. For two days he remained encamped under the walls of Casinum, laying waste all the country-side around. He then marched through Interamna and Aquinum to the Liris River in the territory of Fregellae, where he found that the inhabitants had cut down the bridge in order to delay his march. Meanwhile the cross-ing of the Volturnus had also delayed Fulvius, since Han-nibal had burned all available boats, and a scarcity of timber in the area made it difficult to provide rafts. How-ever, once across the river Fulvius met no further delays on his journey; provisions were willingly offered not only in the towns but all along the road. The eager soldiers exhorted each other to remember they were going to de-fend their homeland and to quicken the pace.

A messenger from Fregellae, who had traveled a day and a night without stopping, caused great consternation in the city. Wild rumors men added to the news they had heard spread through the city and contributed further to the confusion. From every house the weeping of women could be heard, and everywhere matrons rushed into the streets, hurrying to the temples of the gods. Falling to their knees, they swept the altars with their disheveled hair and stretched upturned hands toward heaven to the gods, beseeching them to free Rome from the hands of the enemy and save the women and small children from harm. The senate waited in readiness in the Forum in case mag-istrates should wish to consult them. Some were given duties and left to carry out their assignments; others of-fered to go wherever there should be any need. Guard posts were established in the citadel, in the Capitol, on the walls, around the city, even on the Alban Mount and in the fortress of Aefula. In the middle of this confusion the news arrived that Quintus Fulvius was coming with his army from Capua; since his authority as proconsul would cease upon his entry into the city, the senate passed a decree granting him equal jurisdiction with the consuls.

After ravaging the territory of Fregellae with particular severity because of the destruction of the bridge, Hannibal proceeded into the territory of Labici through the districts of Frusino, Ferentinum and Anagnia. He then set out from Mount Algidus for Tusculum, and there, after being denied entry into the city turned right toward Gabii; he then marched down into the neighborhood of Pupinia where he pitched camp eight miles from Rome. As he came nearer to Rome the Numidians who rode ahead of the army killed more and more people who were fleeing to the city and took more captives of every age and class.

10. In the midst of this uproar Fulvius Flaccus entered Rome with his army through the Porta Capena. He then proceeded through the middle of the city, by way of Carinae and the Esquiline, camping outside between the Colline and Esquiline gates. There his soldiers received provisions from the plebeian aediles; the consuls and senate then arrived and a consultation was held concerning the welfare of the state in the present crisis. It was decided that the consuls, too, should pitch camp near the Colline and Esquiline gates; that Gaius Calpurnius, praetor of the city, should take command of the citadel on the Capitol; and that the full senate should assemble in continuous session in the Forum in case there should be need to pass any emergency measure.

Meanwhile Hannibal established an encampment on the river Anio three miles from the city. From this entrenched position he himself with two thousand horsemen proceeded toward the Colline gate all the way to the temple of Hercules, and rode up as closely as he could to observe the walls and the layout of the city. It angered Flaccus to see him doing this with such leisure and impunity; so he sent out his own cavalry with orders to move the enemy away from the walls and drive them back to their own camp. The consuls were sure that about twelve hundred Numidian deserters who were then located on the Aventine would be the best troops possible for fighting among the hollows, walled gardens, sepulchers, and deep lanes which run all over the Esquiline; therefore they ordered them to cross over at once to this quarter through the middle of the city. However, when the garrison at the citadel and the Capitol saw them galloping down the Publician Hill some cried out that the Aventine had been taken. This created such panic that if Hannibal's camp had not been outside the walls the hysterical population would have rushed out of the city. They fled to their houses and nearby buildings, and whenever they saw their own fellow citizens walking through the streets, showered them with stones and spears, mistaking them for the enemy. Because the streets were full of farmers and their flocks which they had fearfully driven into the city, it was long before the mistake could be explained and the panic allayed. The cavalry skirmish was successful and the enemy driven away from the walls. However, since near riots were cropping up all over the city and constantly had to be suppressed, it was decided to confer consular powers on all former dictators, consuls, and censors until the enemy withdrew from before the walls. For the rest of the day and the following night many disturbances arose needlessly but were effectively subdued.

11. The next day Hannibal crossed over the Anio and drew up his forces in preparation for battle. Flaccus and the consuls were not reluctant to fight, and soon the two armies stood marshaled opposite each other prepared to

compete in a contest for which Rome would be the prize
for victory. Suddenly, however, a downpour of rain
mixed with hail so deluged both armies that the soldiers
could hardly hold their shields. Each side retreated to its
camp, fearing nothing less than the enemy. On the next
day in the same place a cloudburst again separated them.
But as soon as they had retreated to their camp the clouds
broke, and an uncanny serenity pervaded the atmosphere. This prodigy filled the Carthaginians with superstitious awe; it is reported that Hannibal was heard saying that first he was denied the inclination, then the opportunity to take Rome. Two further incidents—one important, the other trivial—deprived him even of hope. He
learned that while he stood in arms before the walls of
Rome, a Roman force had marched out to reinforce the
army in Spain. He also learned from a captive that the
very land on which he had encamped had just been sold
at no loss of value whatsoever. It seemed to him to be
such supercilious insolence for a buyer to have been
found for the very land which he himself occupied that
immediately he summoned a crier and ordered him to
announce the sale of the bankers' offices which stood
around the Roman Forum.

As a result of these events Hannibal decided to withdraw his army to the river Tutia, six miles away from the
city. From there he proceeded to the grove of Feronia,
where at that time there was a temple famous for its treas-
ures. Here the Capenatians and other inhabitants of this
region brought their first fruits and other offerings in proportion to their means and they kept it lavishly decorated with silver and gold. This temple he stripped of all
its riches. However, after Hannibal's departure great
heaps of copper were found which his soldiers had left behind in contrition because of their sacrilege. All authorities agree that this temple was plundered. However,

Coelius testifies that Hannibal turned aside to the temple on his journey from Eretum to Rome, after proceeding from Amiternum through Reate and Cutilae; from Capua he traces his route through Samnium, the territory of the Paeligni and beyond the town of Sulmo into the country of the Marrucini; he then marched through the district of Alba into the territory of the Marsi, and from there to Amiternum and the village of Foruli. There is no difference of opinion about his route; the traces of that great a commander and such a large army can not have been expunged in so short a time. The only question is whether he traveled by this route on his march to the city or as he returned from Rome into Campania.

12. Hannibal did not exhibit so much resolution in defending Capua as the Romans in beleaguering it. He now marched with such rapidity through Samnium, Apulia and Lucania to Bruttium and the Sicilian strait that he almost captured Regium by surprise. Meanwhile, Capua felt the return of Flaccus, even though in his absence the severity of the siege had not been moderated. At first the inhabitants wondered that Hannibal had not returned at the same time. Soon, however, they learned through conversations with the Romans that they were abandoned, and Hannibal had lost hope of retaining possession of Capua. Following this, the proconsul, in accordance with a decree of the senate, made a proclamation which was spread among the enemy that any citizen of Capua who surrendered himself before a certain day would be pardoned. None of the Campanians surrendered, however. They were restrained not by any continued fidelity to Hannibal, but by fear, because their misconduct during their defection had been too great to be forgiven. And, just as no one would desert in the interests of his own safety, there were no measures proposed for the general safety. The aristocracy had rejected all public offices, and the senate could

not be forced to meet. Their chief magistracy was held by a man who had not acquired honor for himself from the office, but by his own unworthiness reduced the office's prestige and authority. Now none of the aristocracy ever appeared in the forum or in any public place. They shut themselves up in their houses and each day awaited the deathblow of the state and with it their own.

The whole burden of public administration had fallen on the shoulders of Hanno and Bostar, the captains of the Carthaginian garrison, and they were worried about their own danger, not that of their allies. They dispatched a stern and outspoken message to Hannibal, accusing him of delivering Capua into the hands of the enemy and betraying themselves and his garrison to every torture. He had gone off to Bruttium, the message said, as if he were turning his back, so that Capua might not be taken before his eyes. But the Romans, by Hercules, could not be drawn away from their blockade of Capua even by an attack on their own city; so much more resolute an enemy was the Roman than the Carthaginian a friend. If he would return to Capua with all his forces, both the garrison and the Campanians were prepared to attack in concert with him. He had not crossed the Alps in order to wage war on Regium or Tarentum. The place for the Carthaginian army was where the Roman legions were. Success had been achieved at Cannae and at Trasumennus by meeting the enemy, opposing him in full force, and trying the fortune of battle.

A letter to this effect was composed and entrusted to Numidian messengers who were hired to carry out the task. Since the prolonged famine in Capua gave anyone a plausible pretext for desertion, they came into Fulvius' camp pretending to be fugitives and intending to abscond when an opportunity presented itself. However, a Campanian woman, the mistress of one of the Numidians, suddenly arrived in the camp. She informed the general that they had come under false pretences and were taking a dispatch to Hannibal. She was prepared to prove it, since one of them had revealed the plan to her. When this man was brought forward, at first he obstinately asserted that he did not know the woman. However, when he was refuted by one fact after another, and when he saw the instruments of torture being made ready, he broke down and confessed the truth. He even added a fact hitherto unknown: other hostile Numidians had free run of the Roman camp pretending to be deserters. About seventy of these were captured and were scourged along with the latest "deserters." Their hands were then cut off and they were driven back to Capua.

13. The sight of this severe punishment broke the spirit of the Capuans. A crowd gathered before the senate house and forced Loesius to call a meeting of the senate. They loudly threatened the aristocrats, who had shunned meetings of the senate for so long, that unless they appeared for a meeting they would go around to their houses and drag them out into the street. This intimidation produced a full senate. When the senate convened, everyone else was for sending ambassadors to the Roman generals, but Vibius Virrius, who had been the instigator of the revolt, said, "Those who advise sending ambassadors to discuss peace and surrender have forgotten what they would have done if they had had the Romans in their power, and the penalty which they themselves must now pay. Do you think the terms of surrender will be the same as we received when we asked for help against the Samnites and surrendered ourselves and all that we owned to the Romans? Have you forgotten what straitened circumstances Rome was in when we defected? How we put their garrison to death with torture in order to show our contempt instead of releasing their

garrison unharmed? . . . I will never look upon Appius Claudius and Quintus Fulvius swollen with arrogant triumph. I will never be chained and dragged as a spectacle through the city of Rome, only then to be thrown into prison or bound to a stake to be scourged and beheaded. I will not see my city destroyed and its matrons, virgins, and free-born children ravished. . . . Thus, for those who wish to yield to fate before seeing such woes I have prepared a banquet in my house. After you have satisfied yourself with food and wine that same cup will be passed to you which is given to me. That toast will spare our bodies torture, our minds insult, our eyes the sight and our ears the sound of the wretched indignities which must befall the conquered. There will be persons prepared to place our lifeless bodies on a great pyre in the courtyard of my house. This is the one free and honorable road to death. The enemy themselves will admire our courage, and Hannibal will know that the allies whom he has deserted and betrayed were brave men."

14. More of the senators heard Virrius' speech with approval than were able to summon courage to carry out his proposals. The greater part were aware of Rome's accustomed clemency in time of war, and did not doubt that now the Romans could be conciliated. Therefore they directed that delegates be sent to surrender Capua to the Romans. About twenty-seven senators accompanied Vibius Virrius to his house and dined with him. So far as they were able they drowned all thought of impending doom in wine, then drank the poison. With the banquet finished they grasped each others' hands and with one final embrace wept together over the fate of their country and themselves. Some then remained to be burned on the pyre, while others left for their homes. Since their veins were filled with food and wine the action of the poison was slow. Most of them lived through the night and

part of the next day, but all breathed their last before
the gates were opened to the enemy.

On the next day the Gate of Jupiter, which faced the
Roman camp, was opened at the order of the proconsuls.
One legion and two companies of allied cavalry under the
command of Gaius Fulvius entered through it. He first
gave orders for all the weapons in the city to be brought
to him and established guards at all the gates to prevent
any escape. He then took into custody the Carthaginian
garrison and ordered the Capuan senators to report to
the Roman generals in the camp. When they arrived there
they immediately were thrown into chains and ordered to
report to the quaestors all the gold and silver they owned.
This totaled 2,070 pounds of gold, and 31,200 pounds
of silver. Twenty-five senators were sent into custody at
Cales and twenty-eight, who had been the primary instigators of the defection, to Teanum.

15. There was great disagreement between Fulvius
and Claudius concerning the punishment of the Campanian senators. Claudius favored leniency, while Fulvius
inclined toward much greater severity. For this reason
Appius wished to refer the whole responsibility to the
senate at Rome. He also thought it proper for the senate to
be given the chance to question the Campanians as to
whether they had communicated their plans to any of the
Latin allies, and if so whether they had received any assistance from them in war. Fabius, however, thought that
at all costs they should avoid worrying faithful allies with
dubious accusations and making them answerable to in-
formers who never gave a thought to what they did or
said. Therefore he would prevent such an inquiry. This
remark ended the conversation. Although his colleague
spoke very vehemently Appius did not doubt that in a
matter of such importance he would await instructions
from Rome. Fabius, on the other hand, was afraid that

just such a delay would frustrate his intentions. Dismissing the council, he ordered the military tribunes and legates of the allies to direct two thousand picked horsemen to be prepared for action at the beginning of the third watch.

With this company of cavalry he set out for Teanum during the night. Just at dawn he entered the gate of the city, and made straight for the forum. As a crowd quickly gathered at the arrival of so many horsemen he ordered the Sidicinian magistrate to be summoned, and this official he directed to produce the Campanians in his custody. All were brought forth, scourged, and beheaded. Thereupon he set out at full speed for Cales. Upon his arriving there he took his seat on the tribunal, and the Capuans who had been brought out were just being bound to the stake. Suddenly an emissary from Rome pulled up in haste before the tribunal, and handed Fulvius a message from the praetor Gaius Calpurnius along with a decree of the senate. A murmur swept through the crowd that the disposition of the Campanians was to be referred to the senate. Fulvius was also sure that this was the case. Putting the dispatches in his breast unopened, he signaled to the herald to order the lictor to carry out the sentence. When the Campanians at Cales had been executed, the message and the decree of the senate were read—too late to prevent the deed which had been hastened expressly so that it might not be prevented.

As Fulvius arose from the tribunal Taurea Vibellius, a Campanian, forced his way through the crowd, calling him by name. As Fulvius sat back down again wondering what the man wished, he cried out, "Order me, too, to be killed so that you can boast that you have killed a much braver man than yourself." Flaccus answered that he must have lost his senses, and that now even if he wished to do so the decree of the senate forbade it. To this Vibellius replied, "My city has been captured, my friends and relatives lost; I have slain my wife and children with my own hand so that they might suffer no indignity. Now I am not even allowed to die as my countrymen; therefore let me seek death courageously as a deliverance from this hateful life." Taking a dagger from beneath his clothing he plunged it straight into his breast and fell dying at the feet of the commander.

After Publius and Gnaeus Scipio were killed in Spain and their armies virtually annihilated, in 210 B.C., a new army was sent to Spain under the command of the younger Publius Scipio, a former aedile, then only twenty-five years old. Upon his arrival in Spain, he learned that all three Carthaginian armies were withdrawn into the interior, and he seized this opportunity to pounce upon New Carthage and take it by surprise.

42. Leaving Marcus Silanus with a garrison of three thousand infantry and three hundred cavalry in command of that area [between the Ebro and the Pyrenees], he crossed the Ebro with the remainder of his forces, numbering twenty-five thousand infantry and twenty-five hundred cavalry. Since the Carthaginian armies had withdrawn into three different areas, certain officers advised him to attack the one nearest. However, he realized that if he should do this all three might unite and prove more than a match for him alone. Therefore he decided at present to attack New Carthage. This city was wealthy in its own right and also contained a large enemy arsenal, the enemy treasury, and hostages from all of Spain. In addition, it was situated very conveniently for crossing into Africa, and commanded a harbor large enough for any fleet—the only one, I believe, along the Mediterranean coast of Spain.

The only person to whom he confided his destination was Gaius Laelius. Laelius was sent with his fleet along the coast with orders to coördinate his arrival with Scipio's in order that he might enter the city's harbor at the same time that the army came into sight by land. On the seventh day after crossing the Ebro the fleet and the army arrived in New Carthage at the same time. Scipio pitched camp to the north of the city, where the side facing the city was protected by a natural fortification; a double rampart was erected along the opposite side.

Now the site of New Carthage is as follows: about midway along the coast of Spain there is a bay, facing the southwest, about two and one-half miles in depth and a little more than twelve hundred yards wide. At the entrance to this bay lies a small island which protects it from all winds except those from the south-west. From the bottom of the bay extends a peninsula, on the headland of which stands the city. To the east and the south it is encircled by the sea; on the west it is encompassed by a lake which stretches northward and which rises and falls with the tide of the sea. A strip of land only about one-quarter of a mile wide joins the city with the continent. Across this the Roman general did not erect a rampart, although it would have taken little labor; either he disdainfully wished to exhibit his self-confidence to the enemy, or he wished to insure an unobstructed retreat after his frequent attacks on the walls of the city.

43. When he had completed all his fortifications he lined his ships up before the harbor as if he intended a blockade by sea as well. He then went around from ship to ship in a boat warning the captains to be especially on the alert during the night watches, saying that when under siege at first an enemy attacks everywhere along a blockade to try its weaknesses.

44. When Mago, the Carthaginian general, saw the blockade drawn up both by land and sea, he arranged his forces as follows. Two thousand of the townsmen he sta-

tioned in the direction of the Roman camp. He occupied the citadel with five hundred soldiers and placed
another five hundred at the highest point in the city to
the east. He instructed the rest of the citizens to be prepared to come with assistance wherever they heard a
shout and wherever a crisis should arise. Then the gate
was opened and he sent out those whom he had stationed
on the road leading to the enemy camp. At the command
of their general, the Romans fell back a little so that they
might be nearer to reinforcements during the battle. At
first the battle was fought evenly on either side. Soon,
however, with the help of reserves continually sent from
the camp the Romans routed the enemy and pursued
them so closely that if the retreat had not been sounded
as they scattered they would have rushed into the city
among the fugitives. The confusion during the battle was
not greater than that now in the city. Many deserted their
stations in panic and fled; the walls were abandoned as
each man jumped down from the point where he happened to be standing.

When Scipio from his position on a knoll called
Mercury's Hill, noticed that the walls were defenseless in
many places, he gave the order to bring forward the scaling ladders and to assault the city in full force. Scipio
himself, protected by the shields of three strong young
men—for missiles of every kind were showering from the
walls—approached close to the walls, giving appropriate
commands and encouragement, and what most inspired
his men to bravery, witnessing the bravery or cowardice
of each man in person. Thus the soldiers charged forward
heedless of wounds into the thick of the falling missiles;
neither the walls nor the weapons of their defenders
could stop them as they eagerly clambered upward. At
the same time an assault from the ships began on
the walls facing the sea. However, the confusion which re-

sulted was greater than the pressure which could be exerted against the enemy. As they put the ships to shore, dragged out the scaling ladders, and rushed pell-mell for the nearest point of land, they impeded each other in their haste and impatience.

45. Meanwhile the Carthaginians had again covered the walls with men, and there were large quantities of arms from the arsenal at their disposal. However, neither men nor weapons nor anything else contributed as much to the defense of the walls as their height itself. Few ladders were as tall as the walls, and these were too weak because of their very length. When the first man up was unable to climb off onto the wall, and others continued to follow him up the ladder, it broke under their weight. Some men, even though their ladders held, became dizzy from the height and fell to the ground. As men and ladders fell down everywhere and success increased the eagerness and daring of the enemy, the signal was given for retreat. This retreat not only gave the besieged hope of an opportunity to rest from the moil of battle, but inspired them with confidence that the city could not be taken by scaling ladders. Siege works were difficult to construct, and this would allow time for their generals to come to their aid.

The din and confusion had scarcely abated when Scipio gave the order for fresh troops to take the ladders and renew the assault with greater vigor. He had previously learned from fishermen in Tarraco that they were accustomed to wade across the lake when their skiffs ran aground, and that at low tide it was easy to reach the walls by foot. Therefore, when he learned that the tide was ebbing he personally led five hundred men down to the water. It was about the middle of the day, and the water already was receding into the sea with the tide; in addition, a blustering north wind had blown up and was driving the water in the same direction as the tide, making it so shallow that in some places it was no more than waist-deep—in places barely knee-deep. This phenomenon, which he had discovered by careful inquiry and calculation, Scipio chose to call a miracle. The gods, he said, were turning back the sea and draining the lake to lay bare a highway for the Romans never before trodden by human feet. Calling upon his men to follow Neptune's lead he gave the order to advance through the lake to the walls.

46. The party attacking from land was in difficult circumstances. Not only were they thwarted by the height of the walls, but the walls' construction exposed them to a cross fire, and their flank proved to be more vulnerable to attack than their front. But the five hundred on the opposite side encountered no difficulty in crossing the lake or scaling the wall. The wall was not completely fortified, since the lake itself had been considered a sufficient defense, and now there were no guards posted there; all were engrossed in defending the position where the danger had manifested itself.

They entered without opposition, and hurried as quickly as possible to the gate around which the battle was raging. There the combatants and the spectators encouraging them were so absorbed in the battle that they had eyes and ears for nothing else. No one really realized that the city had been taken from the rear until a cascade of spears fell on their backs and they were assailed on two fronts. The defenders were routed in confusion and the walls occupied; the gate was being battered from both within and without. Soon it had been smashed and dragged out of the way. Armed men rushed in. A large number scaled the walls and scattered everywhere killing the townsmen, while those who had come in the gate fell into regular order and marched through the middle of the city to the market place. Scipio noticed that the towns-people were fleeing in two directions, some toward the knoll to the east which was occupied by five hundred men, others to the citadel where Mago himself had fled with most of the soldiers who had been driven from the walls. Dividing his forces, Scipio sent some to the knoll while he himself led the attack on the citadel. The knoll was captured with the first charge, and when Mago saw that the whole city was full of the enemy and no hope was left, he surrendered himself and his garrison. Until the citadel was taken, the Romans continued their massacre throughout the city, sparing no adult male whom they met. Then the signal was given to end the slaughter, and they victoriously turned to collecting plunder, of which there was a great quantity.

47. About ten thousand freemen were captured. Those who were citizens of New Carthage Scipio released, restoring to them their city and all their property which had survived the battle. There were two thousand crafts-men, whom he declared the property of the Roman peo-ple; these he offered hope of an early release if they as-siduously applied themselves to the service of the war. All the rest of the young freemen and the huskier slaves he assigned to the fleet as rowers; to the fleet itself he added eight captured ships. In addition to the population of the city there were Spanish hostages toward whom he was almost as attentive as if they had been children of the al-lies. In addition a large quantity of military equipment was taken. . . . Sixty-three freighters also were seized in the harbor, some of which carried cargoes of grain and arms, in addition to brass, iron, sails, hemp and other ma-terials for outfitting a fleet. Amid all this military equip-ment the capture of the city itself was of the least impor-tance.

Book 27

2 1 0 - 2 0 7 B C

After his defeat in the battle of Baecula, in Spain, in 208 B.C. Hannibal's brother, Hasdrubal, succeeded in eluding Scipio and set out for Italy to join his brother with a fresh army. In the spring of 207 he crossed the Alps, and another crisis for Rome was at hand.

40. The consuls departed from the city in different directions, doubling men's anxiety, so to speak, with the threat of two simultaneous wars. They recalled the disasters which Hannibal's arrival had brought upon Italy, and anxiously asked themselves what gods would be so kindly disposed toward the city and the empire as to accord to the Romans success on two fronts at the same time. Up to this time Rome had survived only by offsetting its many defeats with victories. When Rome had suffered disaster at Trasumennus and Cannae in Italy, success in Spain had compensated for these catastrophes. When later in Spain successive blows had destroyed the greater part of two armies and both outstanding generals had been lost, many victories in Sicily and Italy had sheltered the buffeted Roman state. And since that war was waged in a faraway land distance itself afforded Rome room to breathe. But now two wars had found their way into Italy, and two renowned generals threatened the city from either side. The whole weight and burden of the danger was bearing down upon one spot. If one of these should

be victorious then in a matter of days he would join forces with his associate. The disastrous loss of two consuls in the preceding year increased the anxiety of the people. With these fearful misgivings men accompanied the consuls out of the city as they departed for their provinces. Marcus Livius was extremely embittered against the citizens because of his conviction for dishonesty after his first consulship. It is said that as he set out, when Quintus Fabius cautioned him against attacking the enemy before carefully scouting him, Livius replied that he would fight as soon as he caught sight of the enemy. When he was asked the reason for his haste he replied, "I shall either receive great glory for victory over the enemy or have well-deserved, if not creditable gratification at the defeat of my fellow citizens."

Before the consul Claudius Nero reached his province, Gaius Hostilius Tibulus with his light infantry attacked Hannibal as he marched over the borders of the territory of Larinum into that of the Sallentines. He created pandemonium among Hannibal's troops, who were taken by surprise and were not in battle order, killing almost four thousand and capturing nine standards. At the report of Hannibal's approach Quintus Claudius, who had billeted his troops in the various towns of the Sallentine territory, recalled them from winter quarters and prepared to meet the enemy. Therefore, in order to avoid meeting two armies at once, Hannibal withdrew his camp by night from the area of Tarentum into Bruttium. Quintus Claudius then returned into the Sallentine territory while Hostilius marched toward Capua, and met the consul Claudius Nero near Venusia. There from both armies forty thousand foot soldiers and twenty-five hundred horsemen were chosen who accompanied Claudius on his march against Hannibal. Hostilius was ordered to take the remaining troops to Capua and surrender them to the proconsul Quintus Fulvius.

In southern Italy minor skirmishes were fought between Hannibal and Claudius Nero.

43. After Hasdrubal abandoned the siege of Placentia he sent four Gallic horsemen and two Numidians with a message to Hannibal. These horsemen had traveled through the middle of enemy territory across almost the whole length of Italy, and were following Hannibal as he withdrew to Metapontum when they took the wrong road and were carried to Tarentum. There they were captured by Roman foragers and taken to the propraetor Quintus Fulvius. At first they attempteed to confuse him with ambiguous answers, but under threat of torture they were forced to tell the truth and revealed that they were taking a message from Hasdrubal to Hannibal. This dispatch was given still sealed, just as it was, to the military tribune Lucius Verginius, who was instructed to take it along with the messengers to the consul Claudius. Two companies of Samnites were sent along as a guard. After the message had been read to the consul by an interpretor and the captives had been questioned, Claudius decided that in this crisis he should not be bound by the usual rules which limited each general to the boundaries of his own province, his own army, and the enemy appointed for him by the senate. Now, he thought, a daring and unexpected move should be attempted; at first it would cause as much fear among the Romans as among the enemy, but if successful their anxiety would be repaid—with great rejoicing. Therefore he sent the message from Hasdrubal to the senate at Rome along with a dispatch of his own explaining his intentions. Since Hasdrubal wrote that he would meet his brother in Umbria, Claudius also advised the senate to summon one legion from Capua,

levy another at Rome and oppose Hasdrubal with this army in the neighborhood of Narnia.

Into the territories of Larinum, of the Marrucini, the Frentani, and Praetutii, through which he proposed to march, Claudius sent ahead messengers with orders for the inhabitants to prepare supplies for the soldiers and have them brought down along the road. They also were instructed to bring out all their horses and pack animals in order to provide sufficient transportation for the soldiers who became exhausted. From the whole army he chose six thousand infantry and one thousand cavalry, the best troops from among both the Romans and the allies. As a pretext for ordering preparations for a march he announced that he intended to capture the nearest city in Lucania and its Carthaginian garrison; but when he set out after dark he turned towards Picenum. Leaving the legate, Quintus Catius, in charge of the camp he hurried with forced marches to meet his colleague.

44. In Rome there was as much panic and confusion as there had been four years before when Hannibal had pitched camp before the walls of the city. The citizens were unable to decide whether to praise or blame him for daring to attempt such a march. Although nothing is more unfair, it was apparent that the public opinion would judge him according to the success or failure of his enterprise: "After depriving the army of its best soldiers," they said, "he has left it leaderless, encamped near such an enemy as Hannibal. He announced that his destination was Lucania, when he was actually going to Picenum and Gaul. The only protection left to his camp is Hannibal's ignorance that it is leaderless and deprived of part of its strength. What will happen if Hannibal learns of all this and decides to pursue Claudius Nero and his six thousand men with his whole army? Or what if he should choose to attack the camp? Weakened, leaderless, with no one to

take the auspices before battle, it is ripe for the taking."
The Romans were cowed by the previous disasters of the
war, and in particular by the deaths of the two consuls
the year before. "All those things happened with one
enemy general and one army in Italy. Now we have two
Punic wars, two armies, and virtually two Hannibals in
Italy. Hasdrubal was born of the same father as Hannibal
and is an equally able soldier. For many years he has been
trained in Roman tactics. He has distinguished himself
by destroying two Roman armies with their renowned
generals. Indeed, he is entitled to brag much more than
Hannibal of the speed of his march from Spain and of
his success in soliciting the assistance of the Gallic tribes.
Indeed, he was able to recruit an army in the very regions
in which the greater part of Hannibal's troops died from
cold and starvation, the most wretched of deaths." Those
who were familiar with the campaign in Spain added that
Hasdrubal was well acquainted with Claudius Nero. Once
when he happened to be trapped in a cul-de-sac, he had
tricked Claudius like a child by making fraudulent terms
of peace. Thus, under the influence of fear, which looks
on the worse side of everything, they magnified the resources of the enemy and underrated their own.

45. After Nero had gotten far enough away from the
enemy that it was safe to disclose his plans he spoke
briefly to his troops. "No general," he said, "has ever conceived a strategem more daring in appearance or safer in
fact. I am leading you to certain victory. My colleague
refused to move before the senate gave him all of the cavalry and infantry that he demanded—a larger and better-
equipped force than if he were attacking Hannibal himself. Now whatever strength we can add will bring us certain victory. Just let it be heard on the battlefield—and I
will make sure that it is not discovered sooner—that a
second army and a second general have arrived, and we

shall be assured of victory. Battles are won by hearsay, and things of little importance inspire both confidence and fear. You yourselves will win most of the glory for victory; for it always seems that the last thing added determines the whole. You see even now what cheering and applauding crowds have gathered along your line of march."

Indeed men and women thronged together from the fields everywhere and lined both sides of their route shouting their blessings and their admiration. They called them the guardians of their country, the deliverers of the city and the Roman empire. On their swords and right hands rested their own liberty and safety and that of their children. They beseeched the gods to protect them on their journey, be with them in battle, and give them an early victory over the enemy. They prayed that good fortune might obligate them to pay their vows, so that just as they now were following the army with anxiety and solicitude, in a few days they might happily greet them exulting in victory. Each one held out to the soldiers the provisions he had brought, urging, even importuning, them to take the supplies he offered for themselves and their animals. The soldiers, on the other hand, vied with each other in moderation, refusing to take anything more than was necessary. They never halted, or dropped out of their ranks, nor even stopped to eat; day and night they marched on, scarcely allowing themselves the minimum of rest their bodies required. Claudius sent messengers ahead to his colleague announcing his arrival and asking whether he should arrive secretly, by night, or by day, and whether he should come into the same camp or establish another. Livius thought it best for him to arrive quietly by night.

46. Livius thought it imprudent to enlarge the camp, for fear that the enemy would become aware of the sec-

ond consul's arrival. He issued orders quietly that each individual tribune, centurion, foot soldier and horseman should accommodate one of the new arrivals in his own quarters. This crowding of extra men into limited space would be somewhat easier because Claudius' troops had brought almost nothing with them except their arms. However, their numbers had been augmented by volunteers, both veterans who had volunteered and young men who seemed physically fit for military service. Livius' camp was near the town of Sena, about half a mile from that of Hasdrubal. Therefore, when Claudius drew near he halted and waited under cover of some mountains until it was night and he could enter the camp. As they quietly arrived each man was hospitably received by one of his own rank. On the next day the consuls had a consultation which was also attended by the praetor L. Porcius Licinus. He now had united his army with that of the consuls. Before they came he had followed Hasdrubal and harassed him, keeping to the hills. By sometimes blockading a narrow pass to stop the enemy's advance, sometimes picking at his flank or rear, he had hindered the enemy's advance skillfully and efficiently. Many of those present favored postponing the battle for a few days so that Claudius' troops could rest from their long marches and loss of sleep, and he have an opportunity to become familiar with the enemy. Claudius, however, entreated them earnestly not to jeopardize his plan by dawdling after the speed of his march had insured its success. Hannibal, he said, was still idle because of his ignorance of recent events; he had not yet attacked Nero's camp, which was left leaderless, nor had he undertaken to pursue him on his march. But he would soon discover his mistake. Before Hannibal moved Hasdrubal's army might be destroyed and Claudius return into Apulia. By putting off the battle they would be betraying the camp in

Apulia and leaving the way open for Hannibal into Gaul, so that he might rendezvous with Hasdrubal at his leisure. The signal should be given immediately and they should march out to battle. They should take advantage of the delusions of both enemies, while one was ignorant of his opponent's weakness, the other of his enemy's strength. The council was then adjourned, the signal for battle displayed, and at once the army marched out to attack the enemy.

47. The enemy armies stood facing each other on the field. However, now there was a delay. Hasdrubal rode out with a small escort before his lines and noticed weather-beaten shields and lean horses which he had not seen before. The enemy army also seemed larger. Suspecting the truth he sounded the retreat. Subsequently he sent a scouting party to the river where the Romans got their water; they were to take some prisoners, if they could, and to observe whether any of them were unusually sun-burned as they might be after a recent march. He sent another party with orders to ride around their camp and inspect the rampart to see if it had been extended anywhere and to listen whether the bugle calls were sounded once or twice. They reported back that the camp had not been enlarged. There were two camps—one M. Livius', the other L. Porcius'—just as there had been before the arrival of the second consul; the fortifications had not been extended. At first this fooled him. But they also reported that there were three bugle-calls—one in the praetor's camp and two in the consul's. From his long experience with a Roman enemy he realized his worst fears were true; there were indeed two consuls in the camp. He anxiously wondered how the second had escaped from Hannibal, but never even imagined what really had happened—Hannibal had been so baffled that he did not know where the consul was, or the army which

had been camped near his own. Surely Hannibal must
have suffered some major disaster so that he did not dare
to follow. He began to fear very much that he had arrived too late and that all was lost in Italy just as in Spain.
On the other hand he suspected that his dispatch to his
brother had been intercepted and that now this second
consul had hurried there to help overpower him.

Apprehensively he gave orders for the fires to be put
out; at the first watch he ordered his soldiers to collect
their baggage in silence and to march. Because of the general anxiety and confusion caused by the darkness the
guides were not watched closely; one slipped away into
a hiding place, the other swam across the Metaurus at a
shallow spot which he knew. After being abandoned by
its guides the army wandered aimlessly here and there;
many dropped out in exhaustion; soon few were following their standards. Until morning came and he could find
his route, Hasdrubal gave orders to follow the river. However, wandering blindly along the twists and turns of the
winding river, he made little progress; when daylight
came he intended to find an opportune spot to cross. But
the further he advanced inland the higher and steeper the
banks of the stream became. He wasted a day trying to
find a ford, and gave the enemy opportunity to overtake
him.

48. Claudius arrived first with all the cavalry. Porcius
followed next with the light-armed troops. From every
direction they attacked and harried the column of weary
soldiers. Finally Hasdrubal halted his march, which
showed signs of becoming a rout, and undertook to pitch
camp on a knoll overlooking the river. But at this point
Livius arrived with the main body of troops armed and
marshaled in battle array. With all the forces united the
line was reformed; Claudius Nero took charge of the right
wing, Livius the left, the praetor the center.

Hasdrubal saw he would have to fight and abandoned his attempt to fortify a camp. In the center of the first line he placed his elephants. On the left wing opposite Nero he put the Gauls, in whom he had no great confidence, but whom he thought the enemy feared. He himself took the right wing with the Spaniards—veteran troops upon whom he relied most. The Ligurians were placed behind the elephants in the center. His line was long but not deep. The Gauls were protected by a hill rising across their front. The right wing, occupied by the Spaniards, met the Roman left. The Roman right extended beyond the fighting and was idle, for the hill before them prevented their attacking the Gauls in the front or the flank.

The battle between Livius and Hasdrubal raged fiercely, and great losses were suffered on either side. On this front were the generals of both armies, most of the Roman troops, the veteran Spaniards who had a long acquaintance with Roman tactics, and the Ligurians, a race of powerful warriors. The elephants also were sent into the Roman left. With their first charge they threw the front rank into disorder and compelled the column to retreat. Soon, as the battle grew more violent and the clamor louder, they became impossible to manage. They raged back and forth between the two armies as if they had forgotten to whom they belonged, like ships without rudders caught in a storm.

Meanwhile, crying out to his men, "Why did we hurry to complete this long march?" Claudius tried vainly to lead them up the hill in their way. When he saw that he could not get to the enemy in that direction, he withdrew several companies from his right wing where he knew they would be forced to stand idle, and led them around behind the Roman line. Then before the Romans, much less the enemy, realized what was happening, he had attacked the flank of the enemy right wing. He moved so swiftly that he had hardly appeared on the enemy flank before he was attacking its rear. From every side now, the front, the side, and the rear the Spaniards and Ligurians were being cut to pieces. Soon the Romans forced their way through and fell upon the Gauls. Here they met the least opposition. A great number had deserted their standards in the night, lying down to sleep in the fields. And those who remained, being naturally unable to endure hardship, were so exhausted from marching and lack of sleep they could scarcely support the armor on their backs. It was now the middle of the day; gasping with heat and thirst they passively suffered themselves to be killed or captured.

49. More elephants were killed by their drivers than by the enemy. The drivers carried a mallet and a chisel like that used by carpenters. When the elephants began to lose their senses and to charge into their own lines each driver placed the chisel between his mount's ears at the joint between the head and the neck and struck it as hard as he could. That was the quickest way found for killing these great beasts when they had broken completely out of control. It was invented by Hasdrubal himself, who had proven himself a notable general on many occasions, but especially in this battle. Constantly he inspired his men by shouting encouragement and by leading them personally into danger. When they were ready to give up in exhaustion and despair he rallied them again by appealing to them and reproving them. By turning men back from flight in several places he restored the battle after it had been abandoned. Finally, when the enemy's victory was no longer doubtful he spurred his horse and charged into a company of Romans. He did not wish to survive his great army which had followed him in trust of his distinguished reputation. There he died fighting, as was worthy of his father and of Hannibal, his brother.

Never in that war were so many men killed in one battle. It now seemed that Cannae was sufficiently revenged; for the enemy general had been killed and his army slaughtered. . . . The victors were completely satiated with blood. On the next day Livius was informed that the Cisalpine Gauls who had deserted before the battle or had managed to escape had collected together and were retreating in disorder with no leader or standard; it was possible to send a single squadron of cavalry and destroy them all. To this report Livius only replied, "Let some survive to tell of our bravery and the enemy's disaster."

50. The night following the battle Claudius started back to Apulia, marching more rapidly than he had come, and reached his camp on the sixth day. Since no messenger now preceded him fewer people lined his route, but those who did greeted his approach with such rejoicing that they could scarcely control themselves.

It is impossible to describe the anxiety and apprehension with which the people at Rome awaited the outcome, or with what jubilant excitement they received the news of victory. From the day that news of Claudius Nero's expedition arrived, never did a senator leave the senate house or the people the Forum from dawn to dusk. Since there was nothing the women could do to help, they turned to prayer and supplication, wandering from shrine to shrine wearying the gods with their entreaties.

As the citizens waited so anxiously and tensely, at first an unsubstantial rumor spread that at the camp set up to blockade the road to Umbria two Narnian horsemen had arrived from the battle bringing news that the enemy army had been annihilated. When they first heard this rumor they could not believe it; it seemed too great and too fortunate to be true. Even the speed with which it arrived seemed to make it impossible; it was reported the battle had taken place only two days before. But then a message from L. Manlius Acidinus in the camp reached the city confirming the report of the Narnian horsemen. As this message was taken through the Forum to the tribunal of the praetor, the senate hurried out of the senate house. The impatient crowd before the doors of the senate house created such press and confusion that the messenger could not get through. He was dragged back and forth by the people shouting questions and demanding that the message be read from the rostra before it was read in the senate. Finally they were pushed back and held in check by the magistrates, and the happy news, which they could scarcely realize, was able to be announced. The message was read first in the senate, then to the people. Reactions to the message varied, according to individual temperaments. Some considered the good news certain, but others refused to believe before they heard envoys or a report arrived from the consuls.

51. Soon it was announced that the envoys were coming. They were L. Veturius Philo, P. Licinius Varus, and Q. Caecilius Metellus. Everyone, both young and old, ran out to meet them, each wishing to be the first to hear the good news. The crowd extended to the Mulvian bridge in one unbroken procession. As the envoys made their way into the Forum they were thronged by people of every class and description importuning them with questions about what had happened. As each one learned that the enemy army was destroyed, its general dead, the Roman legions safe as well as the consuls, they turned in delight to others to tell them the good news. Finally they reached the senate house and the crowd was removed from the building with great difficulty. After the dispatch was read to the senate the envoys were conducted into the assembly. Here Lucius Veturius again read the message and explained in detail all that had happened. His words were received with great applause and finally were

drowned with cheers; the people could no longer repress their jubilance. Some ran at once to the temples to give thanks; others hurried to announce the happy news to their wives and children.

The senate decreed a three days thanksgiving. Gaius Hostilius announced the decree to the senate and the thanksgiving was celebrated by men and women alike. For three full days all the temples were crowded. Dressed in their finest clothes women offered thanks with their children, as carefree as if the war were over. The economic climate also was affected by the victory. Men now began to do business with each other, to buy and sell, to lend money and repay loans just as though peace had been made.

Nero carefully preserved the head of Hasdrubal and returned with it to his camp. As soon as he had arrived he gave orders for this to be thrown in front of the enemy guard post, for the African captives to be paraded before it in chains, and for two of them to be freed to tell Hannibal all that had happened. Hannibal was so overwhelmed with personal grief and despair for his country that he is reported to have declared that he now recognized Carthage's destiny. He then decamped and undertook to gather together in Bruttium, the farthest corner of Italy, all his allies, whom he could not protect while they were scattered far and wide. The whole population of Metapontum was removed from their city as well as all the Lucanians who recognized his authority.

Epitome of Book 28
207 - 205 BC

Recounted here are the successful operations against the Carthaginians in Spain carried out by Scipio's lieutenant Silanus and by his brother Lucius Scipio, and those carried out by the proconsul Publius Sulpicius in alliance with Attalus king of Asia on behalf of the Aetolians against Philip king of the Macedonians. When a triumph was decreed to the consuls Marcus Livius and Claudius Nero, Livius who had directed the campaign in his own province rode in a four-horse chariot, whereas Nero, who had entered his colleague's province to assist his victory, followed on horseback; even in this guise he enjoyed greater glory and reverence, for he had done more than his colleague in the war. The fire in the temple of Vesta went out by the negligence of a virgin who failed to watch over it; she was scourged. Publius Scipio finished the war with the Carthaginians in Spain in the fourteenth year of the war, in the fifth year after his arrival there; after shutting the enemy out of the possession of that province altogether, he recovered it. From Tarraco he crossed over to Syphax king of the Massylians in Africa, and made a treaty with him. Hasdrubal son of Gisgo dined with him there, on the same couch. He gave a gladiatorial show in honor of his father and uncle at New Carthage; he employed not gladiators but men who undertook to duel in honor of their general or to answer a challenge. In that show princes who were brothers contended for the kingship with steel. When the city of Gisia was under attack the townsmen slew their children and wives upon a pyre they had built and then flung themselves upon it. Once when Scipio was gravely ill part of the army mutinied; upon his recovery he quashed the mutiny and forced the rebellious people of Spain to surrender. He made peace also with Masinissa king of the Numidians, who promised him support if he should cross over into Africa. He made friends with the people of Gades also when Mago, who had received written orders to proceed to Italy, left that city; he then returned to Rome and was made consul. He asked for Africa as his province, but Quintus Fabius Maximus opposed him; he was assigned to Sicily, with permission to cross over into Africa if he judged such a move advantageous to the state. Mago son of Hamilcar wintered in the lesser Balearic island, and from there crossed over to Italy.

Epitome of Book 29
205 - 204 BC

Gaius Laelius, whom Scipio sent from Sicily to Africa, brought back immense booty and gave Scipio a message from Masinissa complaining that he had not yet carried his army over to Africa. A war which Indibilis stirred up in Spain was brought to an end with the Romans victorious. Indibilis himself was killed in battle; Mandonius was surrendered to the Romans at their demand. To Mago, who was at Albingaunum among the Ligurians, a large contingent of soldiers was sent and money with which to engage auxiliaries; he was ordered to unite with Hannibal. Scipio crossed over into the Bruttian country from Syracuse and recovered Locri by expelling the Carthaginian garrison and putting Hannibal to flight. Peace was made with Philip. The Idaean Mother was brought to Rome from the Phrygian town of Pessinus; an oracle had been found in the Sibylline books saying that an alien enemy could be driven from Italy if the Idaean Mother were brought to Rome. She was handed over to the Romans through the agency of Attalus king of Asia. She was a stone which the natives called Mother of the Gods. She was received by Publius Scipio Nasica, son of the Gnaeus who had perished in Spain. The oracle had commanded that the divinity should be received and consecrated by the best man, and the senate adjudged him the best, though he had not yet held the quaestorship. The Locrians sent emissaries to Rome to complain of the intemperance of the legate Pleminius; he had confiscated the money of Proserpina and had violated the chastity of their children and wives. He was brought to Rome in chains and died in the prison. Concerning the proconsul Publius Scipio a false report was brought to the capital, alleging that he was living voluptuously in Sicily, and emissaries were dispatched by the senate to discover whether the charges were true. Scipio was cleared of the slander, and crossed over into Africa with the senate's permission. Syphax married the daughter of Hasdrubal son of Gisgo and renounced the alliance he had made with Scipio. Masinissa king of the Massylians was excluded from the kingship, upon the loss of his father, while he was fighting for the Carthaginians in Spain. He made war to regain it, but was defeated by Syphax in several battles and completely dispossessed. As an exile he joined Scipio with two hundred horsemen, and with him, at the very beginning of the war, killed Hanno son of Hamilcar together with a large force. Scipio was forced to raise the siege of Utica by the arrival of Hasdrubal and Syphax, who had brought almost a hundred thousand armed men; he fortified a winter camp. The consul Sempronius fought a successful battle against Hannibal in the territory of Croton. Between the censors Marcus Livius and Claudius Nero there was a memorable quarrel; Claudius deprived his colleague Livius of his horse because he had been condemned and banished by the people, and Livius deprived Claudius of his because Claudius had borne false witness against him and because his reconciliation had not been in good faith. Also Livius reduced all the tribes but one to the status of mere taxpayers because they had condemned him when he was innocent and subsequently made him consul and censor. The lustrum was completed by the censors; the count of citizens was 214,000.

Book 30

203-201 BC

Following the Battle of the Metaurus River Hannibal remained in southern Italy until 203, still unconquered, but accomplishing little for his cause. The young Publius Scipio invaded Africa, and several Roman victories there forced Carthage to recall Hannibal after sixteen years in Italy.

20. When Hannibal heard the words of the envoys it is said that he groaned and gnashed his teeth, scarcely able to keep back the tears. "So now they are openly

recalling me," he said, "for years they have tried covertly to force my return by refusing me any money and re-inforcements. The Roman people did not conquer Hannibal; many times their armies were decimated and put to rout. It is the senate of Carthage which has defeated me, through hatred and jealousy. Scipio will not exult so much at the grotesqueness of my recall as will Hanno. When he was unable in any other way to destroy my house he did so through the ruin of Carthage."

He already had prepared ships, however, in anticipation of this eventuality. He disposed of the useless masses of his troops by assigning them, ostensibly to serve as garrisons, among the towns of the district of Bruttium; a few of these towns he still held, through intimidation rather than loyalty. Only the experienced and competent nucleus of his army was transported to Africa. Many who were Italians refused to accompany him and fled to the shrine of Juno Lacinia, a sanctuary inviolate until that day; but he mercilessly butchered them in the temple itself. It is said that no exile ever departed his native soil so sadly as Hannibal left this enemy land. Time and again he looked back at the shores of Italy, denouncing gods and men and recriminating himself for not leading his soldiers to Rome while still covered with blood from their victory at Cannae. Scipio, he thought, who during his consulship never saw a Carthaginian foe in Italy, now had dared to attack Carthage, while Hannibal himself, after killing 100,000 warriors at Trasumennus and Cannae, had grown old around Casilinum and Cumae and Nola. With such complaints and self-reproaches he watched Italy, which he had occupied so long, recede in the distance behind him.

The Carthaginians concluded an armistice with Scipio, and ambassadors were sent to Rome seeking terms of peace. Their overtures were rejected, however, and when a Roman supply convoy was seized by the Carthaginians the truce also was broken off.

28. In Rome meanwhile, both hope and anxiety increased day by day. No one knew whether to rejoice or be afraid. "After sixteen years," they said, "Hannibal had withdrawn from Italy, leaving sole dominion to the Roman people; but he has been allowed to escape safely with his army. He has changed his theater of operation, but the peril remains the same. Not for nothing had Quintus Fabius, who died shortly before prophesied that Hannibal would be a more dangerous enemy in his own country than in foreign territory. Scipio will not now be dealing with Syphax, a king of a rag-tag barbarian race, whose general Statorius was little more than a camp-follower; nor will he be dealing with Syphax's father-in-law, the timid Hasdrubal, nor with irregular armies levied from half-armed bumpkins. Now his opponent is Hannibal, who was virtually born in the field-headquarters of his father, and was reared and educated in an army camp. As a boy he served as a soldier, he became a general when scarcely grown; he has now grown old celebrating victories, and has filled Spain, Gaul, and Italy from the Alps to the Sicilian strait with monuments of his mighty exploits. He commands an army of veterans whom he has led through all his campaigns. These men have been inured to almost unbelievable hardships; a thousand times they have been drenched in Roman blood and have carried away spoils taken from the bodies not only of common soldiers but of generals. Many men will face Scipio who have killed Roman praetors, generals, and consuls in battle. Many had been decorated for scaling walls and ramparts. They have wandered at will through captured Roman camps and cities. All the Roman magistrates together do not have as

many *fasces* as Hannibal has captured from fallen Roman commanders and can have borne before him."

By brooding over such forebodings as these their anxieties were intensified. One other consideration added to their fears. They had become accustomed to war; for many years they had watched it drag on in one part of Italy after another, with small hope of any imminent conclusion. Now they looked on in concern as Scipio and Hannibal prepared, as it were, for one final conflict. Even those with great confidence in Scipio and great hope of success grew more apprehensive the more they longed for victory.

The Carthaginians were in a similar frame of mind. When they looked at Hannibal and the magnificence of his deeds they regretted suing for peace. But then again they remembered that twice recently they had been conquered in battle, that Syphax had been captured, and that they had been driven from both Italy and Spain. When they reflected that all this was accomplished through the courage and wisdom of one man, they shrank in fear from Scipio as the avenger destined for their destruction.

29. Hannibal had now arrived at Hadrumetum, where he delayed a few days for his soldiers to recuperate from the rough sea voyage. There frightened messengers arrived, reporting that all the country around Carthage was occupied by the Roman army. At this news he hurried by forced marches to Zama, which is five days journey from Carthage. From there he sent forward scouts who were captured by Roman guards and taken to Scipio. Scipio told them to inspect the Roman camp without fear, and handed them over to a military tribune with orders to show them around wherever they wished to go. When they returned he asked whether they had observed everything to their satisfaction. He then sent them back

to Hannibal under escort. Their detailed report, however, was anything but gratifying to Hannibal. He was particularly disturbed by the confidence of the enemy, which seemed to him entirely justified. Among other things the scouts reported that the very day they were in the camp Masinissa had arrived with six thousand foot soldiers and four thousand horsemen. Accordingly, he sent a messenger to Scipio requesting a conference with him.

He was aware, he indicated, that he himself had started the war, and that his arrival in Africa had destroyed all hope of a peace treaty as well as the truce which had been made; nevertheless he thought that he could obtain better terms while his army was still at full strength than if he waited to seek peace until after he had been defeated. Whether he undertook these negotiations on his own authority or by order of the government I am unable to say. Valerius Antias writes that before suing for peace he met Scipio in battle and was defeated; after this battle, in which twelve thousand Carthaginians were killed and seventeen hundred captured, he went to Scipio's camp as one of ten envoys. At any rate, Scipio did not reject the request for a conference, and the two generals agreed to move their encampments closer together in order to be able to hold meetings more conveniently. Scipio pitched camp not far from the town of Naraggara; in addition to other advantages, a watering place was in spear range of this spot. Hannibal occupied a small hill four miles away; his position was safe and convenient in every respect except that his water supply was some distance away. In order to avoid possibility of ambush a spot was selected halfway between the two camps which was open to view in every direction.

30. When their bodyguards had withdrawn at an equal distance the two generals, each with an interpreter, stepped forward and stood face to face. These two were

not only the greatest generals of their own age; they were equal to all previous kings and commanders in the recorded history of the whole world. For moments each regarded the other in awe. Then Hannibal broke the silence: "It seems that it was destined by fate that I, who began this war and so often had victory almost in my hands, should be the first to sue for peace; if so, then I am glad that fate has appointed you as the one from whom I must ask it. Among your many great accomplishments this will not be the least of your claims to glory: that Hannibal, to whom the gods granted victory over so many Roman generals, capitulated to you; and that it was you who made an end to this war which will be remembered more for your disasters than for ours. I invaded Italy during your father's consulship, and he was the first Roman general with whom I fought. Now fortune has played this burlesque trick: it is to his son that I come unarmed to beg for peace. Surely it would have been best if the gods had granted our fathers forebearance—if yours had been content to be masters of Italy, ours, to rule over Africa. Even for you Sicily and Sardinia are not sufficient return for the loss of so many fleets, so many armies, so many great generals. But the past is more readily lamented than corrected. We coveted the wealth of others and we have had to fight to keep our own. It has meant war for us in Africa, for you in Italy: You have seen the standards of an enemy army almost within your gates and on your walls; in Carthage we can hear the armies of the Roman camp. Now peace is being discussed while you have the upper hand—a thing which we most abhor and you desire above all else. We who are bargaining for peace would benefit most from it, and whatever terms we make our people will confirm. We need only the patience and prudence which is necessary for sober discussion.

"As for me, I am now returning in my old age to a

country which I left as a boy; old age and the vicissitudes of life have taught me to prefer to follow reason rather than fortune. I fear both your youthfulness and your constant success; both are likely to be impatient of calm consideration. It is difficult for a man to whom fortune has never proved false to reflect upon its uncertainties. What I was at Trasumennus and Cannae you are today. When scarcely old enough to be a soldier you received a command, and in even your most reckless ventures fortune has never deserted you. You avenged the death of your father and uncle; from that disaster you won a glorious reputation for courage and filial devotion. You recovered the loss of Spain by driving from it four Carthaginian armies. . . .

"But in a single hour fortune can destroy all the glory you have won and that you hope for. If you make peace everything will be in your power. If not you must accept whatever fortune the gods grant. If in victory Marcus Atilius Regulus had granted our fathers' request for peace he would have been a unique illustration of virtue and prosperity. But he set no limits to his happiness, and refused to curb his mounting aspiration; the higher he had climbed the harder was his fall. It is for him who grants peace, not for him who seeks it to dictate its terms; but perhaps you will not think it presumptuous for us to impose a penalty upon ourselves. We relinquish claim to all the territory disputed in the war: Sicily, Sardinia, Spain, and all the islands between Italy and Africa. Since the gods so will we shall confine ourselves within the shores of Africa and recognize your sovereignty over all the territory beyond, both by land and by sea. Because the recent request for peace was made insincerely and we did not wait for it to be granted, I do not deny that there is reason to suspect Carthaginian promises. However, the inviolability of a treaty depends primarily upon the influ-

ence of the person who negotiates it. I have been told
that your senate rejected our last offer of peace partially
on the ground that our delegation lacked authority. Today it is I, Hannibal, who ask for peace. I should not seek
it unless I thought it in our best interests, and for that very
reason I shall protect its inviolability. Because I was responsible for beginning the war I took care that none of
my countrymen should regret it, until the gods became
jealous of my success. Now I shall spare no pains to prevent dissatisfaction with the treaty which I negotiate."

31. To these words the Roman general answered: "I
realized, Hannibal, that it was the expectation of your
arrival which prompted Carthage to break the truce and
destroy all hope of peace. You yourself acknowledge it
by omitting from the previous terms of peace every concession which has not long been in our power. It is your
concern to show your countrymen how much your intercession can alleviate their misfortunes. But I must make
sure that they are not rewarded for their dishonesty; I
cannot allow conditions which they previously agreed
upon now to be omitted from the treaty. You did not deserve the conditions you received before, and now you
are seeking to benefit from your treachery. Our fathers did
not go to war to gain Sicily, and we did not attempt to
take Spain from you. You were the aggressors in both
instances. Then it was the danger threatening our allies
the Mamertines which aroused us to arms as right and
duty demanded; this time it was the destruction of Saguntum. You yourself acknowledge that you were the aggressors and of this the gods are witnesses. They granted
to us a righteous victory in that war, and shall grant us
victory now.

"As for me, I am sensible of the helplessness of mortals; I am aware of the power of fortune, and I know that
everything we do is subject to a thousand mishaps. If you

had withdrawn from Italy voluntarily, and with your army already aboard ship had come to ask for peace, it would have been arrogant and irresponsible for me to repulse you. As it is, I have dragged you to Africa almost by main force in spite of every kind of resistance; so I am not obliged to show you consideration. You are aware of the terms upon which previously peace seemed about to be concluded. If, in addition to those, some reparation is proposed for the seizure of our supply convoy and the abuse of our ambassadors, I shall have something to refer to my council. But if this seems a heavy penalty to pay, prepare for war—since you cannot endure peace."

Thus without negotiating any peace, the two commanders broke off their conference and returned to their own armies. They announced that their talks had been fruitless; they must settle the difficulty by arms and leave it to the gods to determine the results.

32. When they reached their camps both commanders directed the soldiers to prepare their swords and minds for the final conflict; if they were successful they would be victors not for one day, but forever. They would know by sunset the next day whether Carthage or Rome was to dominate the world, for not just Africa or Italy, but the whole world would be the prize of the conquerors; and the punishment for defeat would be as great as the reward for victory. For the Romans had no refuge in a strange and unknown land; and when Carthage spent her final ounce of energy destruction would be imminent.

The next day the two ablest generals of the world's richest nations led forward their mighty armies to this decisive contest; this would mark the culmination or the forfeiture of their many honors. The soldiers wavered constantly between hope and fear. They looked from one army to the other, estimating their strength with the eye rather than the mind, and seeing reasons for both confidence and fear. The enthusiasm which they could not find themselves their generals tried to inspire with words of exhortation. Hannibal reminded his men of the war they had waged for sixteen years in Italy, of the generals they had killed and the armies they had destroyed, of the deeds of individuals who had won distinction in battle. Scipio spoke to his soldiers of their Spanish campaigns and their recent battles in Africa. He reminded them of the enemy's confession of defeat; their fear had forced them to seek a truce, but their perfidy had not permitted them to abide by it. Moreover, since the conference with Hannibal had been held in private he was free to embellish and interpret it as he wished. He speculated that as the Carthaginians marched out to battle the gods had revealed to them the same auspices which their fathers had received before they fought at the Aegates Islands. This, he said, was the end of the war and their labors. The booty from Carthage was in their grasp, and soon they could return home to their parents, children, wives, and household gods. With shoulders erect, and a light in his eyes, he spoke like a man already victorious.

The battle of Zama (202 B.C.) proved to be an easy victory for the Romans.

37. The next day the Carthaginian ambassadors were called to the Roman council of war and severely rebuked for their treachery. They were admonished to take a lesson from their disasters and in future to have reverence for the gods and the sacredness of oaths. The conditions of peace were then read to them:

They would live as a free people under their own laws. They would retain possession of the territory and cities which they had had before the war and with the same boundaries. That day the Romans would discontinue the plundering and devastation. They were to restore all de-

serters, runaway slaves, and captives to the Romans. They
were to surrender all warships, except for ten triremes, in
addition to all trained elephants which they had. They
were forbidden for the future to train elephants for war.
They were to make war neither within nor outside of
Africa without the permission of the Roman people. They
were to restore to Masinissa all that they had taken and
were to sign a treaty with him. Until their envoys should
return from Rome they were to provide rations and pay
for the Roman auxiliary troops. They were to pay an indemnity of 10,000 talents of silver in equal annual installments over a period of fifty years, and were to surrender one hundred hostages, to be chosen by Scipio, between the ages of fourteen and thirty. Moreover they
would be granted an armistice only if they returned the
transports which they had captured, along with their cargoes. Otherwise there would be no armistice nor any
hope for peace.

These were the terms for peace which the envoys were
ordered to carry back to Carthage. When they recited
them in the assembly, a certain Gisgo came forward and
objected to the treaty. His words were heard by the common people with respect, for they were still recalcitrant
although they were helpless to renew the war. Hannibal,
however, was outraged that such words were even considered at such a crisis; seizing Gisgo by the hand he dragged
him from the platform. This was an unusual spectacle in
a free state, and evoked an outcry from the people. At
this unwonted freedom of expression the old soldier was
nonplussed. "I left you at the age of nine," he said, "I
have returned after thirty-six years. I am well versed, I
think, in the military arts which I began learning from my
father as a boy and continued to learn after being chosen as your general. But you must teach me the rules,
laws, and customs of the city and the forum." After apol-

ogizing for his rashness, he spoke at great length, insisting
that the peace terms were not unfair and were unavoidable. The greatest difficulty was that nothing except the
ships themselves could be found of the supply convoy
which had been seized during the truce. It was impossible to learn much by questioning because those accused
of possession of the cargo also opposed the treaty. It was
subsequently decided that the ships should be returned
and that a diligent search should be made at least for their
crews. Scipio would be requested to evaluate the cargo
and to assess the Carthaginians this amount.

Some authorities say Hannibal went straight to the
coast from the battlefield. There he had arranged for a
ship to be waiting in which he sailed immediately for the
court of Antiochus in Syria. Scipio's first demand was for
Hannibal's surrender, but he was informed that Hannibal was no longer in Africa.

Epitome of Book 31
201-200 BC

The causes of the renewal of the war against Philip
king of Macedon, which had been intermitted, are recounted as follows. At the time for initiates two young
Acarnanians who had not been initiated came to Athens
and entered the sanctuary of Ceres along with other of
their countrymen. For this they were killed by the Athenians on the grounds of supreme sacrilege. The Acarnanians were aroused by the death of their men, petitioned
Philip for help in avenging them, and attacked Athens. The

Athenians asked the Romans for help, a few months after
peace had been granted to the Carthaginians. When the
envoys of the Athenians who were under Philip's siege
asked help of the senate, the senate thought help should
be given, but the people dissented, because the continuous exertion of so many wars was burdensome. But the
authority of the senate prevailed, and the people too enacted that help should be extended to an allied state.
This war was entrusted to the consul Publius Sulpicius,
who led an army into Macedonia and won cavalry battles against Philip. The Abydenes who were besieged by
Philip followed the example of the Saguntines and slew
their families and themselves. In a pitched battle the praetor Lucius Furius defeated the Insubrian Gauls, who were
in revolt, and the Carthaginian Hamilcar, who was stirring
war up in that part of Italy. Hamilcar and thirty-five thousand men were killed in that war. The book also contains
the campaigns of King Philip and the consul Sulpicius and
the storming of cities by each of them. The consul Sulpicius waged war with the support of King Attalus and the
Rhodians. The praetor Lucius Furius celebrated a triumph
over the Gauls.

Epitome of Book 32

1 9 9 - 1 9 7   B C

Recorded here are prodigies reported from various regions, among them the sprouting of a laurel at the stern
of a war ship in Macedonia. The consul Titus Quinctius
Flamininus fought against Philip in the passes of Epirus

with success, put him to flight, and forced him to return
to his own kingdom. Flamininus himself, with Athenian
and Athamanian allies, harried Thessaly, which is ad-
jacent to Macedonia; his brother Lucius Quinctius Flamininus, with the assistance of King Attalus and the
Rhodians, harried Euboea and the seacoast. The Achaeans were received into friendship. The number of praetors was enlarged; now six would be elected annually. A
conspiracy of slaves calculated to release the Carthaginian
hostages was suppressed, and twenty-five hundred were
executed. The consul Cornelius Cethegus routed the Insubrian Gauls in battle. A union of friendship was made
with the Lacedaemonians and their tyrant Nabis. The
storming of cities in Macedonia is also narrated.

Book 33
1 9 7 - 1 9 5 B C

*In 197 B.C. Philip V of Macedon, who had incurred
Roman hatred by his alliance with Hannibal after the Battle of Cannae, was finally crushed by Titus Quinctius
Flamininus at the Battle of Cynoscephalae. The Greek
states over which Philip had gained suzerainty were
restive under his tyrannical rule, and when Flamininus
proclaimed Greek independence at the Isthmian Games of
196 B.C. the announcement was received with wild enthusiasm.*

32. The date set for the celebration of the Isthmian
Games was now approaching. The Games are always
heavily attended, for love of spectacle is deep-rooted in

Greek character. There were contests of artistic perfor-
mances of every kind and tests of strength and speed;
furthermore, the location of the spectacle between two
seas made it a general market supplying every sort of human need, and consequently the common meeting place
of all Greece and Asia. On this particular occasion, however, it was more than the usual attractions which induced
men to come from all parts; they were on edge to learn the
future status of Greece and their own expectations. Men
held widely different opinions and debated openly about
what the Romans would do. Almost no one believed they
would withdraw completely from Greece.

When the spectators had seated themselves, in accordance with their custom, a herald accompanied by a trum-
peter proceeded into the middle of the arena. There the
opening of the games was solemnly pronounced according
to an established ritual. After the trumpet had given the
signal for silence, the herald read the following proclamation: "The Roman senate and their commander, T.
Quinctius Flamininus, as victors over King Philip and
the Macedonians, do solemnly decree that the following
peoples shall henceforth be free, autonomous, and exempt from all foreign taxation: the Corinthians, the
Pherrhaebians, and the Achaeans of Phthiotis." These
were all the states which had been subject to Philip's sovereignty. When these words were heard they seemed too
good to be true. The people could scarcely believe they
had heard aright, and they looked around at each other
in astonishment wondering if this were a dream. Distrust-
ing their own ears they turned to ask their neighbors what
they had heard. The herald was brought back and everyone demanded not only to hear but to see the decree of
their freedom. Again he read the same proclamation. At
this reassurance that the good news was really true a great
chorus of applause swelled forth; from the prolonged repe-

tition of these cheers it was plain that of all human goods nothing is more coveted by a people than its freedom. They then hurried quickly through the games; for the good news so preoccupied their minds that they had neither ears nor eyes for anything else.

33. When the games were ended, everyone flocked around the Roman general, showering him with garlands. He was almost smothered by the crowd which pressed forward eagerly to touch his hand. He was at this time hardly thirty-three years of age; the vigor of youth and his delight at his new-found glory supplied him with strength to survive this encounter. This rejoicing was not just a short-lived burst of enthusiasm; it was cherished for days in grateful hearts and on thankful tongues: "There is indeed a nation on the earth which wages war at its own expense, toil, and labor for the sake of the liberty of others. This altruism it does not reserve to its neighbors alone. It crosses the seas throughout the whole world so that nowhere may tyranny thrive, but that everywhere justice, right, and law may reign supreme."

Epitome of Book 34
1 9 5 - 1 9 3   B C

The Oppian law on limiting female extravagance, enacted during the Punic War by Gaius Oppius, tribune of the people, was abrogated, but with sharp debate, for Porcius Cato was the principal speaker against rescinding the law. He proceeded to Spain and pacified Nearer Spain in a war which he opened at Emporiae. Titus Quinctius

Flamininus ended his war against the Lacedaemonians and their tyrant Nabis satisfactorily; he granted peace according to his own desires, and liberated Argos, which had been under the tyrant's sway. Recorded also are the successful campaigns in Spain and against the Boii and the Insubrian Gauls. For the first time the senate attended games apart from the people. The censors Sextus Aelius Paetus and Gaius Cornelius Cethegus intervened to have it so, and the plebeians were indignant. Many colonies were founded. Marcus Porcius Cato celebrated a triumph over Spain. Titus Quinctius Flamininus celebrated a three-day triumph for his victories over Philip king of Macedon and Nabis tyrant of Lacedaemonia and for liberating all of Greece. Carthaginian ambassadors announced that Hannibal, who had taken refuge with Antiochus, was helping him plot a war. Hannibal was also trying to stir the Carthaginians to war through Aristo, a Tyrian, whom he had sent to Carthage without written letters.

Epitome of Book 35
1 9 3 - 1 9 2 B C

Publius Scipio Africanus was sent as ambassador to Antiochus. At Ephesus he spoke with Hannibal, who had joined Antiochus, to dispel Hannibal's obsessive fear of the Roman people. When, in the course of the conversation, Scipio asked Hannibal whom he considered the greatest general, he named Alexander king of Macedon on the grounds that he routed countless armies with his small force and that he traversed remote countries which it was beyond human hope to see. Upon Scipio's inquiring whom he ranked second, he said that Pyrrhus had taught the art of measuring camps and that no one could choose his ground or deploy his forces with greater niceness. Scipio continuing asked for the third, and Hannibal named himself. Scipio smiled and said, "What would you say if you had beaten me?" "Then," replied Hannibal, "I should have put myself before Alexander and before Pyrrhus and before all others." Among other prodigies, which are said to have been numerous, a cow belonging to the consul Gnaeus Domitius is recorded to have uttered the words, "Rome, beware." Nabis tyrant of the Lacedaemonians, instigated by the Aetolians, who were also inciting Philip and Antiochus to make war on the Roman people, rebelled against Rome; he was killed in a war waged by the Aetolians against Philopoemen, the leader of the Achaeans. The Aetolians also defected from friendship with the Roman people. In alliance with them Antiochus king of Syria made war upon Greece and seized several cities, among them Chalcis and all Euboea. The book also contains operations in Liguria and Antiochus' preparations for war.

Epitome of Book 36
1 9 1 B C

The consul Acilius Glabrio, with the assistance of King Philip, defeated Antiochus at Thermopylae and drove him from Greece; he also subdued the Aetolians. The con-

sul Publius Cornelius Scipio Nasica, the man who was adjudged best by the senate and had brought the Mother
of the Gods to the Palatine, dedicated a temple to her.
He also conquered the Boian Gauls, received their surrender, and triumphed over them. Successful naval engagements against the officers of King Antiochus are also
narrated.

Book 37
1 9 0 - 1 8 9 B C

*In 190 B.C., when Antiochus failed to observe their
terms after the battle of Thermopylae, the Romans sent
an army into Asia Minor with the consul Lucius Scipio
ostensibly in command. Lucius was accompanied by his
elder brother, Publius Scipio Africanus, who was the real
director of Roman strategy in this campaign. The Romans
were supported by Eumenes II of Pergamum, Antiochus'
rival in Asia Minor.*

37. The camp of the king was near Thyatira. When
Antiochus heard that Publius Scipio was ill and had been
taken to Elaea, he sent ambassadors to return his son
(whom Antiochus had captured) to him. This act of kindness was not only gratifying to his fatherly affections; it
was beneficial to his body as well. After embracing his
son he turned to the envoys, "Please convey my thanks to
the king," he said. "I am able to grant him no favor in
return except to urge him not to fight before he hears
that I have returned to camp." Although Antiochus' sixty
thousand foot soldiers and twelve thousand horsemen

gave him reason for optimism, the authority of this great
man prevailed over him; with an eye to the uncertain outcome of the war, upon Scipio he placed hope of support
if his fortune should be unhappy. Therefore he withdrew across the river Phrygius and pitched camp near
Magnesia ad Sipylum. In case his attempts to postpone
battle should provoke the Romans to attack his camp, he
surrounded it with a trench six cubits deep and twelve
cubits wide. Around this trench on the outside he constructed a double rampart; along the trench's inner edge
he raised a wall with many towers from which the enemy
could easily be prevented from crossing the trench.

38. Thinking that Antiochus was in the vicinity of
Thyatira, the consul reached the Hyrcanian plain by
forced marches in five days. When he discovered that
Antiochus had decamped, he set out in pursuit and finally
pitched camp just west of the Phrygius river four miles
from the enemy. There about one thousand horsemen—
most of them Gallograeci, along with some Dahae and
mounted archers from other tribes—charged across the
river and swooped down on the pickets. The Romans
were caught off guard and at first were thrown into confusion. As the battle went on, however, the numbers of
the Romans were augmented by reinforcements from the
camp nearby. The king's forces soon were exhausted and
could no longer withstand the weight of numbers. They
retreated to the bank of the river but before they could
cross many were killed by the Romans attacking their
rear.

For two days more all was quiet, as neither side crossed
the river. The third day all the Roman forces crossed and
pitched camp about two and one-half miles from the
enemy.

While they were still occupied with measuring off and
fortifying the camp, three thousand of Antiochus' picked

troops, both cavalry and infantry, attacked, creating great panic and confusion. The number of Romans on guard was considerably smaller; nevertheless they called for no reinforcements from the troops fortifying the camp, and at first were able to hold their own. As the fighting grew hotter they succeeded in repulsing the enemy, killing and taking prisoner about two hundred. For the next four days both armies stood before the ramparts of their camp, drawn up in battle order. On the fifth day the Romans marched out onto the open field. Antiochus, however, refused to advance, and remained with his rear lines less than one thousand feet from his rampart.

39. It was now apparent that the enemy declined to fight. The next day the consul called a council to discuss what should be done, if Antiochus would not afford them the opportunity for battle. Winter was approaching; either they would have to keep the soldiers in their tents, or, if they wished to retire to winter quarters, the conclusion of the war would have to be put off until summer. No enemy had ever been so scorned by the Romans. Everyone cried out at once that he should lead them out to battle immediately and should make the most of the zeal of the soldiers. They looked upon the battle not as a struggle with many thousand enemies but as the slaughter of so many cattle. If the enemy should not come out and fight they were prepared to storm his camp over trench and rampart.

Gnaeus Domitius was sent with a scouting party to find the best approach to the enemy rampart. When he had returned with a detailed report it was decided to move the camp nearer the next day. On the third day the army again marched out halfway between the two camps and began to form in battle order. Antiochus also thought that he should hang back no longer, for fear that his reluctance to fight would demoralize his own men and give con-

fidence to the enemy. Leading out his troops, he advanced
far enough from the camp for it to be apparent that he intended to fight.

The Roman line was almost uniform with regard to
men and weapons. There were two Roman legions
and two of the Latins and allies, each legion containing
fifty-four hundred men. The Romans occupied the middle of the lines with the Latins on the wings. The *hastati,*
or spearmen, made up the first line; the heavy-armed
principes, the second; and the *triarii,* the reserves, were
in the rear. To the right of the battle line proper, and even
with it, the consul marshaled the auxiliaries of Eumenes
mixed with the Achaean targeteers. Beyond these he placed
the cavalry, which numbered less than three thousand.
Eight hundred of these were troops of Eumenes and all
the rest were Roman cavalry. On the far right Scipio
stationed the Trallianians and Cretans, who numbered
about five hundred each. The left wing was protected by
the sheer bank of the river and did not seem to need such
reinforcements. Nevertheless, four companies of cavalry were posted there.

This was the total of the Roman forces except for a
mixed force of two thousand Macedonians and Thracians
who had volunteered for the expedition. These were left
behind to guard the camp. Sixteen elephants were posted
in reserve behind the *triarii.* These were not put in the
first line because, in the first place, they would not be able
to hold their own against the larger number—there were
fifty-four—of the king's elephants; in the second place
African elephants cannot contend against even an equal
number of Indian, for the Indian elephants are far bigger
and more warlike.

40. The army of the king was an amalgam derived
from many nations, and was much less uniform with respect to either men or armor. There were sixteen thou-

sand men armed in the Macedonian fashion; these were
called "the phalanx." They comprised the middle of the
battle line and their front was divided into ten sections.
Between each two sections were stationed two elephants.
This phalanx extended to a depth of thirty-two ranks and
was the core of the enemy attack. Its appearance was
terrifying in other respects, but especially because of the
elephants, which towered high above the armed men.
They were made to seem even more formidable by the
frontlets and crests on their heads and howdahs on their
backs in which sat three armed men besides the mahout.
On the left flank of the phalanx were fifteen hundred
Gallograeci infantry. To these were attached three thousand armor-clad horsemen whom they call *cataphracti*.
Joined to these was another division of about three thousand horsemen known as *agema*. These were picked men,
mostly Medes, but with horsemen of many other nations
of that same area mixed with them. Placed next to this
cavalry in reserve was a group of sixteen elephants. Next
came the royal guard, called *argyraspides,* or "silver
shields," after the material of their armor. Following these
were the Dahae, twelve hundred mounted archers. Then
came three thousand light-armed troops, about half Cretans and half Trallianians; attached to these were twenty-
five hundred Mysian archers. The end of this wing was
occupied by a mixed group of Cyrtian slingers and Ely-
maean archers

On the left wing, next to the phalanx were fifteen hundred Gallograeci infantry along with two thousand similarly armed Cappadocians sent to the king by Ariarathes.
Then came a force of twenty-seven hundred auxiliaries drawn from all nations. Next to them were three thousand armor-clad horsemen along with one thousand other
horsemen similarly equipped but having lighter armor for
themselves and their horses; these, most of whom were

Syrians along with some Phrygians and Lydians, comprised the royal squadron. In front of this cavalry were stationed chariots armed with scythes and camels of the type which are called dromedaries. Mounted on these were Arabian archers, who also carried swords with narrow blades four cubits long with which they could reach the enemy from the high backs of the camels.

Then followed another large aggregation, equal in size to that on the right wing. First came the Tarentini, then twenty-five hundred Gallograeci horsemen, followed by one thousand Neocretans; next came fifteen hundred Carians and Cilicians similarly armored, followed by the same number of Trallianians and four thousand targeteers; these were Pisidians, Pamphylians, and Lycians. Finally came an auxiliary force of Cyrtians and Elymaeans followed by sixteen elephants stationed not far away.

41. The king himself was on the right wing. His son Seleucus and his nephew Antipater he placed in command of the left wing. Command of the middle of the line was assigned to three men, Minnio, Zeuxis, and Philippus, the master of the elephants.

An early-morning fog, which rose into clouds as the day went on, made it difficult to see. Then a mist coming up from the south covered everything with moisture. This discomfitted the Romans not at all but it hampered the king's forces greatly. For the obscurity was not great enough to prevent the Romans from seeing all of their relatively short line. And the moisture did not hamper the efficiency of the weapons—swords and spears—of the heavy-armed troops who comprised most of the Roman lines. Antiochus' line, on the other hand, was so long that from the center they could not see their own wings, much less see from one wing to the other. More-

over, the slings and bowstrings and thongs of their javelins were softened by the moisture. And the chariots
armed with scythes, which Antiochus had believed would
throw the enemy line into disorder, threw his own into
disorder.

The chariots were armed in this general fashion.
Pointed poles mounted along the tongue extended about
ten cubits from the yoke like horns so that they would
pierce anything they met. At each end of the yoke extended two scythes, one in line with the yoke, the other
lower down, turned toward the ground; the former was
designed to slash anything which approached from the
side, the latter to reach men who had fallen or were going
underneath. In the same way two scythes were attached
to the axle of each wheel. These armed chariots, as I have
said, the king posted in the front rank since, if they had
been placed in the rear or in the center, they would have
had to drive through their own men.

Eumenes was aware how unreliable this type of
weapon could be if you could stampede the horses before
they reached your line. Therefore he ordered the Cretan
archers, the slingers, and the spearmen along with several
squadrons of cavalry to charge out not in close order but
spread out as widely as possible, and to assail the horses
pulling the chariots with missiles simultaneously from
every direction. These missiles fell on the horses like a
storm. Their wounds and the din of the shouting soldiers
terrified them and they stampeded everywhere as if they
were unbridled. The light-armed troops, the lightly
equipped slingers, and the nimble Cretans evaded charges
of the horses easily. Meanwhile the cavalry increased the
uproar by attacking the horses and camels, causing them
to panic; to all this was added the confused shouting of
the multitude stationed nearby. At length the chariots

were driven away from the middle of the field and this idle sport was concluded. Finally the signal was given on both sides and the regular battle began.

42. But this insignificant incident proved the cause of a real disaster for Antiochus. The auxiliaries stationed nearest the chariots had been terrified by the panic of the horses and had fled, exposing the whole line all the way to the armor-clad cavalry. With their auxiliaries dispersed, these horsemen did not even withstand the first attack of the Roman cavalry. Some of them fled, others, because of the weight of their armor, were ridden down and killed. Finally the whole left wing gave way and the auxiliaries between the cavalry and the phalanx were routed; panic now had reached the center of the line. There the ranks were thrown into disorder, the soldiers running back in confusion among their fellows kept them from using their extremely long javelins, which the Macedonians call *sarisae*. Not even the elephants posted between the companies deterred the Romans. They had become accustomed to these beasts during their African wars and knew how to evade their charge and to attack them from the side with spears, or, if they could move closer, hamstring them with their swords. Now the center of the line was almost completely routed in the front; the reserves had been flanked and were being cut to pieces from behind.

Meanwhile from the other side, almost as far back as their camp, the Romans could hear the terrified shouts of their companions who were being routed. Antiochus had seen that the Romans were relying on the river to protect their right wing and had posted no reserves there except for four squadrons of cavalry. This cavalry, in order to remain close to the infantry and keep the line intact, had left the bank undefended. With his auxiliaries and armor-clad cavalry Antiochus directed a frontal attack in this area and at the same time flanked the wing and attacked it from the side. At length the horsemen began to flee, then the nearest of the foot soldiers were routed and driven back to their camp.

43. The tribune Marcus Aemilius, son of the Marcus Lepidus who a few years later became pontifex maximus, was in command of the camp. When he saw the rout he met the fugitives with his whole garrison and ordered them to halt, then to return to battle, upbraiding them for their panic and their shameful flight. He warned them that they were rushing blindly to their own destruction if they disobeyed his orders. Finally he gave the signal to his own men to kill the first of the fugitives, and to force them back toward the enemy with wounds and cold steel. This greater terror overcame the lesser. Assailed from both sides, at first they halted in fear, then returned to battle. Aemilius with his garrison, two thousand brave men, stood firm against the forces of the king, who was following in hot pursuit. On the right wing, Attalus, Eumenes' brother, saw the rout of the troops on the left and the disturbance around the camp. Leading two hundred horsemen he arrived just in time. When Antiochus saw the men at whose backs he had just been looking turn back to battle while others came to the rescue from the camp and the battle line, he turned his horse and fled.

Thus the Romans were victorious on two fronts. They pressed on to plunder the camp struggling over heaps of corpses, especially in the center of the line, where the gallantry of the men and the weight of their armor had delayed their flight. First the horsemen of Eumenes, then the whole cavalry dispersed in pursuit of the enemy, cutting down those in the rear as they overtook them. But still more harm was inflicted upon the fugitives by their own disorder and by the chariots, elephants, and camels mixed among them. When their ranks gave way the troops

rushed blindly one over the other, or were crushed under
the feet of the elephants. In the camp also there was a
great slaughter—greater almost than that on the field.
Most of the first to flee had sought refuge in the camp.
There they had found new confidence in their numbers
and with the camp's garrison had fought stubbornly before the rampart. Consequently, the Romans, after being
stopped short at the gates and the rampart, which they
had expected to take with the first charge, became incensed, and when they finally broke through took harsh
vengeance.

44. About fifty thousand infantry are said to have been
killed that day and three thousand cavalry. Fifteen hundred were captured along with fifteen elephants and their
drivers. A considerable number of Romans were wounded,
but not more than three hundred foot soldiers were
killed and only twenty-four horsemen.

After sacking the camp of the enemy the victors returned to their own camp bearing a large amount of spoils.
The next day they stripped the bodies of the slain and
assembled the prisoners. Ambassadors arrived from
Thyatira and Magnesia and Sipylum to offer the surrender of these cities. Antiochus, meanwhile, had fled
with a few men, but collected more on the road and arrived in Sardis about the middle of the night with a reasonably large band of soldiers. After hearing that his son
Seleucus and several of his friends had proceeded
to Apamea, he too set out for that city with his wife and
daughter at about the fourth watch. The protection of
Sardis was entrusted to Xeno, while Timo was placed in
command of Lydia. Their authority, however, was completely ignored by the townsmen and the soldiers in the
garrison, who sent ambassadors to the consul.

45. About this same time delegations arrived from
Tralles, the Magnesia which lies on the Meander river,

and Ephesus, to surrender their cities. When news of the battle arrived Polyxenidas, Antiochus' admiral, had abandoned the city and had sailed with his fleet as far as Patara in Lycia. Fearing the Rhodian ships stationed near Megiste, he disembarked at Patara and set out with a few men on foot for Syria. The cities of Asia were surrendering themselves to the good faith of the consul and the sovereignty of Rome. Lucius Scipio was now at Sardis, and here Publius also arrived from Elaea as soon as he was able to endure the exertion of traveling.

At about that time a herald from Antiochus obtained permission from the consul through Publius Scipio to send a delegation from the king. A few days later Zeuxis, the former governor of Lydia, and Antipater, Antiochus' nephew, arrived. They first met with Eumenes, whom, because of their long-standing enmity, they expected to find especially obdurate against a peace. When he proved to be friendlier than they had expected, they then approached Publius Scipio, and through him, the consul.

At their own request they were granted an audience before the full council for the purpose of making known their commission. "We ourselves have little say," Zeuxis began. "Our only purpose is to ask you what we may do to make recompense for the error of our king, and how we may obtain peace and indulgence from our conquerors. Always you have exhibited the greatest magnanimity in pardoning other kings and peoples. But now an even greater and more generous liberality is in keeping with this victory, which has made you masters of all the world. It now behooves you to renounce all human quarrels, and to guide and protect all humankind." Even before the legates had arrived it had been decided what answer should be given them. Publius Scipio had been chosen to respond. It is reported that he spoke as follows:

"What we Romans possess was in the power of the gods

and they chose to give us. But our spirits, which are the creature of our minds, have always and shall always remain the same; success has not inflated them nor has failure diminished them. Not to speak of others, I might submit Hannibal to you as a witness of this, if I could not offer you yourselves. Before we crossed the Hellespont and before we saw the king's camp or his army, when the outcome of the war was still in doubt, you approached us concerning peace. Then, as equals to equals, we offered to you certain conditions; those same conditions we now offer again as conquerors to conquered. Stay away from Europe. Withdraw from Asia west of the Taurus mountains. In compensation for the expenses incurred in the war you will pay an indemnity of fifteen thousand talents: five hundred now, twenty-five hundred when the senate and the Roman people ratify the treaty, and one thousand annually for twelve years. In addition, you must pay to Eumenes four hundred talents and the remainder of the grain which was owed to his father. When we have concluded this treaty, you will give twenty hostages of our choosing as security that you will abide by it. But never shall we be certain of your peaceful attitude toward the Roman people as long as you have Hannibal. Above all else we demand his surrender. You will also surrender Thoas the Aetolian who instigated the Aetolian war, and who aroused you and the Aetolians against us by inspiring you with confidence in each other. In addition to him you must surrender Mnasilochus the Acarnanian, and the Chalcidians Philo and Eubulidas. The king's position as he negotiates this peace is worse because he makes it later than he might have. If he wishes now to delay, let him be sure that the majesty of kings is pulled down from the zenith to the middle with more difficulty, than it is precipitated from the middle to the nadir."

Book 38
1 8 9 - 1 8 7 B C

In the lull after the defeat of Hannibal and of An-
tiochus, political rivalry came to the fore. One faction was
headed by Publius Scipio Africanus, who represented the
office-holding oligarchy and supported an enlightened
foreign policy; the other by Marcus Porcius Cato, who for
political reasons advocated isolationism and broader
access to positions of civic and military leadership.

50. All dissension and all concern over the question
of Gnaeus Manlius' triumph were eclipsed by the rise of
a greater controversy, involving a greater and more
famous man. According to the testimony of Valerius, Publius Scipio Africanus was indicted by two tribunes, both
named Quintus Petillius. The meaning of this arraignment
was interpreted by different people in different ways.
Some blamed not the plebeian tribunes but the state itself
for enduring such an outrage. The two greatest cities in
the world, they said, at almost the same time had shown
their ingratitude toward their leading citizens. But Rome's
ingratitude was more blameworthy. Carthage had exiled
Hannibal after defeat, but Rome was banishing Africanus
who had led them to victory. On the other hand, other
men insisted that no single citizen should be so exalted
that he could not be held accountable for his actions according to law. There was no more important safeguard
for equal liberty, they said, than the right to indict any
citizen—even the most powerful. How could anything

at all—not to speak of the very existence of the state—
be entrusted to any man if he could not be required to
render an account of his conduct? If any man could not
endure equality before the law, no measures taken against
him were unjustified.

These opposing points of view were argued until the
day of the trial arrived. No one—not even Scipio himself
when he was consul or censor—had ever been accompanied to the Forum by a larger throng than
was Scipio as he proceeded to his trial. When ordered to
make his defense he did not even mention the charges
against him, but he spoke with such eloquence of all his
accomplishments that everyone felt that no man had ever
been praised better or more truly. He described his career
with the same dauntless self-confidence with which he
had conducted it. No one took offense because he was
speaking to protect rather than to exalt himself.

51. In order to bolster their present charges the
tribunes reverted to the old innuendoes about luxurious
excesses in the winter quarters at Syracuse and the disturbance caused by Pleminius at Locri. They also brought
charges that Scipio had accepted bribes, but these were
based more on suspicion than on proof: when his son had
been captured he had been returned without ransom. In
all other respects Antiochus had paid court to him, as if
peace and war with Rome lay in his hands. He had been
more like a dictator than a lieutenant to the consul (his
brother Lucius) when he had accompanied him to his
province of Greece. In Spain, Gaul, Sicily and Africa it
was firmly believed that he was both the source and buttress of Roman prestige and power; that under Scipio's
protective shadow lay the city which was mistress of the
world; that his nod was as authoritative as a decree of
the senate or an act of the assembly. He had gone with
Lucius for no other purpose than to encourage these opin-

ions in Greece and Asia, among all the kings and peoples
of the East.

When the tribunes were unable to brand him with dis-
honor they attempted to appeal to envy against him.
The speeches ran on into the night, and the trial was adjourned until the following day. The next morning the
tribunes took their places on the rostra at dawn. When
the defendant was summoned he marched through the
assembly to the rostra followed by a long line of friends
and clients. When the assembly became silent, he said,
"Tribunes of the plebs, and you, Quirites, this is the an-
niversary of my successful battle with Hannibal in Africa.
It is fitting, therefore, for us to dispense today with the
bickering of litigation. I shall proceed immediately to the
Capitol to offer my prayers to Jupiter Optimus Maximus
and Juno and the other gods who protect the citadel. I
shall give thanks to them that on this date and many other
times they gave me the ability and the opportunity to
perform great services for the state. All of you, too,
who have the time, come with me, and pray that you
may always have leaders like me. For from the age of
seventeen you have granted me offices before I was of the
legal age for them; but I have always anticipated your
honors by my achievements."

With these words he marched from the rostra to the
Capitol. The whole assembly turned and followed Scipio
out, until even the clerks and pages deserted the tribunes;
no one remained except the slaves attending them and the
herald who summoned the defendant to trial.

Accompanied by the Roman people Scipio visited all
the temples of the gods, not only on the Capitol but
throughout the city. That day he was more exalted by
popular esteem and by a true recognition of his greatness
than on the day he rode through the city in triumph after
his victories over King Syphax and the Carthaginians.

52. This was the last day to dawn in glory upon Publius Scipio. He foresaw further denunciation and further wrangling with the tribunes; and so, after obtaining an extended adjournment of his case, he went into retirement at Liternum, specifically in order to avoid standing trial. His self-respect was too great, and his position in life had been too high, for him now to see himself on trial or be submitted to the indignity of defending his honor.

When the day of the trial came and he was summoned to come forward Lucius Scipio apologized for his absence, saying that he was ill. The tribunes who had indicted him would not accept this excuse and asserted that he refused to stand trial out of arrogance; this same attitude had prompted him to turn his back on the tribunes and walk out of the court. Those same people, they said, whom he was depriving of the right to judge him he had dragged behind him like prisoners of war in a triumph over the Roman people; that day he had led a latter-day secession from the tribunes to the Capitol. "Here you have the reward of your impetuosity: the very man who led you to abandon us now has deserted you. Seventeen years ago when he commanded an army and a fleet, we dared to send an aedile and a tribune of the plebs to Sicily to take him into custody and bring him back to Rome. But our courage has gradually waned to the point that now when he holds no office we do not dare to bring him back from his villa to stand trial."

Lucius Scipio appealed to the tribunes as a whole and they made the following decision: Since a plea of illness had been offered this plea should be accepted and the hearing be adjourned by those who had brought the indictment. One of the tribunes at that time was Tiberius Sempronius Gracchus, who was on unfriendly terms with Scipio. Gracchus forbade his name to be attached to the decree, and everyone expected a more uncompromising decision from him. The decree he issued ran as follows: "Since Lucius Scipio has submitted a plea of illness for his absent brother this seems to me to be sufficient. Moreover I shall not permit a date to be set for a trial before he returns to Rome; and if he then appeals to me I shall prevent his standing trial. Through his own achievements and the honors conferred upon him by the Roman people Publius Scipio has reached a position of great dignity in the sight of gods and men. For him now to be forced to stand before the rostra as a defendant and listen to the scurrility of adolescents would be grotesque. It would be a greater disgrace to the Roman people than to him."

53. After reading his decision he addressed the assembly indignantly: "Is Scipio, the conqueror of Africa, to stand beneath your feet, Tribunes? Was it to this end that in Spain he routed four Carthaginian armies led by Carthage's most renowned generals? For this did he capture Syphax, conquer Hannibal, make Carthage our tributary, and, with the help of his brother, push back Antiochus east of the Taurus Mountains? Did he do all this in order to abase himself before these two Petillii? Will you allow them to triumph over Publius Africanus? Can great men never, by virtue of their own merits and the honors you bestow upon them, reach a safe and sacred refuge where they may rest in old age, if not revered, at least inviolate?" These words, along with the opinion he submitted, excited the sympathy of even the prosecutors; they said that they would deliberate further on the measures their office required.

After the dismissal of the assembly of the plebs, the senate convened. All of the senators, especially the older men and those of consular rank, expressed great gratitude toward Tiberius Gracchus for holding the public good above his personal enmities. The Petillii were virulently attacked for seeking publicity by demagogically maligning another, and for wishing to reap spoils from a victory over Africanus. Henceforth no more was said about Scipio. He passed the remainder of his life at Liternum, without wishing ever to see the city. It is said that when he died he asked to be buried there at his country estate so that his funeral might not be held in his ungrateful native city.

Scipio was a remarkable man, although more noted for his military than his civic accomplishments. He achieved greater fame during the first part of his life than during his old age. His youth was spent amid constant warfare; but with his old age his glory also declined and no further opportunity arose for him to use his abilities. What was his second consulship or even his censorship compared with his first? What honor did he receive from his service as lieutenant in Asia when he was hampered by ill-health and saddened by the misfortune of his son? And after his return he was reduced to the necessity of standing trial or banishing himself from his native city. Nevertheless he won undying glory for bringing to an end the Punic War, the greatest and most dangerous ever fought.

54. With Scipio's death his enemies grew bolder. Their leader was Marcus Porcius Cato. During Scipio's lifetime Cato frequently disparaged Scipio's greatness, and it was thought that it was he who induced the Petillii to indict Scipio. After Scipio's death these same tribunes introduced this motion in the assembly: "Is it your will and pleasure, Quirites, that Servius Sulpicius, the praetor of the city, shall introduce to the senate the proposal that they should delegate one of the praetors to conduct an inquiry concerning the money which was seized and exacted from King Antiochus and his subjects but has not been accounted for to the state?" . . . Lucius Scipio, who obviously was going to speak more in his own defense than against the bill, arose to oppose it. He com-

plained that this motion had been presented only after the death of his brother, Publius Africanus, the bravest and most distinguished of men. It was too little that Africanus had received no funeral encomium at his death; now he was to endure accusations of malfeasance. The Carthaginians had been content to exile Hannibal. But the Romans were not even satisfied with Scipio's death. They must malign his character as he lay in his grave, and his brother must be sacrificed as a sop to their malice. The motion was supported by M. Cato. His speech "On the money of King Antiochus" is still extant, and his influence discouraged the Mummii from opposing the proposal. They withdrew their veto and the motion was passed by a unanimous vote of the tribal assembly.

Book 39

1 8 7 - 1 8 3   B C

The original function of the censorship was to register all citizens and divide them into property classes. In time, however, the censors came to assume for themselves the right to consider qualifications other than that of wealth and to reduce citizens to lower classes on such vague grounds as bad citizenship and moral turpitude. Since the duty of reviewing and revising the membership roll of the senate also rested in their hands this arbitrary power could be felt by the most powerful men in the state. In addition the censors supervised the collection of taxes and were in charge of contracts for public works. Marcus Porcius Cato, Scipio Africanus' old enemy, was elected to this office in 184 B.C. *along with Lucius Valerius Flaccus.*

40. Another election followed, which was of greater importance and involved more numerous and more powerful men. This was the election for the censorship; for this position L. Valerius Flaccus, Publius Scipio Nasica and Lucius Scipio, Gnaeus Manlius Vulso, L. Furius Purpurio, all patricians, as well as the plebeians M. Porcius Cato, M. Fulvius Nobilior, Titus Sempronius Longus and Marcus Sempronius Tuditanus, all contended. But of all of these men, both plebeians and patricians of the most eminent families in Rome, by far the most prominent was Cato. He was a man of such ability and determination that he would have undoubtedly made a name for himself no matter how obscure his origins. He possessed great competence in every phase of business, both public and private. He was equally experienced in farm management and urban affairs. Some men have risen to prominence through their knowledge of law, others through their eloquence, still others through military skill. So versatile was this man's genius that one would say he had been born to any task he undertook. As a soldier he was extremely courageous and distinguished himself in many important battles; when he had advanced to a position of prominence he became an able general. In peace, when consulted on legal matters, he proved most learned in the law. When he had to plead a case he did so eloquently. He was not content to fascinate his contemporaries with his tongue, and to leave no monument of his eloquence. On the contrary, his eloquence still lives and thrives, immortalized in writings of every kind. There are many speeches in his own defense, in the defense of others, and against still others. For he plagued his enemies not only by prosecuting them, but

even when speaking in his own defense. Scores of feuds badgered him constantly, and he in turn allowed them no respite; it would be difficult to say whether the aristocracy toiled harder to suppress him or he to harass them. There is no doubt that he was a severe and uncompromising man, whose tongue was often caustic and too outspoken. But he was never bested by his passions. He was a man of rigid integrity who scorned wealth as well as personal popularity. His habits were sober and thrifty. With iron resolution he inured his body to endurance of toil and danger. Even old age with which everything declines could not vitiate the vigor of his mind. At the age of eighty-six he pleaded a case in which he wrote and delivered his own speech of defense; at the age of ninety he indicted Servius Galba before the assembly.

41. Just as they had done throughout his life, the aristocrats now opposed him as a candidate for the censorship. Except for Flaccus, who had been his colleague in the consulship, all the candidates intrigued to deprive him of the office. They were ambitious for the position themselves, and were indignant at the thought of a man whose father had not even been consul becoming censor; but still more important, they feared that since he had been wronged by many men and was anxious for reprisal his censorship would be a severe one, prejudicial to many reputations. Even in canvasing for votes he assumed an aggressive attitude; he charged that those who were trying to defeat his candidacy were afraid of a courageous and equitable censorship. At the same time he campaigned for Flaccus also; with that colleague alone, he said, he could repress modern immorality and reëstablish traditional moral ideals. With such words he won ardent support; against the opposition of the aristocrats the people not only made Cato censor but gave him Flaccus as his colleague as well.

42. Amid great apprehension the censors Cato and
Flaccus began their review of the membership of the senate. They removed seven names from the roll, including
that of one eminent man, the former consul, Lucius Quinctius Flamininus. It is said that it was once the practice for
the censors to attach explanatory remarks to the names of
those removed from the senate roll. But Cato in addition
made several virulent speeches, which are still extant,
against those whom he reduced from the rank of senator
or knight. The most bitter by far is the speech against
Flamininus; if Cato had delivered this speech in accusation of Flamininus before his election as censor, Flamininus could not have been retained on the senate
roll by anyone—not even if his brother Titus had been
censor at that time. Among other things he charged that
Flamininus had promised huge gifts to a notorious cata-
mite, Philip, a Carthaginian, to accompany him to
his province in Gaul. In order to fetch a higher price for
his favors this boy was accustomed to mock him playfully
and to upbraid him for taking him away from Rome just
before the gladiatorial games. One day when they were
dining and had become heated with wine, it was announced that a Boian noble accompanied by his children
had just arrived as a deserter; he wished to see the consul to receive a personal guarantee of safety from him.
The man was led into the tent and began to address the
consul through an interpreter. While he was speaking
Flamininus turned to his paramour and said, "Since you
missed the gladiatorial show, do you wish to see this Gaul
die?" The boy nodded, thinking he was jesting; but Flamininus immediately seized a sword which hung over head
and struck the Gaul in the head; when the Gaul turned to
flee, imploring the protection of the Roman people and
those who were present, he stabbed him in the side.

43. Valerius Antias, who had never read the speech

of Cato and depended upon a tale of uncertain origin
which was in circulation, gives a version which is different in detail but very similar in its capricious brutality.
Flamininus invited to dinner a woman of ill repute from
Placentia with whom he was infatuated. Bragging to the
courtesan, who lay beside him on the couch, among other
things he told her what a ruthless judge he was and how
many people he had in custody condemned to be beheaded. She mentioned that she had never seen a be-
heading but that she would like to very much. At this the
indulgent lover ordered one of the miserable wretches to
be brought in to him, and he cut off his head. Whether
the incident occurred as the censor says or as Valerius
tells it, it was an atrocious deed. In the midst of feasting
and drinking, when it is the custom to pour libations and
to pray to the gods for blessings, a human victim was
sacrificed and the table spattered with blood—to satisfy a
fickle jade lying in the consul's arms! At the end of his
speech Cato challenged Flamininus to take legal action
if he denied his charges; but if he admitted them, he
asked if he thought anyone would grieve at his disgrace,
since in a frenzy of drunken lust he had entertained himself by shedding human blood.

44. In revising the list of the knights the censors struck
the name of Lucius Scipio Asiaticus from the roll. The tax
rates which they established were oppressive to all classes.
The clerks were directed to assess all women's clothing,
jewelry, and carriages worth more than fifteen thousand
asses at ten times their values. Slaves less than twenty
years old which had been bought within the last five years
for ten thousand *asses* or more were to be listed at ten
times this value; all these items were to be taxed at the
rate of three *asses* per one thousand. All water piped
from a public acqueduct into a private building was shut
off. All private buildings built on public property were

demolished with thirty days notice. Then with money appropriated for these purposes they let contracts to pave reservoirs with stone, cleaning sewers wherever it was necessary, and for constructing others on the Aventine and elsewhere where there still were none. In addition, a highway over the hill at Formiae was built. Independently, Flaccus constructed a causeway over the Waters of Neptune. Cato bought for the state two market buildings, the Maenium and the Titium, and four shops near the Lautumiae; he also erected there a law court known as the Basilica Porcia. The censors farmed out taxes to the highest bidders and let contracts for public works to the lowest. With loud complaints the tax farmers prevailed upon the senate to order the original contracts abrogated and new ones made. The censors, in answer to this, barred from the bidding those who had been instrumental in causing the cancellation of the old contracts, and let new ones at slightly lower rates. This censorship was notable for the bitterness and dissidence it caused. Since Cato was given all credit for all its severity the grudges which resulted plagued him for the rest of his life.

51. In 195 B.C. Hannibal's political enemies accused him before the Roman senate of intrigue with their enemies in Greece and Asia Minor. Because of this Hannibal was forced to flee for asylum to the court of Antiochus III of Syria, where he remained until Antiochus was conquered by Rome in 190 B.C. Again he fled, this time to Prusias, king of Bithynia. When Prusias became involved in war with Eumenes of Pergamum, who solicited Rome's aid, the senate seized upon this pretext, in 183 B.C., to send Titus Quinctius Flamininus as an envoy to Bithynia, to demand Hannibal's extradition.

Prusias was held in disfavor in Rome because he had granted asylum to Hannibal after the flight of Antiochus,

and because he was waging war against Eumenes. Titus
Quinctius Flamininus was sent as an emissary to remon-
strate with him, among other things, for harboring this
man, who of all men living was most hostile to the Roman
people. He had instigated first his own country, then, after
its defeat, King Antiochus, to make war against Rome.
Perhaps because of Flamininus' reproach, or perhaps to
ingratiate himself with the Roman people, Prusias was
persuaded to kill Hannibal or to surrender him to
Flamininus. After the first conference Flamininus' soldiers
were sent to guard Hannibal's house.

Hannibal always had anticipated such an end, for he
recognized the ineradicable hatred the Romans had for
him and distrusted the good faith of kings. He had previously witnessed their capriciousness, and he had anticipated Flamininus' arrival with terror, since he knew it
spelled death for him. Because of his perpetual danger he
wished always to have some route provided for escape.
Therefore in his house he had built seven exits, some of
them secret. But the awful power of kings leaves nothing unexplored; a heavy guard was placed all around the
house to prevent any chance at all of escape. When Hannibal was informed that guards had been stationed in his
vestibule he tried to leave by a side door which was very
well hidden. Finding that this was blockaded by soldiers
he asked for the poison which many years before he had
prepared for just such an emergency. "Since the Roman
people are weary of waiting for the death of an old man,"
he said, "let me relieve them of their tedium. This death
of a man who is unarmed and betrayed will be no memorable triumph for Flamininus. This day will prove how
much the character of the Roman people has changed.
When King Pyrrhus was commanding a hostile army in
Italy, their forefather's admonished him to beware of
poisoning; but they have sent a former consul as an

envoy to induce Prusias to murder his guest." After calling down curses upon the head of Prusias and invoking the gods of hospitality to witness his breach of faith, he drained the cup. Such was the end of Hannibal's life.

52. According to both Polybius and Rutilius, Scipio died that same year. However I do not agree with them.

Book 40
1 8 2 - 1 7 9 B C

After the Second Macedonian war Philip V of Macedon had been allowed to retain his sovereignty. Later, Macedonian relations with Rome again became strained and Philip's younger son, Demetrius, was sent to Rome to try to effect a reconciliation. When Demetrius became popular in the ruling circles of the Romans, Philip's other son Perseus saw in him a danger to his own right of succession, and succeeded in persuading his father that Demetrius was a traitor. At Perseus' instigation Philip executed his younger son, but soon after bitterly repented his rashness.

54. In that year [179 B.C.] Philip, king of Macedon, died, wasted with old age and grief at the death of his son. He was wintering at Demetrias, tortured by longing for his son and by remorse for his own cruel brutality. He also was embittered toward his other son, who now in his own opinion as well as that of others was as good as king. All eyes were turned toward Perseus, and Philip was deserted in his old age; most men merely were waiting for his death,

and others did not even bother to wait. This neglect increased his misery, which was shared by Antigonus, son of
Echecrates. This man was named for his uncle, who had
been Philip's guardian; he had been a man of regal dignity
and was famed for his victory over Cleomenes of Sparta.
He was given the surname "the guardian" by the Greeks
to distinguish him from his royal namesakes. His nephew
Antigonus remained to the end the one true friend
among all the men whom Philip had honored. This
loyalty had made Philip's son Perseus, who was in no wise
a friend, Antigonus' implacable enemy, and he foresaw
how dangerous to himself Perseus' succession to the
throne would be. When he saw that the king was beginning to repent and sometimes to sigh with longing for
his dead son, he undertook to become a companion in his
grief. He sympathetically offered Philip his ear and even
sometimes himself lamented the rashness of the act. And
since truth usually leaves its own traces, he worked
wholeheartedly to discover all the facts in the case.
Apelles and Philocles were suspected of being Perseus'
accomplices; they had been ambassadors to Rome and
had brought back the damning letter which bore the sig-
nature of Flamininus.

55. There were now general murmurings in the palace
that the letter had been forged by a scribe and stamped
with a counterfeit seal. While the matter was still only
suspected and there still was no clear proof, Antigonus
happened to come upon Xychus. He apprehended him
and took him into the palace where he put him under
guard. Then, going to Philip he said, "I am sure, from my
conversations with you, that you would like very much to
know which of your sons was betrayed by the other.
Xychus, the only man in the world who can solve this
puzzle for you, is now in your power. I came upon him
by accident and ordered him taken into custody." Once

in the palace, this man attempted to deny everything; but he was so diffident and apprehensive that with a little pressure he confessed the whole plot. He could not bear the sight of the torturer and the lash, and gave a detailed account of the ambassador's intrigue, including his own complicity in it.

Immediately men were sent to arrest them, and Philocles, who was not far away, was apprehended. Apelles, who had been sent in pursuit of a certain Chaereas, got wind of Xychus' confession and crossed over into Italy. There is no clear account of what happened to Philocles. Some declare that first he stoutly denied the evidence, but that when Xychus was brought into his presence he could hold out no longer; others say that he steadfastly defied even the rack. Philip's grief was redoubled, and he thought himself all the more unfortunate in his children because one of them still remained alive.

56. Perseus was informed that all had been discovered, but considered himself too powerful to make flight necessary. He took care only to keep his distance while Philip was still alive, and to guard himself against his burning wrath. But Philip, since he had no hope of seizing and punishing him, determined at least to prevent his reaping the reward for his crime. On the other hand he was obligated to Antigonus for uncovering proof of the crime, and thought that because of the fame of his uncle the Macedonians would not resent him as a king. He therefore summoned him and said, "I have reached the point that childlessness, which other men so abominate, seems a thing to be desired. I wish to leave to you the kingdom which your uncle protected with faithful care and even enlarged. You are the only one I have left who is worthy of the throne. If I had no one I should prefer it to perish from the earth rather than to fall to Perseus as a reward for his damnable crime. You alone wept with me over De-

metrius' undeserved death. It would seem to me that Demetrius had returned from the dead if I could leave you
in his place." From that time forward Philip labored increasingly to honor Antigonus in every way. When Perseus was away in Thrace he traveled through the cities of
Macedon recommending Antigonus to their leaders. If
he had lived he undoubtedly intended to leave him in
possession of the throne.

After leaving Antigonus he stopped for some time in
Thessalonica. From there, after arriving in Amphipolis,
he was stricken with a serious illness. His illness was not
of the body but of the mind. The image of his dead son
seemed constantly to hound him, and he could not sleep
for his haunted desperation. He died with a curse for Perseus on his lips.

Antigonus might have been warned if he had been
present or if the king's death had been disclosed at once.
But the death was unexpected and Perseus had suborned
Calligines, the physician of the king; when Calligines recognized that there was no hope for Philip, by pre-arrange-
ment he sent messengers to Perseus and concealed the
news of the death from those outside the palace until Perseus arrived.

57. Perseus fell upon all his enemies before they knew
or even suspected, and seized by violence the throne he
had won by crime.

Epitome of Book 41
1 7 8 - 1 7 4 B C

The fire went out in the temple of Vesta. The proconsul Tiberius Sempronius Gracchus defeated the Celtiberians and accepted their surrender. As a monument to his achievements he founded the town of Gracchuris in Spain. The Vaccaei and the Lusitani were subjugated by the proconsul Postumius Albinus. Both men were granted triumphs. Upon the death of Seleucus, who had inherited the kingdom of his father Antiochus III, his brother Antiochus was sent home by the city to succeed to the throne of Syria. Antiochus was a pious man and erected many magnificent temples in many places, including one to Jupiter Olympius at Athens and another at Antioch to Jupiter Capitolinus. Otherwise he cut a poor figure as king. The census was completed by the censors, and the population was reckoned at 258,294. The tribune of the plebs Quintus Voconius Saxa procured the enactment of a law forbidding anyone to name a woman as his heir. This law was supported by Marcus Cato, whose speech urging its passage is extant. This book contains, in addition, accounts of successful expeditions by a number of generals against the Ligurians, Histrians, Sardinians, and Celtiberians. It describes also the beginning of the Macedonian War which was being fomented by Perseus, the son of Philip. To Carthage he had sent an embassy to whom the Carthaginians had granted audience by night. He also was making overtures to other Greek states.

Perseus was a wise and careful administrator, but the Romans came to suspect Macedon's economic growth and increasing influence in the affairs of its neighbors as a military threat. In 172 B.C., when his enemy Eumenes of Pergamum protested Perseus' growing power, the Senate was quick to believe him. Perseus' envoy Harpalus returned to Macedon to announce that Rome was on the verge of declaring war.

15. Perseus himself now believed that war would come and even desired it; for he was sure that he was at the height of his power. He hated Eumenes above all others and resolved to begin the war with his lifeblood. He bribed Evander, a Cretan, the commander of his auxiliaries, and three Macedonians who were experienced at such crimes, to assassinate the king. It had been ascertained that Eumenes intended to go to Delphi to sacrifice to Apollo. Therefore he gave them a letter of introduction to Praxo, a friend of his and a rich and influential woman among the Delphians.

The assassins, led by Evander, arrived ahead of Eumenes, and searched about for a suitable place to finish their undertaking. As you went up the hill toward the temple from Cirrha, the port of Delphi, before you reached the surrounding buildings there was a mud wall to the left of the path. At the foot of this wall the path narrowed, so that people could only pass single file; a landslide had left a precipice of some depth just to the right. They hid themselves behind the wall on steps which they had built up against it, intending to use it as a rampart and hurl missiles from it at the king as he passed. The king disembarked and started toward the temple, surrounded by a large number of friends and attendants. Soon, however, the path began to narrow and fewer could walk beside him. When they reached the point which they had to pass single file, Pantaleon, a leader of the Aetolians, was walking ahead of the king talking to him. Suddenly the assassins rose up and hurled two large rocks at Eumenes, one of which hit his head, the other his shoulder. He was knocked unconscious and fell over the precipice; many more rocks were rolled on him as he lay at the bottom. When they saw the king fall, the rest of his escort fled; but Pantaleon staunchly stood his ground in order to protect the king.

16. The assassins might have made sure of killing the king by running a short distance around the wall. Instead they ran up to the top of Mt. Parnassus as if they had finished their task. In such haste were they that when one of their own companions could not keep up over the rough terrain and was slowing them down, they killed him to keep him from informing against them. At first the king's friends, then his attendants and slaves, ran to his body and raised him up still unconscious. They realized that he was alive from the warmth of his body and his faint breathing, but had almost no hope that he would live. Some of the attendants followed the assassins' tracks, but abandoned the hopeless chase in exhaustion. The Macedonians had undertaken their attack boldly but without sufficient deliberation; as a result they had fled in heedless panic.

The next day the king, who now had recovered consciousness, was carried to his ship by his friends. From there they sailed to Corinth, where they made a portage across the Isthmus and continued on to Aegina. There his wound was treated with such secrecy that the rumor reached Asia that he had died. Even Attalus himself believed it, with an alacrity prejudicial to fraternal concord; he spoke to his brother's wife and the commander of the citadel as if he were the successor to the throne. Eumenes discovered this, but decided to disregard it and to bear it in silence. However, at their first meeting he could not resist rebuking Attalus for his premature hurry to marry his wife. The rumor of Eumenes' death even reached Rome.

17. At about that same time Gaius Valerius was sent to Greece to survey the state of affairs there and to determine Perseus' intentions. He returned with information coinciding in every respect with the accusations made by Eumenes. He also brought back with him from Delphi Praxo, in whose house the assassins had stayed, and Lucius Rammius of Brundisium, who told the following story:

Rammius was an important man in Brundisium. He was accustomed to entertain in his house Roman generals as well as eminent foreign ambassadors—especially those representing monarchies. As a result of this he became acquainted with Perseus, even though Perseus' kingdom was some distance away. Subsequently he received a letter from the king giving him hope of a more intimate friendship and in consequence great riches. After making a trip to see the king, in a short time he began to be on very familiar terms and to be drawn more than he desired into the king's secret deliberations. Since he had been accustomed to entertain all the generals and ambassadors from Rome, Perseus offered him bribes to poison those whose names he would send him in a dispatch. He realized, he said, that the preparation of poison was difficult and dangerous; too many accomplices were necessary and the outcome was uncertain; it was difficult to make it strong enough to be effective and still capable of being safely concealed. However, he would give him a potion which would be detected neither during consumption nor afterward. Rammius was afraid that if he refused, the poison would be tested on him. So he promised to do as he was requested and set out for home. However, he was anxious not to return to Brundisium before seeing Gaius Valerius, who he heard was near Chalcis. When he gave Valerius this information he was ordered to come with him to Rome, where he was presented to the senate and told his story.

18. Because of this information together with the testimony of Eumenes, war was immediately declared against Perseus; for it was evident that he not only was preparing honorable warfare, as befitted a king, but was resorting to the furtive crimes of ambush and poisoning.

Epitome of Book 43
1 7 1 - 1 6 9   B C

Several praetors were condemned for cruel and avaricious administration of their provinces. The proconsul Publius Licinius Crassus took a number of Greek cities by assault and sacked them cruelly. As a result, the senate ordered the restoration of the captives whom he had sold into slavery. Many excesses also were perpetrated against the allies by commanders of the Roman fleets. The book contains accounts of the successful campaigns of King Perseus in Thrace as well as his conquest of the

Dardanians and of King Gentius of Illyria. A rebellion led by Olonicus in Spain, failed when he was killed. Marcus Aemilius Lepidus was chosen leader of the senate by the censors.

Epitome of Book 44
1 6 9 - 1 6 8 B C

Quintus Marcius Philippus made his way through trackless passes into Macedonia. The Rhodians sent ambassadors to Rome to warn that they would aid Perseus unless the Roman people made peace with him. This created great indignation. The conduct of the war was entrusted to Lucius Aemilius Paulus, who was consul for the second time in the following year. Before the assembly he prayed that whatever calamity menaced the Roman people might fall upon his own house. Journeying into Macedonia, he defeated Perseus and subjugated all of Macedonia. Before the conflict he warned the army not to be bewildered by an eclipse of the moon which would occur the following night. Gentius, the king of Illyria, renewed the conflict and was defeated by the praetor Lucius Anicius. Upon his surrender he was sent to Rome with his wife and children. Legates sent by Queen Cleopatra and King Ptolemy arrived from Alexandria to complain that Antiochus king of Syria was making war on them. Perseus had solicited the aid of Eumenes, king of Pergamum and Gentius king of Illyria, but was abandoned by them when he failed to produce the money which he had promised.

Book 45
1 6 8 - 1 6 7 B C

The Third Macedonian War dragged on for three years, with neither side scoring any brilliant successes. Finally in 168 B.C. the Roman consul Lucius Aemilius Paulus met Perseus at Pydna and cut his army to pieces. Perseus first attempted flight, then surrendered to the Romans.

4. While Aemilius Paulus was encamped, as I said above, at Sirae in the Odomantic region of Thrace, three beggarly looking men arrived bringing a message from Perseus. It is said that when he saw these men Paulus shed tears at the caprice of human fortune. Not long before this man had not been satisfied with the kingdom of Macedonia but had invaded the Dardanians and Illyrians, and had called the Bastarnae to his aid. Now with his army lost he was exiled from his country, driven to asylum on a little island, where he was protected by the inviolability of its shrine—not by his own power. But when he read, "King Perseus sends greetings to the consul Paulus," he forgot all his pity in indignation at the man's total disregard of his circumstances. The tone of the entreaties in the rest of the letter were anything but authoritative, but nevertheless he sent the envoys away with no answer. Perseus then realized that since he was defeated he would have to forget his title. In a second message he omitted it and asked that someone be sent to him to discuss his status and his present circumstances. Three en-

voys were sent, Publius Lentulus, Aulus Postumius Albinus, and Aulus Antonius. Nothing was accomplished by this mission, since Perseus clung to his royal designation, while Paulus insisted that he surrender himself and all his possessions to the mercies of the Roman people.

5. Meanwhile the fleet under the command of Gnaeus Octavius dropped anchor at Samothrace. With a show of force he hoped to intimidate Perseus and by threats and promises to persuade him to capitulate. An incident which occurred accidentally, or possibly by contrivance, aided him in this attempt. An able young man named Atilius noticed that the people of Samothrace had gathered to an assembly, and asked their officials to be allowed to say a few words to the people. When permission was granted, he said, "We have heard, Samothracian hosts, that the soil of this island is sacred and inviolable. Is this true?" When everyone answered Yes, he continued, "Then why has this sanctity been violated by a murderer tainted with the blood of King Eumenes? When every participation in all sacred rites is prohibited to those who hands are unclean, do you allow your innermost sanctuaries to be polluted by the hands of an assassin?"

The story of Evander's near-successful attempt to murder Eumenes was well known throughout Greece. The Samothracians thought that this reproach was not unjust; and besides they realized that they and their whole island were in Roman power. Therefore they sent Theondas, their highest magistrate, whom they call "king," to Perseus to announce that Evander the Cretan had been accused of murder. They had a traditional procedure, he said, for trying those accused of entering the sacred confines of the temple with impure hands. If Evander was confident that he could prove himself innocent of murder, he should come forward and defend himself; but if he did not dare to submit to a trial he should free the temple of the pollution and protect himself to the best of his ability. Perseus led Evander aside and urged him not to risk standing trial: his opponents had the advantage of him with regard to influence as well as the merits of their case. (Actually he was apprehensive that Evander would be condemned and would expose him as the instigator of the crime.) What now could Evander do, he asked, but die bravely? Evander did not openly refuse. Saying that he preferred to die by poison rather than by the sword, he secretly prepared to flee; but his plans were discovered and reported to the king. Perseus then ordered that Evander be put to death; he was frightened that the Samothracians would turn their anger on himself, thinking that he had helped Evander escape. When the impulsive murder had been committed the realization immediately came to him that he had drawn upon his own head all of Evander's pollution: Evander had wounded Eumenes at Delphi, but he himself had killed Evander at Samothrace. Thus the two most sacred sanctuaries on earth had been polluted with human blood by one man. However, he avoided the possibility of such an accusation by bribing Theondas to say that Evander had committed suicide.

6. This last outrage alienated everyone from him; he had murdered his one remaining friend, with whom he had shared so many trials, and who had been betrayed because he had refused to betray him. Everyone began to defect to the Romans, and Perseus, left almost alone, was forced to consider measures for escape. There was a Cretan merchant named Oroandes who had traded along the coast of Thrace and knew it well. He requested this man to take him on board and carry him to Cotys. At one of the headlands on Samothrace is a harbor called Demetrium; here Oroandes' ship was docked. At about sunset, all of Perseus' necessary baggage, including as much money as he could carry in concealment, was taken

down to the ship. In the middle of the night the king himself with three accomplices slipped out a back door into
a garden near his bedchamber; after much difficulty in
climbing the garden wall they made good their escape to
the shore. But Oroandes had waited only long enough to
take aboard the money; as soon as it was dark he had set
sail for Crete. When Perseus found the ship gone, for a
long time he wandered aimlessly along the shore. He did
not dare return to his own quarters and at last seeing the
coming dawn, he hid in a dark corner along the side of the
temple.

In Macedonia certain sons of prominent citizens were
chosen as attendants to the king, and were known as the
"royal pages." This group followed the king in flight to
Samothrace; they refused to abandon him until Octavius
ordered a crier to proclaim that all the king's pages
and other Macedonians who surrendered to the Romans
would be guaranteed their personal safety and freedom,
and would be allowed to keep all property both in their
possession and in Macedonia. At this announcement they
defected in a body and gave their names to Gaius Postumius, the military tribune. Ion of Thessalonica also surrendered the king's small children to Octavius. The only
child who remained with him was his eldest son, Philip.
Finally Perseus surrendered himself and his son, denouncing the gods to whom the temple belonged for not
aiding suppliants. Octavius ordered that he and what
money he had left be put in the flagship, and immediately
the fleet set sail back to Amphipolis. From there he sent
ahead a dispatch to the consul, informing him that he had
Perseus in custody and was bringing him to his camp.

7. At this news Paulus offered sacrifice of thanksgiving, justly considering this a second victory. Then, calling
a council, he read them the dispatch, and sent Quintus
Aelius Tubero to meet the king. Everyone else he or-

dered to remain assembled at his headquarters. Never had so large a multitude gathered for any spectacle. In the time of their fathers the King Syphax had been captured and led in custody into the Roman camp. But he was a far less famous king from a far less famous country; besides, his role in the Second Punic War was but a minor one. The same was true of Gentius in the Macedonian War. But Perseus had been the very cause of this war. And he was distinguished not only by his own renown, but by that of his father and grandfather, and his great predecessors Philip and Alexander, who had given the Macedonians sovereignty over the whole world. Perseus entered the camp dressed in mourning, without a single companion to share his misfortune and make it more pitiable. His way was blocked by the crowd surging around to see the spectacle, until the consul sent lictors who pushed the crowd back and made a path to the consul's headquarters. The consul arose to greet him, telling his companions to remain seated, and walked a few steps forward to extend his hand to the king. The king flung himself before his feet; but raising him up, the consul refused to let him touch his knees, and led him into the tent where he ordered him to sit opposite the members of the council.

9. This was the end of the war between the Romans and Perseus, which had been waged for four consecutive years. It was the end, too, of a kingdom renowned throughout most of Europe and all of Asia. From Caranus, the first, to Perseus, there were twenty kings in all. Perseus came to power during the consulship of Quintus Fulvius and Lucius Manlius, was recognized by the senate while Marcus Junius and Aulus Manlius were consuls, and reigned eleven years. The kingdom of Macedon was obscure and unimportant until the reign of Philip, son of Amyntas [359-336 B.C.]. In his time it began to grow, embracing all Greece and parts of Thrace and Illyria; but

it still was confined within the boundaries of Europe. During the reign of Alexander which followed, it extended into Asia. Within thirteen years Alexander brought under his sway the enormous Persian empire; he traveled over Arabia and India, where the farthest limits of the earth are girdled by the Red Sea. At this time the Macedonian empire was the greatest and most famous on earth, but with Alexander's death it was dismembered by the rapacity of his successors, who split it into many kingdoms. From the height of its dominion to its final dissolution it lasted one hundred and fifty years.

Despite the severity of the terms which the Romans had imposed upon Antiochus III after the battle of Magnesia, it is significant that they allowed the Seleucid empire to retain its autonomy and kept none of Antiochus' territory for themselves. This was the key to Roman policy in Asia. By depriving Antiochus of all his territory west of the Taurus and adding to the terms offered by Scipio the condition that he surrender his elephants and most of his fleet, Rome effectually stifled Antiochus' ambitions in Asia Minor. At the same time they strengthened Rhodes and Pergamum by dividing between them the territory taken from Antiochus, and so made it difficult for any single strong power to rise. Similarly after the Second Macedonian War Rome had proclaimed the autonomy of all the Greek states which had been subject to Macedonia, and after the defeat of Perseus by Aemilius Paulus in the Third Macedonian War the Macedonian kingdom had been divided into four separate states.

The intention, and the overall result, of this policy was to minimize Rome's direct involvement in Eastern affairs while at the same time maintaining its position of dominance. As the story of Popilius Laenas' circle demonstrates, Rome now was the real sovereign of the eastern

Mediterranean. Under the leadership of Antiochus IV the Seleucid empire enjoyed a brief period of resurgence. During the Third Macedonian War Antiochus invaded Egypt, and was on the point of taking Alexandria. Disturbed at this prospect, the senate sent an envoy, Gaius Popilius Laenas, to demand that he withdraw from Egypt.

12. When Antiochus was four miles from Alexandria he was met by the Roman commissioners. He saluted them and held his hand out to Popilius. Popilius asked him first to read a document which he handed him. He did so, and said he would call and consult his ministers, whereupon Popilius with customary directness drew a circle around the king with the staff in his hand and said: "Give me your answer to the senate before you step out of this circle." The king was stunned by this peremptory order, but after hesitating a moment replied, "I will do as the senate bids." Popilius then deigned to give him his right hand, as a friend and ally.

Antiochus evacuated Egypt by the prescribed date, and the Romans sailed to Cyprus. From this base they expelled Antiochus' fleet, which already had conquered the Egyptian ships in battle. This embassy became renowned throughout the world. For it obviously had been responsible for Antiochus' withdrawal from Egypt after the country already was in his power, and for the restoration of its ancestral kingdom to the Ptolemaic dynasty.

In 167 B.C. King Prusias II of Bithynia paid a visit to ingratiate himself with the senate. The servility of his approach and the peremptory manner with which the senate refused his most important request indicates how truly the senate had become "an assembly of kings."

44. During this year King Prusias visited Rome accompanied by his son, Nicomedes. Followed by a large reti-

nue he entered the Forum and proceeded to the tribunal
of the praetor Quintus Cassius. When a crowd had assembled from every direction, he declared that he had come
to do homage to the gods who inhabited the city of Rome
and to pay his respects to the senate and the Roman people; he wished also to congratulate them upon their conquest of King Perseus and Gentius as well as the extension
of their dominion over Macedonia and Illyria. The praetor offered to present him to the senate that day if he
wished, but Prusias declined, asking that he be allowed
two days to see the temples of the gods, the city, and his
friends and acquaintances. The quaestor Lucius Cornelius Scipio, who had been sent to Capua to meet him, was
appointed to show him around the city. A house also
was obtained which provided adequate accommodation
for both the king and his retinue.

The third day he was presented to the senate. He con-
gratulated them on their victory and reminded them of
his own services during the [Third Macedonian] war.
He then requested that he be granted permission to dis-
charge a vow which he had made to sacrifice ten full-
grown victims at Rome on the Capitol and one to Fortune
at Praeneste. This vow he had made, he said, on behalf
of the victory of the Roman people. He asked that their
treaty of friendship with him be renewed and that the
territory which had been taken from Antiochus but formally allotted to no one be given to him. This land now
was occupied by the Galatians. Finally, he committed his
son to the protection of the senate.

He was supported by all those who had served as commanders in Macedonia, who were well-disposed toward
him. Accordingly all his requests were granted but one:
with regard to the territory possessed by the Galatians the
senate responded that envoys would be sent to investigate
the matter. If the territory was part of that acquired by

the Roman people and had never been allotted to anyone they considered Prusias eminently worthy of receiving that gift. It was possible, however, that it had not belonged to Antiochus and therefore had not been ceded to
the Roman people, or that it had in fact been given to
the Galatians; in such case they asked Prusias' pardon if
the Roman people wished to injure no one else in order to
grant him a favor. A gift, they added, could not gratify
even the receiver if he knew that the giver would take it
away whenever it suited his convenience. They consented
to accept the tutelage of his son, Nicomedes. . . .

With this response Prusias was dismissed. Gifts were
decreed for him to the value of . . . sesterces and vases
of silver of fifty pounds' weight. They decreed that gifts
should be conferred upon the king's son Nicomedes as valuable as those which had been given to Masgabae, son of
King Masinissa (of Numidia). It was further directed that
victims and other things necessary for sacrifice should be
provided for the king from the public treasury just as they
were provided for Roman magistrates. Finally it was
decreed that twenty ships from the fleet at Brundisium
should be placed at his disposal. Until the king should
reach the fleet provided for him and should embark, Lucius Cornelius Scipio was to accompany him at all times
and to provide for the expenses of the king and his
retinue. It is reported that the king was highly gratified at
the benevolence shown by the Roman people toward him.
He refused to allow presents to be bought for himself but
bade his son accept the generosity of the Roman people.
This is what Roman historians tell us about Prusias' visit.
Polybius, on the other hand, declares that that king was
unworthy of the majesty of his title. He was accustomed
to receive envoys with his head shaved and wearing the
skullcap of a freedman; in explanation he would assert
that he was the freedman of the Roman people and for

that reason wore the symbols of that class. At Rome when he arrived at the senate house he prostrated himself and touched his lips to the threshold, calling the senate his guardian deities and saying many other things which reflected less honor on his listeners than shame upon himself.

The Best of the World's Best Books
COMPLETE LIST OF TITLES IN
THE MODERN LIBRARY

A series of handsome, cloth-bound books, formerly
available only in expensive editions.

MISCELLANEOUS